THE ENGLISHMAN'S HOLIDAY

J. A. R. PIMLOTT

THE ENGLISHMAN'S HOLIDAY

A Social History

A MERMAID.

THE HARVESTER PRESS LIMITED
INTERNATIONAL PUBLICATIONS SERVICE

First published in 1947 by
Faber and Faber Limited
This edition first published in 1976 by
THE HARVESTER PRESS LIMITED
Publisher: John Spiers
2 Stanford Terrace, Hassocks, Sussex
and by International Publications Service
114 East 32nd Street, N.Y. 10016

The Harvester Press Limited
ISBN 0 85527 229 5

International Publications Service
ISBN 0-8002-0159-0
Library of Congress Catalog Card Number 75-16045

Printed in Great Britain by
Redwood Burn Limited, Trowbridge, Wiltshire

TO MY WIFE

NEW INTRODUCTION

In his own introduction to **The Englishman's Holiday**, John Alfred Ralph Pimlott claimed to be dealing with 'one of the most characteristic of modern institutions' the rise of which meant a 'revolutionary advance in the art of living'. The three decades which have elapsed since the book was first published in 1947 have seen both a doubling in the number of holidays enjoyed by the English and a spectacular boom in world tourism, now the largest single item in world trade. Nobody would wish to revise this judgement about the importance of the subject. Hence, the reprint of this book, which remains not only the best scholarly introduction to the history of holidays — all the more remarkable in that it was also the first — but also displays attitudes to the philosophy of holidays which are already of historical interest in themselves.

Before Pimlott, holidays had been neglected by professional historians, apart from a few isolated examples. J. L. Hammond had described the 'growth of common enjoyment', Sir John Clapham had seized on seaside piers 'as symbolic of what archaeologists call a culture' and E.W. Gilbert had begun his geographic studies of the growth and multiplication of Victorian watering places including **Brighton Old Ocean's Bauble**, recently re-issued by Harvester Press in its Flare Books imprint. When Pimlott began his book in the late 1930s, however, the place of holidays, especially of holidays with pay, was under growing public discussion and the Amulree Committee was investigating the question as a prelude to legislation in 1938. Pimlott gives a valuable account of these deliberations, appropriately enough since he himself declared that the social historian of the recent past should not hesitate to draw conclusions relevant to current questions. The war interrupted the completion of the book, although the debate about holidays carried on, and **The Englishman's Holiday** was eventually published in the same year the British Tourist and Holidays

Board was founded to be responsible for developing the holiday and tourist business, in itself a significant step in the history of holidays and of government involvement in the affairs of the industry.

Pimlott subtitled his book 'a social history' and, in terms of academic history, it was not only the theme of **The Englishman's Holiday** that was novel but also some aspects of the author's approach to the subject. Today, social history, or history levelled to 'the general surface of life' (Pimlott's phrase), has virtually established itself as an independent discipline. Pimlott would have welcomed this development and acknowledged in this bibliography to this book the need to find an effective way of describing and analysing the social behaviour of the mass of the people. Indeed, by using the census and newspaper materials, he employed, however cautiously, two of the basic sources of the new social history. He also accepted the relevance to history of the social sciences and incorporated the results of contemporary economic surveys into his account of the holiday industry, with his plea that it be regarded as equal to the 'great industries of production'. Yet, whilst his mind was orderly and perceptive, Pimlott was not a natural generaliser and his approach to history remained broadly chronological. Happily, his descriptions remain surprisingly fresh today. It is perhaps inevitable that his harsh judgement on Victorian architecture — 'a period of low aesthetic standards' — should seem dated, but otherwise only the overdrawn account of the jollities of the Victorian seaside really jars the modern reader.

The book describes the evolution of the holiday as a social institution, analysing many of its formative influences as well as the changing context of holidays. The European perspective is always kept before us and, thus, Pimlott can argue that in the seventeenth century the English were relatively backward in their interest in water as a cure or a pastime. Medical considerations were less important to the rise of English spas than the social awakening of the English landed classes, newly affluent in the eighteenth century, and in search of 'company and diversion'. Two of Pimlott's points are worth emphasizing. Spas were really part of the 'pre-history' of holidays, and represented a phase in the social routine of an older society — 'as long as visits to the spas were confined to the leisured it is difficult to regard them as holidays'. Pimlott also underplays the personal importance of such famous individuals as Dr.

Russell of Brighton in the development of seaside spas and argues that the enormous popularity of the inland spa made it inevitable that sea-water would eventually supplement inadequate supplies of mineral water.

For Pimlott there was nothing inevitable about the transition from spa to holiday resort and he dwells on the theme of the depression in the 1830s which hit the leading spas so very hard that many never really recovered. He might have added that the competition of the cheaper and more raffish continent also depressed some of the seaside spas, even successful Brighton for whom the decade of the 1830s was the only one during the nineteenth century in which her population did not grow. **The Englishman's Holiday**, therefore, devotes some of its most thoroughly argued pages to the influences affecting the rise of resorts, ranging from the 'pulmonary interest' and the shift in natural elixirs from water to air during a 'sulphurous century', to the new sensitivity to the needs of children, changing patterns of work and settlement, the influence of benign employers, the advancing technical possibilities of travel, rising incomes, fashion and chance. Pimlott also reminds us about regional variations, with the acceptable generalisation that wakes were most prolonged where unauthorised holidays were not permitted, and perhaps the most interesting section of the nineteenth-century part of the book deals with the efforts to establish a prevailing sentiment of work and the conflicts over the growth of annual and weekly holidays, and, for some workers, holidays with pay.

Pimlott also makes the development of holidays with pay the central theme of his discussion of twentieth-century holidaymaking. The judicious handling of the policy issues involved in this problem, and that of 'peaking', is one of the real pleasures of the book and a happy consequence of the fact that the author of **The Englishman's Holiday** was not by profession an academic historian but a civil servant, and a very successful one to boot. John Pimlott was born in 1910. After Oxford, where he won the Stanhope History Prize, he lived for a while at Toynbee Hall, a residential settlement in London, Chiefly for Oxbridge graduates who wished to share the life and experience of the East-End poor. He came to notice in the war as the Private Secretary to Herbert Morrison and his career took him through the Board of Trade, the Monopolies Commission and the Ministry of Education. 'A stylish administrator', his principal successes were in the Further Education sector where he fought for 'more positive and socially just policies', especially the rise of polytechnics and the establishment of the Council for National Academic Awards. His first book was a history of Toynbee Hall. He also wrote **Public Relations and American Democracy** and a general history of recreations. His death in 1969 prevented him completing a history of the Reform Club.

For twenty years after **The Englishman's Holiday** the subject was barely touched by academic historians. Of those who might have been inspired to research the subject further, the social historians preferred to chronicle the blacker legacy of the industrial revolution and the economic historians, in their efforts to explain the phases and causes of the material progress in Victorian England, neglected the rise of invisible services and the growth of holidays, and concentrated on work and the visible achievements of manufacturing industry. More recently the neglect has been repaired, although mainly by studies which approach the subject only tangentially. Thus, the recent interest in urban history has given us building histories of Bath, with more to come on Brighton, Bournemouth and Blackpool. The transition from spa to resort has been scrutinised in a thorough local study of Kent and there have been brave attempts to generalise about estate-building policies and patterns of holiday-making in the North West. The social and political dynamics of a Victorian boom town have also been analysed for Blackpool and an economic historian has even studied the rising importance of the holiday business from the point of view of Britain's relative economic decline in the later nineteenth century. Little of this new work, however, has meant revising Pimlott's basic narrative. By the same token, foreign historians, especially the busy French, have elaborated in detail the history of the Englishman's holiday abroad. One fascinating account of the rise and fall of an English community in France concerns Pau, popular with the hunting set — its countryside was rather like Leicestershire — and served since 1856 by the first golf course on the continent. Between 1878 and 1887, however, the British medical press condemned its climate for pulmonary illnesses, a fatal charge, since it came at a time when Biarritz presented a strong social challenge to Pau and the new mountain resorts of Switzerland were establishing their rival medical reputation. Another detailed study concerns the change which came over the Riviera between 1905 and 1935 as a result of the displacement of the holiday season from the winter to the summer and the rise in sun-bathing (there is regrettably little on this twentieth-century elixir in Pimlott) which created a summer trade and 'achieved in a decade what capital and enterprise had failed to do in a century'. One startling result was the closure of 106 hotels in Nice, many of which changed into *logements,* mostly those in the hills away from the sea, and another result was the rise of beach resorts which filled every gap on the coastline from Marseilles to 'Monte Carlo encanaillé'.

As with so many civil servants of his generation John Pimlott combined an ideal of public service with a concern for social justice not inappropriate for the historian of Toynbee Hall. For him the rise of popular holidays was a certain sign of social progress, and, although the enthusiasm of his optimistic account may read somewhat blandly today, one sympathises with his lionising Thomas Cook in whom 'educational, enthusiasm and outstanding business capacity' combined in such spectacular effect and public benefit. At the time he wrote, however, despite his hopes for the influence of such improving voluntary associations as the Co-operative Holidays Association and the Holiday Fellowship, Pimlott was disappointed with the use to which the increased number of holidays was being put, more for 'mere relaxation' than for the 'development of the human personality'. He was not alone in worrying about the 'problem of leisure'. In 1935, J. L. Hammond feared 'to see the organisation of man's life outside his work put under the same power of progress through profit-making and competition'. The great liberal intellectual, Beveridge, argued that it was the duty of the state to ensure a 'national minimum', but he also advocated strengthening voluntary associations, which could 'reconcile the responsibilities of the state with the rights and responsibilities of individuals', especially in the field of leisure. In the choosing between the corrosive influence of profit and a further extension of the overweening power of the state, however, Pimlott seems to have had rather more faith in the benign influence of business. He saw Billy Butlin, indeed, as a modern Thomas Cook and was pleased to record that the San Carlo Opera Company had been engaged in 1946 by the Butlin organisation, whose holiday camps were 'the most significant innovation of the century'. He also perceived a trend towards 'communal holidays', or 'social tourism', which would reinforce the influence of the voluntary organisations and improve the general standard of holidaymaking.

Only a few of Pimlott's hopes have been subsequently realised, and maybe not the important ones. Since **The Englishman's Holiday** was published in 1947, the amount of leisure time available for holidays has not increased as much as was at one time expected. The number of hours worked each week by manual workers, for example, 47.8 in 1951, had only fallen to 45.6 hours in 1973 and annual holidays remained small by European standards; 81 per cent of workers enjoyed more than three but less than four weeks a year in 1973. **Political and Economic Planning** had estimated in 1942 that, soon after the war, there might be 45 million holidaymakers, amounting to 90 per cent of the total population. Pimlott thought this an overestimate — 'there will always be some who do not want to go away' — and he was proved right for even today 40 per cent of the population does not take a holiday. Nevertheless, between 1951 and 1972, the growth in the number of Englishmen's holidays has been huge, at home from 25 million to 37.5 million, and abroad an even more impressive jump from 1.5 million to 8.5 million. Pimlott expected the sea and mountains to maintain their attraction in the pattern of holidaymaking and this has proved broadly to be the case, except that traditional holiday resorts have lost some of their relative appeal to new areas and new types of holidays. In particular, the sun has drawn more people to the South West (22 per cent of holidaymakers in 1970) and the rise of car ownership has made individual touring holidays much more popular (·68 per cent of holiday journeys were made by car in 1970). The car, indeed, shattered Pimlott's dream of 'social tourism' at home and the changing popularity of various types of holiday accommodation confirms the same trend towards individual holidays. Holiday camps were the scene of seven per cent of all holidays in 1972, but self-catering holidays, 12 per cent of the total in 1951, had risen to 43 per cent by 1972, 19 per cent by caravan.

Holidays abroad have also been strongly influenced by the pull of the sun. Almost all such holidays now involve travelling south in Europe and Spain has become especially popular as the destination of over 30 per cent of British tourists. Whilst Pimlott compared continental tourists in his day to the grand tourists of the eighteenth century, who pursued abroad the roots of classical civilisation, more recently the pursuit of good health has replaced education as the principle driving force of holidaymakers. Of course, it is also the case today that almost 50 per cent of tourists do travel abroad communally in 'inclusive tours'. Yet, the taste for 'social tourism' and an eagerness to submit to guidance in the correct 'tradition of leisure' are, perhaps, less convincing explanations of the attraction of package holidays than cheapness and simple convenience. Most readers of The Englishman's Holiday, however, will be in a position to judge this point for themselves, which is proof enough of one aspect of the very social progress in the field of holidays that John Pimlott described in such stylish phrases, and with such historical skill and sincerity.

University of Sussex, November 1975 *John Myerscough*

INTRODUCTION

'None can properly be said to write history, but he who understands the human heart, and its whole train of affections and follies. Those affections and follies are properly the materials he has to work upon. The relations of great events may surprise indeed; they may be calculated to instruct those very few, who govern the million beneath, but the generality of mankind find the most real improvement from relations which are levelled to the general surface of life. . . .'

Thus Oliver Goldsmith introduced to the public in 1762 his biography of Richard Nash of Bath, whose contribution to the development of the modern English holiday resort is perhaps greater than that of any other individual.

It is no longer necessary to justify the levelling of history to 'the general surface of life', or the admission of the 'affections and follies of mankind' to the historian's pages. There have been histories of pastimes, fashions, even of vices. Yet the historian has neglected one of the most characteristic of modern social institutions—the migration of holidaymakers to the sea, the countryside, the mountains, which is as typical of Western European culture in the twentieth century as were bread and circuses of ancient Rome and pilgrimages of the Middle Ages. The crowds on the beaches of Blackpool and Brighton, the hiker, the 'Butlineer', the wealthy winter visitor to St. Moritz and Monte Carlo, the thousands who in normal times seek adventure and change in other lands under the safe guidance of the great tourist organizations, are as representative of the age as were the gladiator and the pilgrim of theirs. And though it is now international, the annual holiday is largely British—indeed English—in origin; like the week-end, like the seabathing which has been so important in its development, it ranks high amongst our cultural exports.

The revolutionary advance in the art of living which the annual holiday represents has had far-reaching consequences. It has been an important factor in the improvement of health and in the decline of drunkenness and other social evils. It has influenced manners and has created fashions. It has brought into being a new and still growing industry of which the ramifications are innumerable, and the number of persons employed in which equals or exceeds the number engaged in the great industries of production. It has played its part in international relations. It has led to the rise of great towns, like Brighton, of which Cobbett said that it was 'a place of no trade; of no commerce at all; it has no harbour; it is no place of deposit or of transit for corn or for goods or for cattle', towns which, along with the great seaports and manufacturing centres, were somewhat contemptuously dismissed in the Report on the Census of 1851 as 'of an inferior order' but having 'acquired an adventitious but extraordinary importance and magnitude'.

What has perhaps been the most extraordinary development of all has occurred only in the last generation. This is the admission of the annual holiday with pay to a place amongst the minimum living conditions which in a progressive community the worker is entitled to expect. It has come about by general consent, preceded by little agitation or party strife. Mr. Ben Riley, M.P., seconding the Second Reading of the Annual Holiday Bill in 1936, expressed an almost unanimous view when he told the House of Commons:

'There is an overwhelming body of opinion in favour of this long-delayed social reform becoming a reality. No one for a single moment disputes the desirability, both on physical grounds and on grounds of social amenity, that every worker should have the opportunity without great inconvenience of getting away at least once a year from the scene of his daily toil to a change of environment and a change of scene.'

The cordial reception of this Bill led the Government to appoint a Departmental Committee under the chairmanship of Lord Amulree to investigate the extent to which holidays with pay were given to employed workpeople and the possibility of extending the provision of such holidays by statutory enactment or otherwise: and in 1938 the Amulree Committee's Report endorsed the principle of holidays with pay for all. Since they reported, paid holidays have been conceded to millions of workers. Abroad they are compulsory in some countries, and special Departments of State have been set up to facilitate their use.

It is singular that at any rate in this country—and, as far as I have been able to trace, abroad—historians have paid little attention to the annual holiday and the uses to which it has been put. There are a number of histories of particular holiday resorts, and there is an abundance of literature, much of it of doubtful value to the historian, on the fashionable inland and seaside resorts of the eighteenth century and the Regency. But useful though the former may be on the presence or absence of Roman remains and the date of erection of places of worship, or the latter on the personal lives of notabilities, both are usually superficial and uninformative on matters of more general significance. There is a large undigested mass of primary material—newspapers, correspondence, memoirs, diaries, guide books, official reports—but an almost complete lack of scientific monographs undertaken not as propaganda nor from local pride, but as essays in social and economic history, and even in general works in this field the references to holidays and holidaymaking are incidental and scanty.

The present work attempts to fill the gap for England and Wales—to have included the Scots would have further complicated an already complicated story—but only as an introduction to a subject the comprehensive study of which would require the collaboration of many hands. The treatment has, therefore, been deliberately selective. Yet I hope that it may not be without value to those who are interested in the historical background to what will undoubtedly be one of the most important of the social problems of the generation—the utilization of leisure and in particular of the annual holiday with pay. And, though it is primarily historical, I have tried throughout to see the past in its relationship to the present, and while doing my best to preserve a proper detachment, have not hesitated to draw conclusions which are relevant to current questions. It seems to me indeed that this is one of the functions which should be performed by a social historian who is dealing with the recent past.

One deficiency from which, as I am aware, the volume suffers is due to a difficulty of language.

The word 'holiday' is made to serve so many purposes that it is often ambiguous.[1] It is in particular a drawback that it is used both for a period of time—normally of absence from work—and for the way in which that period is spent. In addition it still retains its old sense of a religious festival, while there is no convenient way of distinguishing between a short holiday such as a day excursion and a more prolonged break such as a middle-class family's fortnight by the sea or a millionaire's world cruise. These disadvantages are considerable, and it will be found that of necessity the term 'holiday' is used in a variety of senses in this book; though it is hoped that ambiguity has been avoided and that the particular meaning which is intended will be clear from the context. While, however, it would be convenient that the different senses should be easily distinguishable, that they are not has at least the advantage of emphasizing the complexity of the subject. The medieval saint's day, the weekly half-holiday, the observance of Sunday, the unauthorized holiday, the school vacation, the bank holiday, the holiday with pay, all have their place in the story we are trying to tell, which is the story of how it has come about that the typical English family expects to go away for a holiday at least once a year, and why this takes the forms it does. More briefly, why 'summer holidays' and why Brighton and Blackpool?

J.A.R.P.

Wimbledon
February 1947

[1] The *Oxford English Dictionary* gives the following meanings: (1) A consecrated day, a religious festival; (2a) A day on which ordinary occupations are suspended; a day of exemption or cessation from work; a day of festivity, recreation or amusement; (2b) A time or period of cessation from work, or of festivity or recreation; a vacation; and (2c) Cessation from work; festivity; recreation.

ACKNOWLEDGEMENTS

I hope that I may be excused if I do not mention all who have helped me in the preparation of this book. The list would be very long, and I will confine myself to saying that I am most grateful. There are a few, however, whose help has been such as to call for special acknowledgment.

First among these are my friends, Mr. W. K. Pyke-Lees, Mr. G. D. Ramsay, and Mr. John Ross, each of whom went through the MS. and made valuable criticisms and suggestions, most of which I have adopted; in addition Mr. Pyke-Lees helped me with the proofs and index. I am also particularly indebted to Dr. J. J. Mallon for the encouragement and help which I have had from him since I started work on the book some years before the War.

Other individuals to whom my special thanks are due are: Mr. Joseph Burke; Mr. Francis Cheetham, who supplied me with some useful unpublished material about Southport; Mr. E. W. Gilbert; Miss Winifred Haward; and Mr. A. L. Rowse. Mr. James Laver of the Victoria and Albert Museum and Mr. E. F. Croft Murray of the British Museum gave me valuable help in connection with the illustrations. Amongst individuals connected with the voluntary organizations I should mention in particular Mr. A. V. S. Lochhead and Mrs. Orr of the Industrial Welfare Society, both of whom kindly supplied me with information in the possession of the Society, and Mr. E. St. John Catchpool of the Youth

Hostels Association. Messrs. Butlin's not only supplied me with much useful information, but kindly arranged for me to visit their holiday camp at Clacton-on-Sea.

To my wife I am greatly indebted for encouragement and practical help.

For the rest I will only say again how grateful I am to all from whom I have had help. Apart from those I have mentioned by name, they include the officials of various voluntary organizations interested in holidays, the principal travel agencies, railway companies, and many local authorities. The International Labour Office also supplied useful material. And I could never have written this book without the help of that great institution—the London Library.

My thanks are due to the following for permission to reproduce or for supplying copies of illustrations: Sir Patrick Abercrombie and Mr. R. S. Nickson (Plate No. 24b); Birmingham City Museum and Art Gallery (Plate No. 13); Blackpool Corporation (Plate No. 12a); Bournemouth Municipal Libraries (Plate No. 12b); Brighton Art Gallery and Museum (Plates No. 9a, 9b and 11a); the British Museum (Plates No. 3, 4, 5, 8, 10, 14, and illustrations on pp. 39 and 47); Messrs. Butlin's, Ltd. (Plates No. 18c, 22a and 22b); Messrs. Thomas Cook and Son, Ltd. (Plates No. 18a, 20a and 20b); the Co-operative Holidays Association (Plates No. 16b and 18b); *Country Life* (Plate No. 17a); Exclusive News Agency (Plate No. 16a); Folkestone Corporation (Plate No. 23); the proprietors of the *Illustrated London News* (Plate No. 15 and illustrations on pp. 125 and 165); the proprietors of the *Lady* (illustrations on pp. 181 and 183); Mr. Frank H. Lloyd (Plate No. 21b); Messrs. Longman (illustration on p. 205); the proprietors of *Punch* (illustration on p. 255 and small illustrations used as chapter endings, all of which come from the *Punch Summer Number* for 1912); Mr. T. W. Thompson (Plate No. 21a); Topical Press Agency (Plate No. 17b); Mr. Evelyn Waugh and Messrs. Duckworth (Plate No. 19); the Workers Travel Association (Plate No. 24a). F. Anstey's poem, *The Joys of the Seaside*, is reproduced by permission of Messrs. Methuen.

J.A.R.P.

CONTENTS

PLATES

Plates

ILLUSTRATIONS IN THE TEXT

NOTE

Every effort has been made to reduce the number of footnotes. References have accordingly not been given for information which is to be found in easily accessible authorities, such as the extensive literature on Bath and the other great English watering places or the histories of the railway companies, or for quotations the origin of which is shown by the context and which can be traced without much difficulty. Where, too, a quotation about a particular resort is given without a reference to its origin it may be assumed that it is to be found in one of the standard histories of the resort. It is hoped that the periodical notes about the sources which have been used in dealing with particular questions will to some extent compensate for the lack of references; the Bibliography will serve as a guide to sources which are not given in the text.

I

BEGINNINGS

Holidays are as old as human society. The forms which they have taken in different societies have reflected the economic and political conditions of those societies, but until modern times their ostensible purpose was usually religious. In ancient Egypt popular superstition forbade work on about one fifth of the days of the year. In classical Athens there were fifty or sixty days of festival annually, and in Tarentum at its greatest period feast days outnumbered working days. In the old Roman calendar there were 108 days on which nominally for religious reasons no judicial or other public business could lawfully be transacted, while in the Julian calendar the number of such days was still greater. The Jewish lawmakers provided for a weekly day of rest, sanctified by the story of the Creation. The account in *Genesis* gives a good illustration of the economic motive which underlay the religious observance: 'And on the seventh day God ended His work which He had made.'

The Christian Sunday derives from the Jewish Sabbath and is still the weekly rest day of the Western world. Particularly in Roman Catholic countries popular holidays continue to be associated with religious celebrations. The English bank holidays, with one exception, are traditional holidays occurring at the great

religious festivals, and the 'wakes weeks' of the North of England are descended from the village wakes which in the Middle Ages were held on the eve of the patronal festival. It is not the least novel feature of the holidays with which we are concerned that they are secular in character and are employed in the pursuit of pleasure, individually or in family units, instead of in religious observances or communal festivities of a religious or semi-religious character.

The dissociation of the notion of a holiday from religion has been a gradual process, which is not yet wholly at an end, but it was one of the prerequisites for the development of holidays in the modern sense. The other main prerequisite was economic and social: there had to be reasonably good facilities for travel and a considerable section of the population in the position to use those facilities. In other words the annual holiday would not have developed but for the secularization of social life and the technical conquests which are features of our modern civilization. As the sphere of religion has narrowed, as wealth has increased and has been more widely disseminated, and as communications have improved, so conditions have become more congenial for its growth.

The increasing secularization of social life, of which this change in the conception of holidays was an aspect, and the economic and social changes, which, beginning with the Renaissance and the Reformation, reached their climax with the Industrial Revolution, provide the background for the present story. They do not explain, however, how and why the practice of taking holidays away from home developed, or why it took the form it did. They were favourable to the spread of travel and to the growth of secular amusements such as the theatre, and they created a new outlook towards pleasure and infinitely more diversified opportunities for its enjoyment. But, however favourable the conditions, some positive stimulus was necessary before so revolutionary a change in social habits could come about. In the time of Elizabeth, for example, there were already many travellers on the roads of England, lawyers following the Judges on their circuits, students going to the Universities, adventurous young men making their way to seek their fortunes in London, members of Parliament, courtiers, officials, merchants, players, vagabonds. The beginnings may even be seen of the tradition of foreign travel which has been so distinctive a feature of Anglo-Saxon civilization. But there were virtually none who were travelling either, like the modern tourist, because they loved travel for its own sake or, like the visitor to the modern holiday resort, to go to strange places for rest and recreation.

That people should come to do these things involved two important innovations; a change of mental attitude, and the coming into existence of places which were attractive to and made provision for the accommodation and entertainment of the pleasure seeker. The first was unlikely to occur in advance of the latter, and the latter might seem to presuppose the former. Until there were centres which it was attractive to visit, there would be no incentive to travel, especially as long as travelling conditions were unfavourable. In the absence of such an incentive why should provision be made for the visitor?[1]

In these circumstances the first holiday resorts might well have been London and other large towns, to which in any event people came for business or social reasons; and in a sense this is what in fact happened. Country gentlemen and wealthy citizens from the provinces were susceptible to the lure of the capital, with all its glamour and excitement and prestige, and provincial cities such as Exeter and York were social centres for the surrounding districts, partly serving for the middle elements in society the same purposes as London and the great watering places in the life of the nation as a whole.

What neither London nor the provincial cities could give was a change of environment for their own population, and, as far as London was concerned, this included the circles which were

[1] The change of outlook which was required is suggestively brought out by Samuel Butler: 'There are Canterbury Pilgrims every Sunday in summer who start from close to the old Tabard, only they go by the South-Eastern Railway and come back the same day for five shillings. And, what is more, they are just the same sort of people. If they do not go to Canterbury they go by the *Clacton Belle* to Clacton-on-Sea.' (*Notebooks*, ed. Henry Festing Jones (1912), 262.)

socially most influential, the Court, the Diplomatic Corps, members of both Houses of Parliament, the high officials such as the Judges, and the wealthy merchants of the City. Thus neither London nor the provincial cities could permanently satisfy the need.

By a curious accident the solution of the problem came as an incidental result of a seemingly irrelevant advance in medicine—the trust which in the sixteenth and seventeenth centuries the medical profession began once again to place in the therapeutic qualities of the mineral waters.[1] This was not an innovation, because, as the ruins of Roman Bath bore witness, they had been much used in the ancient world, and they had not been wholly deserted in the Middle Ages, during which pilgrimages were made to springs credited with magical properties, and Bath itself was frequented by the sick of all classes. Their revival in popularity was attributable to the Renaissance. It was the counterpart of a similar trend on the Continent, where, as was pointed out in 1562 by Dr. William Turner, 'the father of English physicke',[2] the

[1] The best and indeed the only full account of the revival of the mineral springs and their transformation into pleasure resorts will be found in Reginald Lennard's essay on the watering-places in *Englishmen at Rest and Play: Some Phases of English Leisure, 1558-1714*, edited by him (1931). The debt which the present and the next chapter owe to this essay is great. As regards Bath, it should be supplemented by reference to P. Rowland James, *The Baths of Bath in the Sixteenth and Early Seventeenth Centuries* (1938). For a more complete list of the sources used, see the Bibliography; but it may be convenient to mention here that, apart from the works referred to above, standard authorities on Bath are the French historian A. Barbeau's *Life and Letters at Bath in the XVIIIth Century* (1904), and L. Melville's *Bath under Beau Nash* (1907). On the early history of Tunbridge Wells there is little to be added to the first *History* by Benge Burr (1766), who, if not always reliable, gives a reasonably good account of the main outlines of its development. L. Melville, *Society at Royal Tunbridge Wells* (1912), and Margaret Barton, *Tunbridge Wells* (1937), are useful modern authorities; both are illustrated. The information about the other spas in the seventeenth century is decidedly fragmentary.

[2] In his famous work on 'the natures and properties as well of the bathes in England as of other bathes in Germany and Italye very necessary for all seik persons that cannot be healed without the helpe of natural bathes'.

appointments of the spas were greatly superior to those of Bath, the only English spa which he mentioned at all.[1]

None the less, the Corporation of Bath, who had taken over the baths from the Abbey at the Reformation, were doing their best to develop the city as a resort for the sick. Bath and Buxton were mentioned in the Poor Law Act of 1572 as places of great resort by poor and diseased people, in connection with a provision making certain exemptions from the severe restrictions which the Act imposed on the movement of the poor. As far as importance was concerned Bath and Buxton were in a class apart, but there are references to a few other spas. Harrison in his *Description of England* (1577) mentioned St. Vincent's Bath near Bristol, 'Halliewell' (probably the Holywell at Shoreditch), and St. Winifred's Well in Flintshire. In a later edition (1586 or 1587) he added three springs said to have been discovered in 1579 at King's Newnham near Coventry, at Newton, near St. Neots, and at Rugby. Of spas subsequently famous Harrogate (then known under the name of the neighbouring village of Knaresborough) seems to have been rediscovered in the latter years of the century.

The limits of the advance which had been made by the end of the century may be illustrated from the example of Bath. It was still a town of only about a thousand inhabitants, looking backward to the prosperity which it had lost as a centre of the woollen industry rather than forward to a future in which its greatness would flow from its mineral waters. On the other hand, benefactions had helped the citizens to remedy some of the deficiencies of which the father of English physic had complained. The spa treatment was minutely regulated, there was a considerable literature about the waters, there were an ample number of doctors, and there was a rudimentary tourist industry, as was shown by the touts who accosted newcomers on behalf of the quack physicians and the lodging-house keepers. The citizens were in a position to spend a substantial sum of over £1,000 on the three visits paid by James I's Queen. This is evidence of their acumen as well as

[1] According to the *Oxford English Dictionary* 'spa' or 'spaw' was first used for a mineral spring in 1626, but despite the anachronism the term is used here for convenience.

of their affluence. The repute in which the waters were held may be judged from the decision of the Queen's physicians to send her to Bath, and from the large number of other distinguished visitors.[1]

But the spas were not yet holiday resorts. They were visited for reasons of health by the sick of all classes, who placed their faith not only in the medicinal qualities of the waters, but often, as some of the names suggest, in spiritual virtues which may well have been as effective. The provision which was beginning to be made for the amusement of the patients is, however, significant in retrospect. Physicians were already aware of the value of exercise and recreation as aids to treatment, and, modest though they were by later standards, the steps which were taken at sixteenth-century Bath and Buxton to entertain the visitors prepared the way for their transformation into pleasure resorts. The best London companies of players visited Bath, amongst them Alleyn and Burbage, and possibly Shakespeare himself. Out of doors there were bowling greens and for the more energetic there was a tennis court. At Buxton in 1572 there were galleries for walking, there were bowls (then and for long to come the most popular of outdoor games), and shooting at garden butts, 'that noblest of exercises'; indoors there was a game called 'Troule in Madame', which seems to have been rather like a mixture of bowls and bagatelle.

It is not, however, the character or the quantity of the entertainments which matters: it is that provision was made at all. For 'as surely as the holy day was destined to become a holiday, the health resort, whether it started as a holy well or not, was destined to become a pleasure resort, the home of revelry rather than of religion'.[2]

At first sight the transition may not seem so simple. As Goldsmith said, 'To a person, who does not thus calmly trace things to their source, nothing will appear more strange, than how the healthy could ever consent to follow the sick to those places of spleen, and live with those, whose diseases are ever apt to create a gloom in the spectator.' The pleasure-seeker might have been

[1] Rowland James lists over 150 well-known visitors between 1569 and 1625, not all, however, to take the waters.

[2] Lennard, 13–14.

expected to avoid the invalid. Yet the borderland between health and sickness is narrow. The illnesses of many of the visitors to the spas were psychological rather than physical, and the more exalted were accompanied by a fashionable entourage with time on their hands. The spas were the only places of general resort outside London, and as they began to cater for pleasure it was natural that people of wealth and fashion should find in them attractive alternatives to London and their country estates. The transition is hardly perceptible: all that can be said with any certainty is that before the Civil War pleasure-seekers were mingling with the sick. John Evelyn, for example, paid what may loosely be called a holiday visit to Bath in 1639.

Bath benefited most from this change, but it had two disadvantages which were to be of assistance to its competitors. It was relatively far from London. Secondly, owing to the belief that its waters were not good to take in the summer, it had only spring and autumn seasons. Partly because of the drawbacks to Bath, but also of growing demand, there developed two great watering places in the vicinity of London, Tunbridge Wells and Epsom, both with summer seasons.

Tunbridge Wells is of special interest. Unlike Bath it had no history except as a watering place, and its rise illustrates the interplay of three of the main factors in the development of a fashionable resort—the approval of the medical profession, Court patronage, and local enterprise. Its story began in 1606 with the accidental discovery of the springs. Dudley, Lord North, returning from a stay in the country which had been recommended by his doctors as a method of repairing the health which he had undermined by fast living in town, noticed a spring whose appearance reminded him of the waters which he had seen at Spa when he had been campaigning on the Continent. He took a sample to his physicians, who found that it contained chalybeate, and sent him back to drink the waters.

North had been threatened with consumption. This was a prevalent disease, but the springs were on private property, and they were not generally accessible until their owner, Lord Abergavenny, opened them to the public. He cleared the surroundings, sank two wells over the springs, and built a road to Tonbridge. The benefit which North had derived from them was well known, they were near London, and, though as yet there was no accommodation for visitors, they began to be visited by fashionable invalids. In 1619 they were said to have been frequented for three or four years, 'especially this year by many great persons, in so much that they who have seen both say that it is not inferior to the Spa for good company, numbers and other appurtenances'. By 1630 their reputation was such that on the advice of the royal physicians Queen Henrietta Maria visited them for six weeks. This was a landmark in their history. On the strength of the visit the name 'Queenes Welles'—which never, however, gained acceptance—was taken, setting a precedent which has been followed at least once, in the case of Bognor Regis, in the present generation.

Another important step in their evolution was the erection in 1636 of two cottages as resting places for those who came to drink the waters, one for ladies and one for gentlemen. These were precursors of the assembly rooms without which no spa was soon to be complete. Gentlemen paid the substantial subscription of half a crown for the use of pipes and other conveniences; physicians recommended smoking, provided that the patients held the smoke in their mouths for a long time before exhaling it. At about the same time tradesmen began to attend during the water-drinking season to display their wares, and in 1638 a promenade was laid out. There was still, however, no accommodation for visitors nearer than the village of Tonbridge, and it is probable that, like the Queen in 1629, many of them lived in tents. The erection in 1639 of a number of cottages at Southborough, two and a half miles away, partly met the deficiency; but demand still exceeded supply, and high prices were charged for inferior accommodation.

It was fortunate for the spas that on the eve of the Civil War they were still primarily health resorts. Had they been identified with pleasure, they might have fared more hardly at the hands of the various Puritan Governments. As it was, there was little to which the Puritans could object, and, though it was found necessary to place certain restrictions on travel to the spas to prevent them from becoming centres of Royalist intrigue, otherwise they suffered no direct interference. Evelyn's account of Bath in 1654 shows that there had not been an end to 'idle diversions', and a ballroom is said to have been built at Epsom in 1649.

The spas may have marked time, but despite the uncongenial conditions, they survived. They were, therefore, in a position to take full advantage of the changed circumstances of the new reign. These were as favourable as those of the previous twenty years had been unfavourable. The contrast between the thought and practice of the two periods is often exaggerated, but the joy with which Charles II was welcomed on his return from the Continent was a spontaneous expression of the relief of all classes at their emancipation from Puritan restrictions. For the upper strata of society at least, an age of frivolity and pleasure opened, and the young resorts shared in the benefits which this brought to the theatres and other purveyors of amusement.

This was not the only change from which they gained. The fashion for scientific inquiry enhanced the interest in the mineral waters and stimulated the search for new springs. The Royalists returned with a widened acquaintance with the Continental spas and a greater readiness to accept new modes of thought. The close connection which was maintained with the Continent was reflected in an increasing refinement of manners and sophistication of amusements. With growing wealth came new tastes and new demands. Unfamiliar luxuries such as tea and coffee were becoming common on the tables of the well-to-do, and craftsmen from the Continent and rich fabrics from the East added to the comfort of their homes. This was fertile soil for the growth of the resorts. They satisfied not only the craving for remedies for the ills, often imaginary, chronic in any leisured class and aggravated by the reaction from Puritan austerity, but also the desire for novelty and change, for new ways of expending wealth and obtaining excitement, characteristic of an idle society bent chiefly on pleasure in an age of economic expansion. They offered a cure-all for the ills, and a pleasant alternative to the life of the city when the palate for urban life was jaded.

The extent of the vogue for medicinal waters is exemplified by the discovery of more than a hundred mineral springs in the second half of the century. The claims made on their behalf in the medical and pseudo-medical literature which flowed from the presses lost nothing in extravagance, and, despite the spread of the scientific spirit, an uncritical public accepted the most preposterous assertions. It was modestly claimed of the Scarborough waters by a local physician, Dr. Robert Wittie, in 1669, that they were 'good against diseases of the head, as the Apoplexy, Epilepsie, Catalepsie, Vertigo', diseases of the nerves, lung and stomach disorders, asthma, scurvy, 'the Jaunders both yellow and black', and leprosy, and were also a 'most Soveraign remedy against Hypochondriack Melancholly and Windiness'.

Such claims were typical. One of the most widely credited was that the waters were an aid to fecundity and a remedy for gynaecological disorders; and the plausible suggestion has been made that this was responsible for the strong feminine element in spa society.[1] The birth of the Old Pretender to Mary of Modena was attributed to the Bath waters. Queen Henrietta Maria had visited Wellingborough in the hope of an heir, and Tunbridge Wells to recover from a confinement. Scarborough was much frequented by 'ladies that have a desire to be gott with child'.[2] The benefits to be derived from the waters in this respect were psychological as well as physical. The Tunbridge waters rendered 'those who drink of them fruitful and prolific; by reason of their spirituous ferment, they enliven, invigorate and actuate the whole mass of blood, the nobler parts of the body and spirits thereof; likewise reduce them from a saline or sulphureous dyscrasy, and sometimes from both to a sweet balsamick, spirituous and sanguineous temperament; which naturally incites men and women to amorous emotions and titillations, being previous dispositions enabling them to procreation'.[3] The happy results which sometimes followed the treatment must have seemed ample confirmation of the theory.

[1] Barton, 150.

[2] *The Life of Marmaduke Rawdon of York* (Camden Society, 1858), 146.

[3] Dr. Madan, quoted by Barton, 112. Similar claims continued to be made even in the nineteenth century. In 1864 the Tunbridge waters were being recommended as 'peculiarly suitable in maladies relating to the female constitution'. (R. H. Powell, *Medical Topography of Tun-*

In the development of the spas as social centres the Court again took the lead. A concourse of fashionable folk followed the King and Queen to Bath and Tunbridge Wells in 1663, and attended the races at Epsom, which were under the King's patronage. Those who visited Tunbridge Wells in quest of amusement were said in the 'sixties to have outnumbered those brought by motives of necessity. Constraint and formality were banished, and the life was generally delightful. To Bath at the same period many people of fashion came 'solely to amuse themselves in good company. There are music, play, promenades, balls, and perpetual amusement.' Pepys heard almost as good music as he ever heard in the Metropolis, and though there was as yet no permanent theatre, good touring companies paid occasional visits. In the train of the pleasure seekers there came the parasites of fashionable society in full force. The women of the town accompanied their clients, and sharpers and quacks found profitable hunting grounds. Even at Bath and Tunbridge Wells there was also a proportion of 'citizens', merchants and tradesmen anxious to establish themselves in good society, and Epsom, despite its royal connections, appears to have catered largely for the middle class. Anticipating the future, some of the richer citizens of London came down for weekends, others lived at Epsom in the summer and went up to business every day, and there were some day trippers.

At the end of the century the three great watering places, like the Cross Bath at Bath, were 'more fam'd for Pleasure than Cures', but a reminder of the importance which the waters still retained is provided by the fate of Epsom, which despite its apparent prosperity was already on the point of decline.

One reason seems to have been the misguided attempt of John Livingstone, the quack doctor who is chiefly associated with this unhappy phase in its history, to pass off as efficacious the waters of the 'New Wells', which he established in opposition to the old and authentic Epsom Wells. Livingstone was to go down to posterity

bridge Wells (1846), 56), and the internal and external use of the Bath waters in cases of sterility and in functional uterine disorders in 1890 (J. B. Yeo, *Climate and Health Resorts* (1890 ed.), 629.) It is not of course suggested that the claims were without foundation in some cases.

with a reputation for knavery. This may have been deserved. But little is known about him, and if he had been luckier history might have regarded him as a noteworthy pioneer instead of as a charlatan. He was one of the first to make a large-scale attempt to attract pleasure seekers. The prospects must have seemed good. The reputation of Epsom was established, and as Celia Fiennes[1] had recorded in the 'nineties, it was well equipped. It had an abundance of good lodging houses and the usual amusements, and, in addition to the horse racing for which it was famous, a weekly feature in keeping with its tradition was racing with boys, rabbits and pigs.

In 1706–8, contemporaneously with Richard Nash's earliest enterprises at Bath, Livingstone built the 'New Wells', which were part of an amusement centre in the grand style, complete with an assembly room for music and dancing, gaming rooms, shops for the sale of luxuries, a bowling green and a grove. For a time his enterprise flourished and the old wells were deserted for the new ones. Soon, however, it was discovered that the latter were deficient in medicinal properties and they began to lose custom. Threatened with ruin, Livingstone in 1715 adopted the desperate and mistaken course of buying and closing the old wells, thus securing a monopoly. At first this policy paid. There was a brief period of prosperity, coincident with the South Sea Company boom, during which Epsom was filled with every kind of adventurer, 'that vermin called Sharpers', 'alchemists, Dutchmen, Germans, Jews'. It did not last long. Epsom soon sank into the second rank and almost the only memorial of its great days as a watering place is linguistic.

The other spas were numerous but mostly unimportant. Canterbury, Alford in Somerset, Enstone in Oxfordshire, Brill in Buckinghamshire, Astrop in Northamptonshire—the latter described in 1697 as 'grown so Famous as (almost) to Emulate *Tunbridge* itself'[2]—were amongst the many which were destined to

[1] Celia Fiennes, *Through England on a Side Saddle in the Time of William and Mary* (ed. the Hon. Mrs. Griffiths, 1888), is one of the most important seventeenth-century sources on the spas. Miss Fiennes was an unusual woman, a Dissenter of noble birth, who had an exceptional curiosity and interest in detail.

[2] Lennard, 38.

obscurity. The London spas, which included Barnet, Islington, Dulwich, Sydenham, Streatham, Richmond and Hampstead, were principally places of evening or weekend resort, and their role in social life was rather like that of Hampton Court to-day, the Crystal Palace in the last century, and Vauxhall Gardens in the eighteenth century. 'Les Gens de qualité ne vont guères là,' said a foreign observer of Islington in 1697.[1] 'As the Nobility and Gentry go to *Tunsbridge*, the Merchants and Rich Citizens to *Epsome*; so the Common People go chiefly to *Dullwich* and *Stretham*,' wrote Defoe in 1724.

Of spas later famous, Cheltenham and probably Leamington were unknown. Malvern was mentioned by John Evelyn in 1654. The Hotwells at Bristol were much frequented in the 'nineties, and a pump room was built in 1695. The bath at Matlock was built in about 1698. Buxton was recovering from the eclipse which it had suffered possibly as a result of its association with Mary Queen of Scots. Harrogate with its 'stinking waters' had more than twenty bathing houses, which were fully employed in the 'nineties. Scarborough, where Miss Fiennes found that all the diversion was walking on the sands, was greatly favoured by the gentry of the county and the citizens of York, and even by persons of quality from further afield.

The population of England and Wales in 1700 was about 5½ millions, of whom more than 600,000 lived in London. The population of Bath probably did not exceed 2,000. The other watering places were much smaller. Travel was slow and costly: at a time when the income of a squire was estimated to fall within the range of £280 to £450 a year the journey from London to Bath cost £1 5s., including living expenses, and took three days, 'if God permit'. During Queen Anne's visit to Bath some visitors paid a guinea a night for accommodation.

The number whom the spas could accommodate and the number who could afford to stay at them were thus both small. The fashionable watering places counted for little except in the lives of the highest strata of society. The lesser ones were frequented by the provincial gentry and the citizens from the immediate vicinity.

[1] Henri Misson, quoted by Lennard, 37.

For the rest of the community except in the special case of London they served only their primary purpose as a cure.

Yet, when every allowance has been made, there had been great progress, and the lines of future development had been laid down. The spas had emerged from obscurity. They enjoyed the confidence of the leading physicians, and in their new capacity as centres of social life the patronage of the Court and the nobility. They were small; their amenities were primitive; their entertainments were unorganized and not always entirely reputable. But they were advancing rapidly. It would be anachronistic to speak of them as holiday resorts, but they had an established place as resorts for pleasure as well as health. It was ill-defined as yet, but their future was assured.

II

AN AGE OF DIVERSION[1]

'An age of watering-places.' So the eighteenth century in England has been described by a modern historian.[2] The infant spas were growing into flourishing towns whose importance in social and cultural life was second only to that of London. Their significance in the lives of the articulate classes is shown by their extraordinary prominence—unparalleled before or since—in every branch of literature: and correspondence and memoir confirm the impression given by verse, fiction and drama. At the spas the plutocracy created by the overseas expansion of Britain intermingled with the landed aristocracy whose hegemony had been established by the Revolution of 1688; matchmaking mothers found husbands for their daughters, and impoverished gallants sought heiresses for wives; fortunes were won and lost at the gaming tables; aspirants to political and ecclesiastical preferment courted the favour of Ministers of State and Bishops; Grub Street waited on its patrons. 'One would think that the English

[1] 'It is an age of diversion, and not staying at their own habitations' (Gen. Hon. Sir Charles Howard to Lord Carlisle, July 1753, Hist. MSS. Comm. *Carlisle*, 207).

[2] R. B. Mowat, *England in the Eighteenth Century* (1932), 70.

were ducks; they are for ever waddling to the waters,' wrote Horace Walpole in 1790.[1]

In the seventeenth century the growth of the watering places had been haphazard and largely undirected. What they had to learn was that if the patronage of the fashionable pleasure seeker was first to be secured and then to be retained, the accommodation and amenities which they provided had to conform to his standards; and it is significant that it was not a Bath innkeeper or a Tunbridge tradesman who taught them this lesson but a man who, while he was professionally interested in the spas, also belonged to fashionable society.

Their teacher was Richard Nash. This odd man, so bizarre and yet so commonplace, left the stamp of his personality not only on Bath and Tunbridge Wells, at both of which he was Master of the Ceremonies, but on all the other resorts which looked to them as examples and recognized his suzerainty.

Great, however, as was Nash's personal contribution, the way had been prepared for him by others, and fortune was kind to him, not least in providing Goldsmith as his biographer. His work had been partially anticipated by enterprising individuals; the importance of making the most of the spa treatment had long been appreciated; at Bath itself after the triumphant successes of Queen Anne's visits in 1702 and 1703, a Master of the Ceremonies, Captain Webster, had been appointed with a view to the better organization of social life. This seems to have been the first appointment of the kind, and was directed to an object which Nash was to make pre-eminently his own.

[1] There is an extensive literature on the matters dealt with in this chapter. Lennard's essay on the watering places in *Englishmen at Rest and Play* (see above, p. 24) covers the first half of the eighteenth century; Barbeau, Melville and Barton continue to be useful; Goldsmith's *Life of Nash* is still the best account of Nash; and there are histories of most of the chief watering places. As for general literature, there is hardly a well-known eighteenth-century writer in whose works references to the spas will not be found, but special mention may be made of Horace Walpole's letters, the letters of Elizabeth Montagu, *Humphry Clinker*, Fanny Burney's *Evelina*, Sheridan's plays, and later of course the novels of Jane Austen.

Webster was killed in a duel in 1705. Nash, then just over thirty, and one of the needy adventurers and gamblers who were familiar at the spas, was appointed in his place. He already had a reputation as an organizer and as an eccentric. After a chequered career at Oxford, in the Army and at the Bar, in which despite a humble origin and chronic financial difficulties he contrived to obtain admission into the fashionable world, he had found his métier when he was asked by the Inner Temple to organize a pageant and revels in honour of the accession of William and Mary. He was so successful that, according to a story which may be apocryphal but is none the less illustrative, the King offered him a knighthood, and Nash replied: 'Please your Majesty, if you intend to make me a knight, I wish it may be one of your poor knights of Windsor, and then I shall have a fortune, at least able to support my title.' Nash's reputation as an eccentric, to which this episode, if it occurred, must have contributed, was established by his famous exploits of riding through a village naked on a cow, and standing outside York Minster clad only in a blanket for a wager of fifty pounds.

Nash was not a great man, but in a limited sphere he almost achieved greatness. Thanks to his eccentricity and his inside acquaintance with the fashionable world, he was able, with the collaboration of the citizens of Bath, who wisely deferred to his expert judgment, to accomplish what they could never have brought about unaided. He persuaded the Corporation to undertake the substantial expenditure necessary for the fuller development of the amenities of the city which had begun under Webster. In 1705 a somewhat primitive theatre had been built: within a few years an assembly room and pumproom were added, a London orchestra was installed, the lighting of the streets and the night watch were put in order, and a large sum of money raised at his instance to improve the Bath road, the wisest investment of all. Soon, thanks rather to men such as John Wood and Ralph Allen than to Nash himself, remarkable changes for the better began to be made in the public buildings and the accommodation for visitors; as for the details, carpets, wainscoting, better furnishings, marble slabs, and even, said Wood, chimney pieces were becoming common. The measure of the advance, in Wood's words, was that twenty-one years before he wrote in 1727, 'the best Chambers for Gentlemen were then just what the Garrets for Servants now are'.

Nash's own flair was shown to best advantage by the measures which he took to introduce discipline into the social life. Aided, as Goldsmith said, by 'a genteel address, much vivacity, some humour, and some wit' (the last two distinctly coarse), he waged war on the lax manners which were prevalent and set to work to establish the rules of good behaviour which were observed in London. For he saw that while the majority sought a change of air and environment they wanted no fundamental change in their mode of life.

'Mr. Nash . . . first taught the people of fashion how to buy their pleasures, and to procure that ease and felicity they sought for, without diminishing the happiness of others.'[1] This task required courage and determination. Without both Nash could not have imposed his will on the company and made himself an autocrat whose authority the most exalted did not challenge with impunity. He enforced his famous Rules[2] as sovereign laws at Bath and Tunbridge, and these, imitated elsewhere, shaped the life of all the English watering places, and contributed to a general improvement of manners. 'He was the first who diffused a desire of society, and an easiness of address among a whole people who were formerly censured by foreigners for a reservedness of behaviour, and an awkward timidity in their first approaches,' said Goldsmith with pardonable exaggeration.

It was chiefly as an organizer that Nash asserted himself. His originality lay not in the introduction of new pastimes or amusements, but in the introduction of some element of order into the anarchy which previously existed. He attacked and broke down social exclusiveness: he did his best to suppress irregularities in dress such as the wearing of boots by men and aprons by women on social occasions: he forbade duels and by forbidding the carrying of swords earned the praise of Lecky for setting in train a

[1] Burr, 112.

[2] These are reproduced in the note at the end of this chapter.

COMFORTS OF BATH—AN ASSEMBLY (*Rowlandson*)

salutary change of fashion which did not become general until about 1780.

Respectfully as well as ironically nicknamed 'King of Bath', Nash lived up to the title. 'His equipage was sumptuous,' said Goldsmith, 'and he usually travelled to *Tunbridge*, in a post chariot and six greys, with outriders, footmen, *French* horns, and every other appendage of expensive parade. He always wore a white hat, and, to apologize for this singularity, said, he did it purely to secure it from being stolen.' This parade of splendour may have been no more than an expression of Nash's vanity. There is no evidence that it had any deeper motive. Yet like his emphasis on order and discipline it showed a conscious or unconscious insight into his contemporaries, and corresponded to the curious craving for authority which in some matters characterized a professedly liberty-loving age.

It may seem strange that the social life of the spas should have been susceptible of organization down to points of detail. This is to be explained by the comparative fewness of the visitors, by the fact that they came on the whole from the same social milieu, and by the sociable character of their amusements; and it was a corollary of the existence of a master of ceremonies. They knew one another, and their favourite modes of entertainment were communal—dancing, music, gambling, conversation, party games. Hence there developed naturally a set routine whereby certain times were set aside for taking the waters, other for promenades, and others for assemblies. 'The course of Things is as mechanical as if it went by Clockwork.'[1] The eighteenth-century watering place may be likened in this respect rather to a cruising liner or a winter-sports hotel, where the company is small and self-contained, than to a modern seaside resort, where the individual is submerged in the multitude.

Nash's first rule was that the visitor should live in public, and newcomers were welcomed to Bath by a peal of the Abbey bells, for which they paid the ringers half a guinea,[2] and by 'the voice

[1] *English Magazine*, December 1737, quoted by Barbeau, 49.

[2] This was an old custom and was practised in the sixteenth century (James, 95).

and music' of the city waits, who received half a crown or more according to the stranger's fortune or generosity. The object of this custom was to introduce new arrivals, and, though disturbing to the sick, it was popular with the healthy. Its existence implied that every newcomer was acceptable and would participate in the social life of the company. The same assumption underlay the subscriptions expected of the visitor—two guineas towards the balls and music in the pumphouse, covering the cost of dance tickets for every ball night, five shillings, half a guinea or a guinea according to rank and quality for the privilege of walking in the private walks belonging to Simpson's assembly house, five shillings or half a guinea to a bookseller for borrowing books, and a subscription to a coffee house for pen, ink and paper. The ladies often subscribed to a lending library and to a reading-room of their own.

The day usually began with bathing in one of the five baths, the water in which was changed every morning. This lasted from six to nine a.m. Afterwards there was a general rendezvous at the pumphouse, where some drank the hot waters, and all talked and listened to the band. At one time it was customary to drink large quantities of the waters—two quarts, or 'eighteen pretty good glasses', a day; but medical opinion became more conservative and not more than a pint was usually recommended by the middle of the century. After visiting the baths, the ladies and gentlemen separated and went to their respective coffee houses to read the papers, to talk or to write until breakfast. As in London, there was considerable entertaining at breakfast, which was often taken at the assembly houses or at Spring Gardens on the opposite bank of the Avon, and the breakfast parties were sometimes enlivened by private concerts, lectures on artistic and scientific subjects, or dancing.

After breakfast came church, which was attended not only by the devout but by others for whom church attendance was a pleasant interlude occupied with conversation and other irreverent pursuits:

You all go to church upon hearing the bell;
Whether out of devotion yourselves can best tell.

There was always, however, a strong religious element, which increased after the Wesleys and the Countess of Huntingdon came to 'attack Satan at his headquarters'.

At noon the company appeared in public again, some promenading on the walks, visiting the milliners and toyshops, taking the air in coaches or on horseback, others reading or exchanging gossip in the bookshops, which next to the pumproom and the coffee houses were the most important meeting places. In the afternoon there was dinner, which was taken earlier than in London, followed by evening prayers and a second visit to the pumproom. A further promenade preceded tea at the assembly houses, and the evening would be spent at the theatre (which after a chequered early career became a nursery for the London stage), entertaining, visiting friends, gambling, or dancing. There were public balls twice weekly, and private balls on other evenings. Thus, said Goldsmith, Bath catered for all 'even from the libertine to the methodist', and 'the manner of spending the day there must amuse any, but such as disease or spleen had made uneasy to themselves'.

Of the other spas—apart from the many with no social pretensions—it may be said that, as J. Melford remarked of Harrogate in *Humphry Clinker* (1771), 'they trod upon the heels of Bath in the articles of gaiety and dissipation—with this difference, however, that here we are more sociable and familiar'; and that, as Lord Verulam observed of Clifton in 1769, 'the method of spending time here is so much the same with that of other places that I shall not think it necessary to give a description of it'.[1] There were minor differences, but the spirit was essentially the same. Though smaller and quieter, Tunbridge Wells most nearly resembled Bath, and Nash, taking advantage of the fact that the season was in the summer when Bath was out of season, accepted an invitation to become Master of the Ceremonies in 1735. The other spas tended to be more provincial.[2] The difference showed

[1] Hist. MSS. Comm. *Verulam*, 250.

[2] Cf. the lines written on a pane of glass at Malvern Wells, May 1776, quoted by John Chambers, *A General History of Malvern* (1897), 282.

Ye nymphs oppress'd by Worcester's stagnant air,
To Malvern's high aerial walks repair.

itself in plainer living, less formality, and lower prices. 'There is a certain rural plainness and freedom mixed, which are vastly pleasing.'[1] The distinction was of degree rather than of kind, and it diminished as time passed.

It is difficult to assess the importance which still attached to the cure. There was always a nucleus of unmistakable invalids—'wretched beings, some with half their limbs, some with none, the ingredients of Pandora's box *personifié*, who stalk about, half-living remembrances of mortality, and by calling themselves human, ridicule the species more than Swift's Yahoos'.[2] There were others whose ailments were less easy to specify—'*bon-vivants* with decayed stomachs, green-sickness virgins, unfruitful or miscarrying wives'.[3] For the majority, however, said Defoe in 1724, 'the coming to the Wells to drink the Waters was a mere Matter of Custom; some drink, more do not, and few drink physically. But Company and Diversion is, in short, the main business of the Place.' There were always some sceptics, like Matthew Bramble, who, doubtless expressing Smollett's own views, questioned whether the curative quality of the waters was not more than counteracted by the contamination due to their use by sufferers from unclean and infectious diseases. And there were many who thought with Lord Boyle, 'Under the Rose, I believe the renowned Wells are not of any great use. We are ordered down here commonly *pour la Maladie Imaginaire*, for the spirits and the melancholy to which our whole Nation are too subject. The Diversions and Amusements of the Place send us home again chearfull, and the foggy Air of London with the Common Disappointments of Life urge our Return the following Year.'[4] 'Half of us come here to cure the bodily evils occasioned by laziness,' wrote Mrs. Montagu from Tunbridge Wells in 1749, 'the other half to remedy the mental disease of idleness and inoccupation, called *l'ennui*'.[5]

[1] Quoted by J. S. Fletcher, *Harrogate and Knaresborough* (1920), 81.

[2] John Lord Hervey, 1728, quoted by Mrs. Stone, *Chronicles of Fashion* (1845), II, 286–7.

[3] Dr. Arbuthnot to Lady Suffolk, 6th July 1731, quoted by Melville, *Royal Tunbridge Wells*, 173.

[4] Lord Boyle to Mrs. Salkeld, 29th July 1728 (Melville, 169).

[5] Mrs. E. Montagu to her husband, 1749 (Melville, 198–9).

Fashion was the main motive force. 'Bon Ton,' said a newspaper in 1787, was 'Bath: for not to have been at Bath is not *bon ton*'.[1] Spa life was London life in another environment. 'Now the squire's lady comes from whisk in assemblies, miss from Ranelagh, and the bonne bourgeoise from Marybone Gardens,' 'it is but the same scene on another stage,' wrote Mrs. Montagu in 1754.[2]

In these circumstances those were right who feared that the intrusion of the socially undesirable would ultimately bring disaster. The future of the spas as fashionable pleasure resorts depended on the continued participation of all the visitors in the necessarily intimate social life.

In practice, however, it was impossible to exclude the less desirable elements who waited or preyed upon good society, and the parvenus who missed no opportunity of gatecrashing into it. The attention which these elements attracted was disproportionate to their numbers but they were numerous enough to be a serious danger. At the extremes of respectability, they included at the one end ambitious doctors and clergymen, eager to establish themselves in the great world, literary men, artists, actors and musicians, sedulous to cultivate their patrons, and wealthy tradesmen and Colonials, anxious to improve their social status, and at the other end sharpers, pickpockets, procurers and other adventurers. There were some Continental visitors, and all nationalities were represented, 'Hungarians, Italians, French, Portuguese, Irish and Scotch', not to mention 'a great many Jews, with worse countenances than our friend Pontius Pilate, in a bad tapestry hanging'.[3]

Smollett had no mercy upon the intruders. On the occasion of the Melfords' visit, the company at Bath was decidedly mixed. An eminent cowkeeper of Tottenham had arrived to drink the waters for indigestion. A mulatto heiress, a broken-winded Wapping landlady, a brandy merchant, and a paralytic attorney from Shoelane mixed without distinction of rank or fortune with Ministers

[1] Mrs. Stone, II, 290.

[2] Mrs. Montagu to her husband, 30th August 1754 (Melville, 213-14).

[3] Mrs. Montagu to the Duchess of Portland, 27th August 1745 (Melville, 176).

of State, Judges, Generals, and Bishops. Ill-gotten wealth attracted by the opportunity of mixing with birth was represented by 'clerks and factors from the East Indies, loaded with the spoil of plundered provinces; planters, negro drivers, and hucksters, from our American plantations, enriched, they know not how; agents, commissaries, and contractors, who have fattened, in two successive wars, on the blood of the nation; usurers, brokers, and jobbers of every kind'. The same point was made more sympathetically by Benge Burr. At Tunbridge Wells, 'an attentive listener to the several parties would this moment fancy himself at the royal-exchange, and the next at the palace; now at an Indian factory, or an American plantation, and then with the thrifty citizen securing a plum, or the country gentleman improving an estate; this instant on board the fleet in the ocean, or with the brave and generous Granby pursuing victory in Germany, and then in the twinkling of an eye you are wafted from the rough hoarse voice of war to the broken accents and tender warblings of love'.

The watering places performed a useful function in easing the entry of successful members of the middle classes into good society, but their capacity was limited. Nash was able to welcome each arrival in person, and the number of visitors to Bath in a season was variously estimated at 12,000 individuals, 8,000 families, and 8,000 individuals. The other spas were still small in comparison. In 1785, there were about ninety lodging houses in Tunbridge Wells, some of which were split into smaller apartments. Cheltenham in 1760 consisted of two or three hundred houses; at the time of George III's visit in 1788 it was 'almost all one street', and there were 374 visitors in 1780, 1,140 in 1786, and 1,320 in 1787. There were about two hundred houses at Clifton in the middle 'sixties. About a thousand names were given in a list of visitors to Scarborough in 1733. Smollett in *Humphry Clinker* referred to five inns at Harrogate, one with fifty guests and another with thirty-six. At Matlock in the middle of the century all the company breakfasted, dined and supped together in one room; at Great Malvern in 1758 there was one lodging house, with accommodation for fifteen persons; and there were three inns at Buxton in the 'eighties.

A social life so intimate as this could not long survive the intrusion of outsiders in any numbers. The watering places were capable of much further expansion, but the price was inevitably the loss of the exclusiveness on which Nash had set such store, and hence a change in character which boded decay sooner or later. With their invasion by the middle classes the time is approaching when it will be possible to speak of holiday resorts in something like the modern sense. As long as visits to the spas were confined to the leisured it is difficult to regard them as holidays—they were rather phases in the social routine like Ascot and Goodwood in the life of London Society to-day—but when they were made by City merchants and professional men as breaks in the routine of counting house and office they at last began to assume the character of holidays properly so called.[1]

NOTE

Nash's Rules are so revealing that it has seemed worth while to reproduce them in full. Goldsmith says that they were first promulgated in 1707, and they are so much in character that there seems no reason to doubt his statement that Nash wrote them himself. The heading will be noted.

By General Consent Determin'd

1. That a Visit of Ceremony at coming to Bath and another at going away, is all that is expected or desired, by Ladies of Quality and Fashion,—except Impertinents.
2. That Ladies coming to the Ball appoint a Time for their Footmens coming to wait on them Home, to prevent Disturbances and Inconveniences to Themselves and Others.
3. That Gentlemen of Fashion never appearing in a Morning

[1] The leisured also of course spent part of the year on their estates in the country, and in the case of public men and others who had duties to perform in London the return to the country after the season served to some extent the same purpose as the modern summer holiday.

COMFORTS OF BATH—THE BALL (*Rowlandson*)

before the Ladies in Gowns and Caps, shew Breeding and Respect.

4. That no Person take it ill that any one goes to another's Play, or Breakfast, and not their's;—except Captious by Nature.

5. That no Gentleman give his ticket for the Balls to any but Gentlewomen. N.B. Unless he has none of his Acquaintance.

6. That Gentlemen crowding before the Ladies at the Ball, shew ill Manners; and that none do so for the Future;—except such as respect nobody but Themselves.

7. That no Gentleman or Lady takes it ill that another Dances before them;—except such as have no Pretence to dance at all.

8. That the Elder Ladies and Children be content with a Second Bench at the Ball, as being past, or not come to Perfection.

9. That the younger Ladies take notice how many Eyes observe them. N.B. This does not extend to the *Have—at—alls*.

10. That all Whisperers of Lies and Scandal, be taken for their Authors.

11. That all Repeaters of such Lies and Scandal be shun'd by all Company;—except such as have been guilty of the same Crime.

N.B. SEVERAL Men of no Character, Old Women and Young Ones of Questioned Reputation, are great Authors of Lies in this place, being of the Sect of Levellers.

III

THE RUSH INTO THE SEA

Your prudent grandmammas, ye modern belles,
Content with Bristol, Bath and Tunbridge Wells,
When health required it would consent to roam,
Else more attached to pleasures found at home.
But now alike, gay widow, virgin, wife,
Ingenious to diversify dull life,
In coaches, chaises, caravans, and hoys,
Fly to the coast for daily, nightly joys,
And all, impatient of dry land, agree
With one consent to rush into the sea.

—COWPER, *Retirement* (1782)

The latter years of Nash's long life were the midday of the history of the English spas. Though many years of greatness still lay before them, the shadows were lengthening. Their ascendancy was soon to be challenged and then to be overthrown by the insignificant fishing villages, decayed seaports and uninhabited seaside heaths to which visitors were already beginning to flock in pursuance of the new fashion for seabathing.[1]

[1] For the best account of the early phases of the movement described in this chapter see the essay by Lennard in *Englishmen at Rest and Play*. Otherwise there are virtually no secondary authorities except histories of particular resorts, as to which reference should be made to the Bibliography.

It might be thought that in a maritime nation bathing would have been a popular sport from early times. But, though the value of swimming as a personal precaution and for military purposes was recognized, the prejudice against bathing on moral grounds, which went back to the excesses associated with it in the Roman Empire, was slow to disappear, and it was discountenanced as a pursuit for pleasure at least until the Stuart period. In the sixteenth century, the penalty for a Cambridge undergraduate who bathed in any river, pool, or other water in the county was a double flogging for a first offence and expulsion for a second.

This lingering inhibition did not long survive the Restoration. Bathing in pools and rivers became more common, and there arose a school of medical opinion which advocated cold bathing as a cure, irrespective in some cases of the mineral properties of the waters used. That it was influential is shown by the erection of cold baths at various watering places, including Bath itself, but, ironically, its chief importance was that it prepared the way for the discovery of the seaside, and hence ultimately for the decline of the spas. Sir John Floyer, with whose name the cold-bathing school is usually coupled, went so far in anticipating the future as to point out in his *History of Cold Bathing*, which, first published in 1702, had reached its fifth edition by 1722, that 'since we live on an Island, and have the Sea about us, we cannot want an excellent Cold Bath, which will both preserve our Healths, and cure many Diseases, as our Fountains do'. In a previous work, *An Enquiry into the Right Use and Abuses of the Hot, Cold, and Temperate Baths in England* (1697), which was written with special reference to Buxton, 'the most Excellent, Temperate, and safe Cool Bath in *England*', Floyer had listed seawater baths as the most common 'salso-acid Baths', and had mentioned a number of conditions for which they were valuable—ulcers, scabs, scaled heads, itching and leprosy, corns, tumours, pains of the limbs, hydrophobia, all inflammations, all catarrhal effects, nephritis, gonorrhoea, arthritis and many others. And he even said that for drinking as well as bathing 'the Sea-Water will yield the best salt *Bath*'.

There were other pointers in the same direction. In the sixteen-twenties an artificial bath of sea water sodden with herbs was advised for those who were too poor or too sick to come to Bath itself.[1] Seabathing was orthodox treatment for melancholia and hydrophobia. It was recommended for gout by Dr. Wittie, the author of *Scarborough Spa* (1667), but as a seaside practitioner he is necessarily suspect. Evidently, however, the time was not ripe for Sir John Floyer's forecast to be realized. Special fears continued to be entertained of the 'saline effluvia', and in the seventeenth century seabathing did not establish itself either as a cure or a pastime. Why is not clear, but one reason was no doubt the adequacy of the newly discovered inland watering places to satisfy a still restricted demand.

The first references to seabathing resorts do not occur until the seventeen-thirties, and it is noteworthy that the earliest to be mentioned was Scarborough, which was already established as a spa. It was described as the custom for both ladies and gentlemen to bathe in the sea, the former from dressing-rooms, the latter naked from boats. The well-known engraving by Setterington gives a vivid impression of Scarborough in 1736, with the company parading on foot, on horseback, in carriages, in sedan chairs, and the bathers in the sea; while Chesterfield, who stayed there in 1733—at the time of the controversy over Walpole's excise scheme—referred to an alleged proposal to tax seabathing on the ground that it had become the general practice of both sexes. 'The people of this town are at present in great consternation, upon a report they have heard from London, which, if true, they think will ruin them. I confess I do not believe it; not but that there is something probable enough in it. They are informed that, considering the vast consumption of these waters [the spa waters] there is a design laid of *excising* them next session; and moreover, that as bathing in the sea is become the general practice of both sexes; and as the Kings of England have always been allowed to be masters of the sea, every person so bathing shall be gauged, and pay so much per foot square as their cubical bulk amounts to.'

Contemporaneously, a regular bathing season was starting at

[1] James, 128.

the little fishing village of Brighthelmstone (as Brighton was commonly called until the nineteenth century). Other places visited for the sake of seabathing in the first half of the century included Deal, Eastbourne, Portsmouth and Exmouth. Living was cheap, and life was simple. Two parlours and two bedrooms with other rooms could be rented at Brighton for five shillings a week, and the following extract from a letter written in July 1736 gives a charming picture of how the time was spent: 'We are now sunning ourselves on the beach, at Brighthelmstone. . . . My morning business is bathing in the sea, and then buying fish; the evening is, riding out for air; viewing the remains of old Saxon camps; and counting the ships in the road, and the boats that are trauling.'[1]

Yet the baby seaside resorts were not to be compared with the inland watering places, and sea water had an entirely subordinate role in medical practice. Hence Dr. Richard Russell's famous *Dissertation on the Use of Sea Water in the Diseases of the Glands, particularly the Scurvy, Jaundice, King's Evil, Leprosy, and the Glandular Consumption*, which was published in 1752,[2] came upon the public with all the advantages of apparent novelty.

Russell, who was a fashionable London physician, advocated the internal and external use of sea water for the same purposes as the spa waters. The sea, he said, with its four principal qualities, Saltness, Bitterness, Nitrosity, and Unctuosity, or Oilyness, seemed to have been designed by the 'omniscient Creator of all Things' as 'a Kind of common Defence against the Corruption and Putrefaction of Bodies'. It was particularly efficacious against '*the Consumption* which greatly afflicts our Island, and in the Cure of which, our Physicians find the greatest Difficulty', and by its assistance it was possible to relieve 'the Disorders of the internal Glands, and seasonably procure a Remedy in the *Beginning* of this most Dangerous Disease; and preserve the Lungs, that noble Part, from an Impostume'. He had found that it was effective against cirrhosis, leprosy, scrofula, gonorrhoea, scurvy, dropsy and other diseases, and he supported his thesis with judiciously chosen passages from the ancient physicians. Gout was, inevitably, another

[1] J. Evans, *An Excursion to Brighton, etc.* (1821), 37.

[2] It had been published in Latin in 1750.

A

DISSERTATION

On the USE of

SEA-WATER

IN THE

DISEASES of the GLANDS.

PARTICULARLY

The *Scurvy*, *Jaundice*, *King's-Evil*, *Leprosy*, and the *Glandular Consumption*.

Translated from the *Latin* of

RICHARD RUSSEL, M. D.

The THIRD EDITION, Revised and Corrected.

To which is added,

A COMMENTARY on SEA-WATER,

Translated from the *Latin* of

J. SPEED, M. D.

Both by an EMINENT PHYSICIAN.

LONDON:

Printed for W. OWEN, at *Homer*'s Head, *Temple-Bar*.

MDCCLV.

condition for which it was specially recommended. Indeed, like the spa waters, it was regarded as a panacea. 'Were I to enumerate half the diseases which are every day cured by seabathing', wrote young Melford in *Humphry Clinker*, 'you might justly say you had received a treatise, instead of a letter.'

Russell's work was timely. Four editions were called for by 1760, and:

> *Then all, with ails in heart and lungs,*
> *In liver or in spine,*
> *Rush'd coastward to be cured like tongues,*
> *By dipping into brine.*[1]

Yet it would be wrong to ascribe to Russell the main responsibility for the popularity of the seaside. As we have seen, seabathing had been practised for some time, and it was Scarborough, the only spa which was also on the coast, which was chiefly associated with the new pursuit. Floyer and his followers had prepared the way by their advocacy of the cold-water cure, and Floyer himself had foreseen to what this would lead. The search for mineral waters was continuous, and it was inevitable that sooner or later the most abundant of all the mineral waters should be discovered as such. 'Sea water is in fact a *mineral water* to all intents and purposes,' said Dr. A. B. Granville, the leading authority on the spas in the middle of the next century, and Russell and his contemporaries looked upon it in the same light. Russell was the owner of a mineral spring at Hove, and in a later edition of his work he included an 'Account of the Nature, Properties and Uses of all the remarkable Mineral Waters of Great Britain'.

The popularity of the seaside was thus a natural consequence of that of the spas, and Russell's contribution was to add impetus to a process which had already begun. The scientific merit of his work was slight, and in so far as it was original—in his emphasis on the internal use of sea water—its effect was on balance harmful.

[1] Stone, II, 271.

In the circumstances it is understandable that the new resorts should not have been thought to constitute a serious threat to the inland watering places. There were some who considered that the vogue for the seaside would pass—'while this practice prevails', said Matthew Bramble—but even if it had come to stay the spas were so firmly established that they seemed to have little to fear from the upstart fishing villages with their mean streets, humble lodgings in fishermen's cottages, and crude and unorganized social life. 'As to the lodgings in this place,' wrote a visitor to Brighton in 1763 in language which recalls early accounts of Bath, 'the best are most execrable, and what you would find now, I believe, not habitable.'[1] Benge Burr, writing at about the same time, welcomed the improvement of the communications between Brighton and Tunbridge on the ground that 'as Tunbridge has confessedly the advantage of her rival in every respect, she cannot suffer, but must, on the whole, be an infinite gainer by such a close comparison as will, while it sets off her perfections to the greatest advantage, make her adversary's deficiencies but the more conspicuous'.

Burr protested too much. The truth was that the advantages of the inland watering places over their 'adversaries' were superficial, and the deficiencies of the seaside resorts could be quickly remedied. Adequate for the needs of a privileged minority, and reflecting in their highly organized and confined social life the tastes of this narrow section, the spas depended for their prosperity on the monopoly of a limited number of mineral springs, and they were inadequate to meet the rising demand which resulted from the expansion of trade and industry. The capacity of the sea coast, on the other hand, was unbounded. While social life at the spas was necessarily focused on the pumproom and baths, and there was no satisfactory alternative to living in public, the sea coast was large enough to absorb all comers, and social homogeneity mattered less. Also important in weighting the balance was the reaction in the second half of the century against the ordered conception of life of which the spas under Nash were an expression.[2] Nash himself was not taken seriously in his later

[1] Melville, 25. [2] For a fuller account of the causes of the ascendancy of the seaside, see Chapter VI.

years and in 1749 was said to have lost 'most of his power and prerogative':[1] his successors such as Samuel Derrick were derided rather than obeyed, and before long two rival Masters of Ceremonies competed at Bath. Dyarchy succeeded monarchy, a sure sign of decline. The fashion for mountain scenery was one symptom of the change. The fashion for the sea with all its turbulence and majesty was another.

At first, however, love of the sea as such does not seem to have been an important factor. Visitors came to the seaside for the same reasons as to the spas, and amongst them health and pleasure are not easily disentangled. There were three ways in which the health might be benefited—'in air, drinking the water, and bathing. Some use all three, but all use the first.'[2] All these methods of restoring health had been used at the spas. This is obvious as regards drinking and bathing. As for air, Benge Burr devoted a chapter to the air of Tunbridge Wells, adducing as 'solid proof of its sweetness and purity' 'the multitude of sweet herbs, as wild thyme etc., with which the whole country is overspread'. He thought that the importance of good air was self-evident. 'Air is undoubtedly such a necessary instrument of life, that without it we cannot subsist for more than a few moments; and it is very obvious to every reflective mind, that, where it is impregnated with undue mixtures, it must of course produce, or aggravate diseases.'

The continuity with the spas is also illustrated by the extravagance of the claims which were made on behalf of the sea water and in particular by the faith which under the influence of Russell was placed in its internal use. There were authoritative stories of the almost miraculous cures which were effected. The blind regained their sight; cripples threw away their crutches; the paralytic were made whole.

Some of these stories were doubtless well founded. Faith is a

[1] Mrs. Montagu to the Duchess of Portland (Hist. MSS. Comm. *Bath*, I. 331).

[2] W. Hutton, *History of Blackpool*, 23. In 1773 Chatham described the air at Lyme Regis as 'the purest he ever breathed'; he had gone there for the health of the younger Pitt (C. Wanklyn, *Lyme Regis* (1922), 98).

great healer, and in minor disorders the unpleasantness of the remedy was naturally conducive to speedy recovery. The drinking of sea water is said, not surprisingly, to have caused great thirst and nausea, and some stomachs were too weak to take it at all. It may have been for such as these that the admixture of new milk was recommended as an alternative to administration neat. Certainly the quantities which were sometimes drunk must have had a disturbing effect even on the strongest stomachs. One prescription was twenty-five gallons at a pint a day, and a visitor to Lyme Regis in 1791 recorded that many people went down to the beach three or four times in as many hours and drank a pint on each occasion.[1] Sea water was used as a purgative: it also acted as an emetic. Like the spa waters before it, it was bottled and sold in London, and Russell gave a recipe for making it artificially by dissolving bay salt, or common salt and Epsom salts, in soft water.

But it was with bathing that the seaside was chiefly associated, and it was usual to speak of 'seabathing' resorts. The value which was attached to seabathing by the medical profession is illustrated by the establishment at Margate in 1796 of the Royal Sea Bathing Infirmary, which was a specialist hospital where poor patients could take the sea-water cure. As with the drinking, there developed a code of rules by which its use was governed. It was considered advantageous to bathe before breakfast; the reduction of the system by powerful aperients beforehand was recommended; bathing in winter was thought to be specially efficacious, though for some complaints warm baths were advised; and it was regarded as preferable to use towels which had been dipped in sea water and dried, 'as by this simple expedient, the saline particles are less likely to be entirely removed from the skin, than by the means usually employed'.[2]

While, however, the belief in seabathing as an aid to health was important, its chief importance in the life of the resorts was social. Like the pumproom at the spa, the beach was the focus of the activities of the visitors, and bathing was the activity in which all

[1] James Lackington, *Memoirs* (1791), 333. Wanklyn, 136–7.

[2] W. Harwood, *On the Curative Influence of the Southern Coast of England; especially that of Hastings* (1828), 73.

were interested even if all did not take part. Indeed the majority of the ladies were probably never more than spectators, and, since seabathing was English in origin, it is curious to find the English criticized in the eighteen-forties for their lack of a propensity for bathing, particularly in the sea, 'for which they have such ample means. Their propensity is not that way; or, at all events, it is, as compared to the *balneomania* of the Parisians for domestic baths, and of the continental nations dwelling near the seashore for sea-bathing, very greatly inferior.'[1]

Hence the importance of that odd invention, the bathing machine, the object of which was to protect modesty against the too inquisitive eyes of the company, who turned out in full force to watch the bathers. It made an early appearance on the seaside scene. There is a machine in Setterington's picture of Scarborough; Russell mentioned 'bathing chariots'; Bishop Pococke saw bathing carriages at Margate and Brighton in the 'fifties; and it is probable that Benjamin Beale of Margate, to whom the invention of the bathing machine has been attributed, was the inventor only of the canvas screens or umbrellas which were fitted at some places. These led from the machine to the water, thus concealing the bather from observation until he had taken the plunge, and enabling the pleasure and advantages of seabathing to be enjoyed in a manner 'consistent with the most refined delicacy'.[2] Men bathed naked, women frequently did so, and by the use of the bathing machine it was possible, as a later writer said, for both sexes to 'enjoy the renovating waters of the ocean; the one without any violation of public decency, and the other safe from the gaze of idle vulgar curiosity'.[3] As a further precaution mixed bathing was usually forbidden. Rules that men must not go on the beach during the time set apart for the ladies to bathe—at Blackpool the penalty was a bottle of wine—provided yet another safeguard for

[1] A. B. Granville, *The Spas of England and Principal Sea-Bathing Places* (1841), II, 9.

[2] W. C. Oulton, *Picture of Margate* (1820), 53. At Brighton, unlike Weymouth, Margate and Scarborough, the bathing machines were without awnings.

[3] Kidd's *Picturesque Companion* (?1840), 81.

female delicacy. The nature of the penalty at Blackpool is an illustration of the sociable character of the occasion.

Fashioned in the image of Bath and Tunbridge Wells, the seaside resorts developed at first on parallel lines. The patronage of royalty played an analogous part in their history. They were mainly frequented by the same class of visitor. The stamp of Nash was upon them. With their assembly rooms, subscription balls, promenades, circulating libraries, orchestras, scientific and literary lectures, the new watering places imitated the old. Strict rules governed dancing and cardplaying, and a Master of the Ceremonies often presided over the entertainments. Brighton openly modelled itself on Tunbridge Wells. Like Tunbridge Wells it shared for a time the same Master of the Ceremonies as Bath, and took over some of the characteristic customs of both places such as the ringing of bells to greet newcomers. William Hutton proposed a set of seven Rules for the 'infant commonwealth' of Blackpool, the first of which required every visitor to register his name, 'as at Buxton', and subscribe a shilling. As late as 1820 the Master of the Ceremonies at Margate, in the true Nash tradition, was to be found entreating the ladies to enter their names and addresses at the libraries so that he might take an early opportunity of being introduced to them and be enabled 'to pay every individual that attention which it is not less his inclination than his duty to observe'. At Margate at the same time there were public breakfasts sometimes attended by as many as 800 persons.[1]

Brighton, owing to its accessibility from London, the special favour in which it was held by Russell, its natural advantages, the enterprise of its inhabitants, and a fair share of good fortune, quickly established for itself a pre-eminence amongst seaside resorts which was nearly as marked as that of Bath amongst the spas. In 1760, when it consisted of six streets, it was still primarily a fishing port looking back to happier days, for the passing of which the new summer visitors appeared to offer but little compensation:

[1] Oulton, 36–8, and *passim*. Margate in 1820 shared the services of a Master of the Ceremonies with Ramsgate and Broadstairs. There was a Master of the Ceremonies at Aberystwyth in 1833 (S. Lewis, *A Topographical Dictionary of Wales* (1833)).

by the end of the century it was a flourishing and cosmopolitan pleasure resort with fifteen streets and some 7,000 inhabitants, about double the population as recently as 1780 and nearly three times what it had been in 1770. The 'sixties and 'seventies had seen the provision of accommodation suitable for 'the concourse of people who come to it to bathe and to drink the sea waters, under the persuasion that the water is better here than at other places, concerning which a treatise has been written by Dr. Russell'. New property had sprung up and old property had been renovated, one of the finest public rooms in England was built, and in 1765 there came the first royal visitor in the person of the Duke of Gloucester.

The next and most resplendent phase in the history of Brighton began with a short stay by the Prince of Wales in 1783, followed by a longer one in 1784 when he took a course of seabathing for glandular trouble. Subsequently he paid regular visits, bringing with him smart folk of many nationalities, whose extravagant habits made Brighton a byword for fast living: in their train came criminal and semi-criminal elements, and the *corps d'amour* was fully represented.[1] 'Between 1788 and 1823 Brighton', according to Miss Barton and Mr. Sitwell, 'was, no doubt, the gayest, most fashionable place not only in England, but in all Europe.' Be this as it may, it was certainly the gayest and most fashionable place in England.

'Morning rides, champagne, dissipation, noise and nonsense,' said the *Morning Post* in July 1785, 'jumble these phrases together and you have a complete account of all that's passing at Brighthelmstone.' Already before the Revolution members of the French aristocracy were coming over for the races; and a local newspaper claimed that it was 'the center *luminary* of the *system* of pleasure'.[2] The tone was set by the Prince, whose grotesque Pavilion, begun in 1784 and added to at great expense over the years, reflected the eccentricity and uncertainty of his tastes. He took the leading part in the whirl of events which made up the season, the military

[1] *Morning Post*, 4th August 1785. Quoted in Y. Cloud, *Beside the Seaside* (1934), 72.

[2] Quoted by J. Ashton, *Florizel's Folly* (1899), 66.

pageants, the races and prizefights, the balls, the banquets, the escapades of all kinds for which the 'dandies' were notorious. Yet there was always another side to Brighton life, represented by the genuine invalids and by such visitors as William Pitt, Burke, and Lord Mansfield. The town was more than Vanity Fair. It was taking the place of Bath as the chief centre of fashion outside London, and the speed of its advance is witnessed by the rapid rise in the charges for accommodation. Whereas in 1785 a single room could be had for a guinea a week, two beds and a dining-room and parlour for three guineas, and a house on the Steyne for eight or ten guineas, the charges in 1796 were said to range from 2s. 6d. a night for a stable to £20 a week.

Great though Brighton's debt to the Prince Regent was, its other advantages would probably have sufficed to make it the leading seaside resort. Weymouth, on the other hand, might well have remained insignificant but for the patronage of the King. It had a valuable asset in its fine sandy beach, but its distance from London was a serious drawback. The inhabitants were, therefore, wise in according an enthusiastic reception to the King on his first visit in 1784. Every child, as Fanny Burney recorded, wore a bandeau with the slogan 'God save the King'. The same loyal slogan appeared on cockades worn by the boatmen, on the girdles of the bathing women, on almost every shop and house, and in golden letters on most of the bathing machines. And when the King bathed, his machine was followed into the sea by another filled with fiddlers, who played the national anthem as he took the plunge. The reward for these demonstrations of loyalty came in regular visits by the King, followed in due course by the much prized grant of permission to add 'Regis' to the name of the town.

These were the outstanding instances of royal patronage, but there were others of lesser importance. A visit by the King in 1791 started a minor vogue for the village of Sidmouth. Worthing, hitherto consisting of a few miserable cottages, owed much to visits at the end of the century by Princess Amelia, the Princess of Wales and Princess Charlotte. Southend leapt into temporary fashion after the royal physicians sent the five-year-old Princess Charlotte there in 1801.

On the whole royal favour was responsible only for transitory deflections of the stream of fashion. The most important permanent factor was proximity to London. With a few exceptions the largest resorts were in Kent and Sussex. Of these the most interesting in a number of respects were Margate and Ramsgate, which could be reached from London by boat, and hence were accessible to sections of the London population which could not afford other means of travel. Except Gravesend and the London spas—possibly, too, late seventeenth-century Epsom—Margate and Ramsgate were the first resorts which were popular in the strict sense of the word, and it is significant that the reason should have been ease of communications. It was for the same reason that they had been amongst the earliest seaside places to be frequented, and though Margate could do no better for a royal patron than the poor discredited Duke of Cumberland, it quickly established itself in fashionable favour. In 1769 the fine new Assembly Room, the largest building of its kind, had a subscription list of 930 at 5s. a head, and in 1791 numbers of the nobility were said to visit the town in the bathing season. At the same time the famous Margate 'hoys', which were primarily cargo boats but carried some passengers, did 'incredible business', landing 18,000 people in 1800. But at first at least persons of wealth were not deterred. In 1807 Margate and Ramsgate were mentioned with Brighton as the places to which rich Londoners who had no country seats retired during the summer; and in 1823 Cobbett was no less scornful of Margate than of Brighton and Cheltenham and dismissed it as a settlement of 'stockjobbing cuckolds'.

Of the other South Coast resorts, the most important at the end of the century were Worthing and Hastings, both of them rising rapidly. The rest were none of them of particular note. They included Dover, Deal, Folkestone, Seaford, Portsmouth, Lymington and Southampton. The Isle of Wight was beginning to be discovered, and its inhabitants were found to be civil and hospitable;[1] Bognor, at first called Hothampton after the London hatter Sir Richard Hotham who developed it, is of interest as an early though abortive experiment in planning.

[1] J. Hassell, *Tour of the Isle of Wight* (1790).

Farther west only Weymouth was of national importance. Lyme Regis, later to be immortalized by Jane Austen's *Persuasion*, owed a transient prosperity chiefly to being connected with the main London to Exeter road in 1757 and with Bath in 1770. The South Devon watering places, Sidmouth, Exmouth, Dawlish, Teignmouth and Torquay, were small and mainly frequented by the local gentry and the richer citizens of Exeter. Exmouth seems to have been the first to be visited and Teignmouth the first to be fashionable, but both were soon to be outstripped by Torquay, whose fame dates from the Napoleonic period, when it was a rendezvous of the Fleet.

North Devon, where Ilfracombe consisted of one street in 1810, Somerset, where at the same time a speculative innkeeper was beginning to develop Weston-super-Mare, and Wales, where the chief seaside resorts, Swansea and Aberystwyth, were both insignificant, were but little known as yet to visitors from other parts of the country. Cornwall, which was accessible only by packhorse, was almost like a foreign country, and in 1803 a Cornishman in London found himself exhibited 'as a kind of outlandish curiosity'.[1]

In the north-west, Southport in 1800 consisted of little more than an inn and a bathing hut, both erected in the 'nineties. Blackpool, however, had been one of the earliest of the seaside resorts, and though still a village, was described with some justification as a 'celebrated watering place' by Joseph Aston in his *Lancashire Gazetteer* in 1808. A boarding house had been opened in 1750. A contemporary print shows six hotels or boarding houses on the cliffs in 1784. In August 1788 the company was estimated at four hundred, and the amenities included a theatre in a barn, diminutive bowling greens, and 'butts for bow-shooting', an odd reminiscence of the early days of the spas. Prices were low, and, according to several authorities, some of the visitors were working people.

The east coast resorts were overshadowed by Scarborough, which was the northern equivalent of both Bath and Brighton, and long remained a hybrid. Though it had been the first sea-

[1] A. K. H. Jenkin, *Cornwall and the Cornish* (1933), 180.

bathing resort, two visitors in the 'sixties mentioned the great numbers who flocked to the chalybeate spring but did not refer to the seabathing,[1] and Sheridan in 1777 still spoke of 'this northern spa' in *A Trip to Scarborough*. With its excellent theatre, its two assembly rooms, its numerous bathing machines, its circulating library of four thousand books, its spa and its fine sands, it was handsomely equipped, and could bear comparison with the great resorts of the south. Its neighbours, Redcar, Whitby and Coatham, were of purely local importance. In Lincolnshire there was Freestone Shore, which enjoyed a certain popularity amongst the farmers and townspeople of the county; in Norfolk Cromer already had a reputation for being select; and nearest to London on the east was Southend, which with what were charmingly described as 'its terraqueous beauties' was an asylum to 'the lovers of quiet and retirement'.[2] For a time it was highly fashionable, but unluckily—as readers of *Emma* (1815) may recall—it had a reputation for being damp and promoting agues and fevers.

The century ended with the seaside resorts at much the same stage in their development as the inland watering places at the beginning of the century. There was no longer any doubt that they had come to stay. Like the Cross Bath in 1700, they were more 'fam'd for Pleasure than Cures'. Though obviously derivative from the spas they had distinctive features of their own which were increasingly to mark them off from their parents. Yet Brighton—which stood to the other seaside resorts in the same relationship as a hundred years before Bath had stood to the lesser spas—had a mere 7,000 inhabitants, and few of the others were more than villages. Quality, however, counted for more than quantity, and the favour the seaside resorts enjoyed with the world of fashion made it certain that they would enjoy an ever-increasing prosperity in the new society which the Industrial Revolution was beginning to shape.

[1] George Beaumont and Captain Henry Disney, *A New Tour thro' England perform'd in the Summers of* 1765, 1766 and 1767 (undated), 132.

[2] Evans, 274.

IV

IN THE DAYS OF THE GRAND TOUR

For more than two centuries the English tourist has been a familiar figure on the Continent. Insular often to the point of being offensive and ridiculous, he has sometimes had a mixed welcome, but his wealth has compensated for the deficiencies in his manners, and it is in large measure due to the English that Mediterranean fishing villages, Swiss mountain valleys and German mineral springs have been transformed into cosmopolitan resorts which still reflect their tastes and foibles. The stream of cross-Channel visitors has grown almost without interruption except in times of war, and such has been its economic importance that governments have sought to influence the direction which it has taken.

The Continental holiday in its various modern forms shows unmistakable traces of its descent from the Grand Tour. Just as the seaside holiday may be traced back to seventeenth-century medical thought and practice, so the holiday abroad derives from the educational thought and practice of the same century.[1]

[1] Standard works on English travel abroad in the seventeenth and eighteenth centuries are E. S. Bates, *Touring in 1600* (1911), Constantia Maxwell, *The English Traveller in France 1698–1815* (1932), and W. E. Mead, *The Grand Tour in the Eighteenth Century* (1914), and I have made

The custom of sending young men to the Continent in the charge of a tutor to complete their education began in the time of Elizabeth, whose government subsidized the travels of promising youths as part of their training as officials. It was a method of introducing the young aristocrat to the manners and customs of the Continent, especially of France and Italy, and pleasure as such had no place in it. It was purely educational in object, and it was not specifically English. The same practice was common abroad. At first the element of danger was considerable. Odds of five or three to one against travellers returning were laid in the early seventeenth century, and in the Litany 'all that travel by land or by water' were grouped with women labouring of child, sick persons, and young children as in particular need of prayers for their safety. Foreign travel was subject to strict Governmental control. All except merchants needed a permit, and, though this could usually be obtained without difficulty, the conditions imposed normally included a time limit for absence, prohibition of communication with disloyal countrymen or entry into a State at war with England, and a ban on visits to Rome and other places, such as St. Omer, where there were seminaries for English Roman Catholics. Travel was costly, and three years was a normal period of absence.

These were some of the factors which limited travel abroad in the seventeenth century. Others were the unsettled condition of Europe, and the prejudice at home against foreigners and foreign influences. Continental travel was, therefore, confined to a few. There were some adventurous spirits—the type is still familiar—such as Fynes Morison, who 'could not see any man without emulation and a kind of vertuous envy, who had seene more Cities, Kingdomes and Provinces, or more Courts of Princes, Kings and Emperours, than myselfe'. There were invalids who in the search for a cure braved the perils of the journey to Baden, Spa, and other health resorts, where, as at the spas at home, there were already 'many having no disease but that of love, however they faine

full use of these. *The Grand Tour* (ed. R. S. Lambert, 1935), a more popular work, to which a number of well-known writers contributed, also contains much interesting information, especially about the places ordinarily visited on the Grand Tour. It is effectively illustrated.

THE GRAND TOUR.

Containing an Exact

DESCRIPTION

Of most of the

CITIES, TOWNS, and Remarkable PLACES of *EUROPE*.

Together with

A Distinct ACCOUNT of the POST-ROADS and STAGES, with their respective DISTANCES,

THROUGH

HOLLAND,	*SWEDEN,*	*FRANCE,*
FLANDERS,	*RUSSIA,*	*SPAIN,*
GERMANY,	*POLAND,*	And
DENMARK,	*ITALY,*	*PORTUGAL.*

LIKEWISE

DIRECTIONS relating to the MANNER and EXPENCE of Travelling from one Place and Country to another.

AS ALSO

OCCASIONAL REMARKS on the Present State of *Trade*, as well as of the *Liberal Arts* and *Sciences*, in each respective Country.

By Mr. NUGENT.

In FOUR VOLUMES.

LONDON:

Printed for S. BIRT, in *Ave-Mary-Lane*; D. BROWNE, without *Temple-Bar*; A. MILLAR, in the *Strand*; and G. HAWKINS in *Fleetstreet*. MDCCXLIX.

sickenesse of body'. There were merchants and officials whose business took them to the Continent. There were political and religious refugees. But travel for pleasure was almost a contradiction in terms.

The idea of the Grand Tour gradually, however, gained ground. The first recorded use of the term is in 1670, and the intellectual atmosphere of the Restoration and the more stable political conditions which followed the Peace of Utrecht in 1713 were favourable to its spread. It was a short stage from educational to pleasure travel, and it was inevitable that, unless the young tourist was unusually serious or his tutor exceptionally strict, study should merge into the pursuit of pleasure.

Gradually others joined the Grand Tourists properly so called, until by the middle of the eighteenth century pleasure had come to prevail—pleasure to be found at the great spas, in the society of Paris and Rome, in the monuments of antiquity, or in the satisfaction of having accomplished what convention demanded and of returning home with duty done and a stock of reminiscences to last a lifetime. By this time, too, most of the paraphernalia of a tourist industry existed on the Continent, and the English were its wealthiest customers. There were regular cross-Channel services by a number of routes. Dessein, the proprietor of the famous 'Hotel d'Angleterre' at Calais, was said to have made £50,000 profit in ten years. Coach proprietors catered specially for English travellers; guide books, most of them hack productions following a stereotyped pattern, like Nugent's *Grand Tour* and Andrews', *Letters to a Young Gentleman*, ran into many editions; wherever the English went local society opened its doors, and clubs, reading-rooms and similar institutions catered for their needs. Forty thousand English travellers, according to Horace Walpole, were estimated to have passed through Calais alone in the two years after the Peace of Paris in 1763; a visitor to France in the 'eighties calculated that thirty thousand of his fellow-countrymen were there;[1] Gibbon, also in the 'eighties, was told—though he found it hard to believe—that there were more than forty thousand Englishmen, including servants, on the Continent. These figures

[1] J. Cradock, *Literary and Miscellaneous Memoirs* (1828), II, 22.

are to be taken with all reserve, but evidently the numbers were impressive.

As for the motives of the growing army of English tourists, those who regarded foreign travel as 'the high roade of Vertue, and Knowledge'[1] regretted that 'the majority of our travellers run over to France from no other motives than those which lead them to Bath, Tunbridge, or Scarborough. Amusement and dissipation are their principal, and often their only, views.'[2] The controversy over the value of the Grand Tour, which had begun in the previous century, still smouldered, and a common opinion was that, far from educating, it corrupted the young. The Macaroni Club, the qualification for membership of which was foreign travel, was cited as evidence of the ill effects on the immature. 'There is indeed a kind of animal, neither male nor female, a thing of the neuter gender, lately started up amongst us. It is called a Macaroni. It talks without meaning, it smiles without pleasantry, it eats without appetite, it rides without exercise, it wenches without passion.'[3] The critics included Smollett and Adam Smith. The Grand Tourist, said the latter, 'commonly returns home more conceited, more unprincipled, more dissipated, and more incapable of any serious application, either to study or to business, than he could well have become in so short a time had he lived at home'.

The *Annual Register* for 1773 classified the reasons for foreign travel under three heads: 'polite education, the love of variety, the pursuit of health.' Sterne in *The Sentimental Journey* (1768) classified them as: 'infirmity of body, imbecility of mind, inevitable necessity,' and the desire to save money. In his first two categories, he included 'all those who travel by land or water, labouring with pride, curiosity, vanity or spleen, subdivided and combined in infinitum'. The third comprised 'the whole army of peregrine martyrs', especially those who set out 'with the benefit of the clergy, either as delinquents, under governors recommended by

[1] James Howell, author of *Instructions for Forreine Travel* (1642), quoted by Lambert, 55.

[2] J. Andrews, *Letters to a Young Gentleman* (1784), 2.

[3] *Oxford Magazine*, June 1770, quoted by Mead, 397–8.

the magistrate, or young gentlemen, transported by the cruelty of parents and guardians', and travelling under tutors.

The main group consisted of those who, according to Sterne, travelled through imbecility of mind and laboured with pride, curiosity, vanity or spleen. They travelled chiefly because it was fashionable, but they were influenced by a genuine curiosity about the monuments of the ancient world and the Renaissance, and to a lesser degree the oddities of foreign manners and customs, and increasingly by a love of the picturesque and a taste for medieval art and architecture.

On the whole, however, the curiosity was superficial. The tourist rarely made any serious attempt to learn the languages of the countries he proposed to visit, and his preparation did not often go beyond the purchase of a guide book. Nor as a rule was he sympathetic to foreign customs and ideas. Hazlitt complained that the English tended to make their own defects a standard for general imitation and found fault with what was French because it was not English. There were few who followed his excellent rule for foreign travel—'to take our common sense with us, and leave our prejudices behind'. Like Goldsmith, the average Englishman tended to devote an undue proportion of his time to 'scolding everything we meet with and praising everything and every person we left at home'. The gentleman who returned to England immediately on seeing a French kitchen was exceptional, as was the visitor who had determined to spend the rest of his days on the Continent but stayed only one night 'on finding at Calais that he could not have beef stakes well dressed',[1] but there were many who would have concurred in the resolve of another, 'Not to spend more money in the Country of our Natural Enemy, than is requisite to support with Decency the Character of an English Man.'[2] Almost all sighed:

[1] D. Jardine, *Letters from Barbary, France, etc.* (1788), 232.

[2] *The Gentleman's Guide in his Tour through France*, 'Wrote by an Officer in the Royal Navy' (1770). This remarkable little book ran into many editions. It is an entertaining digest of information of all kinds culled from many sources, not least valuable because of the light it throws on the mentality of the average English tourist.

Oh, the Roast Beef of Old England:
And oh! the Old English Brown Beer!

echoed on their return the sentiment: 'Hail, happy land! Hail, ye white cliffs of favoured Albion!' and thanked God for bringing them back:

Once more I'm safely brought to England's shore
For which, my gracious God, I thee adore.[1]

The lack of anything which can be called a philosophy of travel, as the conception of the Grand Tour became more and more diluted, helps to explain another characteristic of the English traveller. He hustled from place to place, stopping only long enough to dispose of the sights specified by the guide books, travellers' wonders such as the great machine of Marli and the floating bridge at Rouen. He had the excuse that travel was so slow as to necessitate the utmost economy in the use of his time. There were so many palaces, statues, pictures, antiquities which it was obligatory to see that he was under a constant urge to press on.

'The greater part of travellers tell nothing,' said Samuel Johnson in the *Idler* in 1760, 'because their method of travelling supplies them with nothing to be told. He that enters a town at night and surveys it in the morning, and then hastens away to

[1] *Mrs. Bousquet's Diary*, 1765, ed. Mrs. Tindall (1927), 64; J. C. Villiers, *Tour through Part of France, etc.* (1789), 321; Cornelius Cayley, *A Tour through Holland, Flanders and France for the year* 1772 (1777), 108. The type was not peculiar to the eighteenth century. As Havelock Ellis said of the present age (*Questions of Our Day* (1936)), 'there are those (often English) who go about suffering obvious discomfort in their unfamiliar surroundings and craving (if they are men) for a mutton chop and a bottle of Bass's ale, or (if they are women) for a boiled egg for breakfast'.

another place, and guesses at the manners of the inhabitants by the entertainment which his inn afforded him, may please himself for a time with a hasty change of scenes, and a confused remembrance of palaces and churches; he may gratify his eye with variety of landscapes, and regale his palate with a succession of vintages; but let him be contented to please himself without endeavouring to disturb others.' The reputation of the English in France was that they were 'in such a violent hurry upon the road, that if some little delay is occasioned, they will rather leave their money behind than stay to recover it'.[1] 'In a hundred', wrote a Frenchman, 'there are not two that seek to instruct themselves. To cover leagues on land or on water; to take punch and tea at the inns; to speak ill of all the other nations, and to boast without ceasing of their own; that is what the *crowd* of the English call travelling. The post-book is the only one in which they instruct themselves.'[2]

Thus the tourist contrived to cover as much ground as possible on what was often his only trip to the Continent. Few strayed from the well-trodden paths. None but eccentrics were interested in exploring the little-known hinterland of the main tourists' routes, and the opinion which had been expressed to John Evelyn 'by divers curious and experienced persons . . . that there was little more to be seen in the rest of the civil world after Italy, France and the Low Countries, but plain and prodigious barbarism' was still generally held. The only important additions were Switzerland and the Rhineland, and they were on a route favoured by many return travellers from Italy. The cities and monuments of Italy and France, the fountain heads of Renaissance civilization, remained the chief attractions until Romanticism supplanted the Renaissance tradition.

Conservatism, fashion and lack of curiosity were not, however, the sole reasons for keeping to the accustomed routes. There were good practical reasons for avoiding ventures into the unknown. The inferior quality of the by-roads, the uncertain honesty of the countryfolk, the lack of inns and the primitive character of

[1] Jones, *Journey to France* (1776), II, 117, quoted by Mead, 107–8.
[2] Dupaty, *Lettres sur l'Italie*, 87, quoted by Mead, 108.

such as there were, made it safer and more prudent to go with the stream which flowed along the main roads. Even in France, where the main roads had a high reputation, and compared favourably with those in England, important cross-country roads might be trackless sand, and it might be necessary to drive through cornfields or vineyards when the road disappeared altogether or to enlist small armies of peasants to extricate carriages which had stuck fast. In the remoter parts of France, in Italy and Germany, and above all in Eastern Europe, the roads were notoriously bad. In France the danger to an armed traveller from highwaymen was small, but elsewhere it was substantial. Most Continental inns were bad by English standards, and off the main routes were sometimes intolerable.

By the time of the French Revolution Continental travel for pleasure was an established institution amongst the upper classes. Like going to Bath it was *bon ton*, and the original educational object was almost completely obscured by other motives. The foundations had been laid of a new tradition, which was to be profoundly important in the future, and the eighteenth-century 'milord' is the archetype from whom the English tourist of each succeeding generation has been obviously descended.

V

THE THRESHOLD OF THE RAILWAY AGE

The rise of the watering places was rapid in relation to the state of communications and the social and economic structure in the seventeenth and eighteenth centuries. These set a limit to the possible number of visitors at any given time. But the saturation point was never reached. It tended rather to recede. Improvements in communications kept pace with the demand, and the traffic on the roads of England continued to increase. The growth of wealth, the infiltration of the habits and tastes of the upper classes into the classes immediately below them, and the rise of new families into their ranks brought more and more visitors to the spas and seaside.

In theory it was possible that supply and demand would ultimately reach equilibrium—there is some evidence of a tendency in this direction in the eighteen-thirties—but this possibility was disposed of indefinitely by the social and economic changes which accompanied the Industrial Revolution, and by the revolution in communications which culminated in the development of the railway. The Industrial Revolution produced a large and prosperous middle class and in due course a still larger and relatively prosperous urban proletariat; the railway made travel cheap, quick and easy as never before. Both changes were of decisive importance for the future of the holiday resorts.

The second was the more tangible factor.[1] We have seen how important communications were in the development of the spas, and the spas in their turn had made a notable contribution to the development of communications. Ralph Allen, the Bath postmaster, was responsible for important advances in cross-country posting arrangements. The introduction of mail coaches was due to John Palmer, the manager of the Bath theatre. It cannot have been wholly coincidence that John Metcalf, one of the greatest of road builders, came from Knaresborough.

Particularly in the second half of the eighteenth century and the first quarter of the nineteenth progress in road improvements was rapid. None the less, road travel continued to be slow and expensive, uncomfortable and often dangerous. In the seventeen-fifties communication between London and Brighton was by carrier's wagon and the journey lasted two days. At the same period three days were required for the journey to Bath. These times were substantially reduced, especially after the introduction of the mail coaches in 1784. The journey to Bath could be done in twelve and a half hours in 1827, and by a triumph of organization, an express coach did the journey from London to Brighton in five and a quarter hours in the same decade. The express services were, however, only within the means of the well-to-do, and only they could afford to use private conveyances or to travel post. In 1840 it cost as much to travel post from St. Leonards to Tunbridge Wells, a distance of less than thirty miles, but involving the payment of three postmasters and post boys and twelve turnpikemen, as to stay a whole fortnight at the former.[2] As for the public coaching services, the average inside fare in the late 'thirties was from about twopence halfpenny to fourpence a mile, excluding living expenses.

[1] There is an extensive literature on the coaching age. The most useful general history covering both this period and the railway age is probably W. T. Jackman, *The Development of Transportation in Modern England* (1916). Extensive use has been made in this chapter of the numerous official reports on the early railways and the histories of the chief railway companies. For a fuller list of sources, see the Bibliography.

[2] Granville, I, xliv.

A less important but not negligible deterrent to travel was the discomfort, and increased speed often meant added discomfort. 'To travel in stage coaches', said Cobbett (admittedly not speaking of the most comfortable form of transport), 'is to be hurried along by force, in a box, with an air-hole in it, and constantly exposed to broken limbs, the danger being much greater than that on shipboard, and the noise much more disagreeable, while the company is frequently not a great deal to one's liking.'

These circumstances help to explain the relatively small number of pleasure travellers at the end of the coaching age. In 1834 six coaches were licensed to ply between London and Bath, making forty trips a week. It was considered remarkable in the previous year that the coaches should have taken 480 passengers to Brighton in one day, and in 1837 the number of travellers to Brighton by coach in the whole year was just over 50,000. Long-distance travel was negligible. On the basis of coach and mail traffic the Committee on Railway Communications between London and Scotland estimated in 1841 that 9,282 passengers per annum could be expected for the whole journey from London to Edinburgh if of the alternative routes the coast line were chosen, and 14,199 if the inland line were chosen. When Mr. Woodhouse and Mrs. John Knightley in *Emma* discussed the relative merits of Cromer and Southend, one argument which weighed with them was the greater distance of the former. Elizabeth Woodhouse had never been to Bath or to the sea. There were boys in Arnold's sixth form at Rugby who had never seen the sea. 'Sanditon', the seaside place which was the subject of Jane Austen's unfinished novel, claimed as one of its advantages that it was a whole mile nearer London than Eastbourne.

In the 'thirties the sands at Southport in the season gave an impression of solitude.[1] It was adduced as proof of the popularity of Blackpool that there were 800 to 1,000 visitors at the height of the season.[2] Upwards of 1,500 persons came to reside in Aberystwyth in the months of August, September and October, though

[1] Sir G. Head, *A Home Tour* (1836), 46.
[2] *New Description of Blackpool*, 10.

there were several thousands of casual visitors as well.[1] At Harrogate in the late 'thirties the average number of visitors annually was estimated at 7,000—8,000.[2] At Brighton the visitors at the height of the season were estimated at about 20,000.[3] Interesting figures given in the 1841 Census Report showed that in June of that year there were 590 visitors at Blackpool, 1,586 at Margate, 89 at Shanklin, 186 at Cleethorpes for the 'annual feast' and for seabathing, 65 at Seaton, 49 at Budleigh Salterton, 50 at Cromer, 44 at Skegness, and 60 at Bridlington.

Yet there was one important indication of the transformation which was soon to occur. An early use of the steamboat was for pleasure excursions on the Clyde, and in 1815 it was introduced to the Thames with a similar object, to carry passengers to London's nearest watering place, Gravesend, and soon to Margate. By the 'twenties the Margate hoys, which had taken from ten to seventy-two hours on the trip, had been superseded by luxurious steamers, 'to be compared to a London coffee house', and furnished with books, newspapers, cards, backgammon, chess, and a band. These did the journey in eight hours for certain. Certainty was considered the great advantage of the steamboat, and the speed and certainty offset for most the 'unpleasant monotony' of the vessel's motion and 'the constant vibration of the timbers'.[4]

The passengers dealt with at Margate and Ramsgate by the Margate Pier and Harbour Company rose from 17,000 in 1812–13 to 21,931 in 1815–16, 43,947 in 1820–1, 98,128 in 1830–1, and to the record total of 105,625 in 1835–6.[5] At Gravesend the pier tolls amounted to £7,000 in 1836, and an additional pier had to be built because of the volume of traffic. Pleasure steamers also plied from Liverpool, Manchester and the other great cities on the coast and the navigable rivers, and steamship services accounted for a considerable proportion of the long-distance travel

[1] Commission on Municipal Corporation Boundaries (1837).

[2] Granville, I, 62.

[3] Freeling, *Picturesque Excursion* (undated, about 1840), 156.

[4] Oulton, 104 *et seq.* E. W. Brayley, *Isle of Thanet* (1817), I, 67. For an entertaining account of a steamer trip to Margate in the 'thirties see *Aquatics: Mr. Jorrocks at Margate* in Surtees' *Jorrocks' Jaunts and Jollities.*

[5] Select Committee on Ramsgate and Margate Harbours (1850).

from London to Scotland and the South-West of England. From Liverpool the pleasure boats went to the Isle of Man and North Wales as well as to the Lancashire and Cheshire watering places, bringing the Isle of Man into the category of a holiday resort for the first time; and in 1845 it was stated that 20,000 people were taken across 'to breathe a pure atmosphere' on the Cheshire bank of the Mersey on summer Sundays.[1] As compared with the coach—and indeed the railway—one of the chief advantages of the steamer was the low fares which were charged. The excursion fare to Gravesend was only sixpence; the return trip from Liverpool to Rhyl cost 4s. or 2s. 6d. according to class. In 1846 the return fares to Margate and Ramsgate from London were from 5s. to 7s., to Dover and Deal 5s. and 6s., to Southend and Sheerness 3s. and 3s. 6d.

The development of the pleasure steamer began the era of cheap holiday travel for the masses, and the process which was thus begun for the towns with access to the sea coast by water was to be immensely accelerated by the railway.

This is, however, only half the story. It does not automatically follow from the existence of a modern system of transport that it will be used for pleasure, still less for holidays away from home. Whether these developed amongst the mass of the population depended upon other factors—not necessarily connected with the new facilities for travel. Firstly it depended upon industrial conditions, particularly earnings and the opportunities which were afforded for absence from work.

It cannot be said that at the beginning of the nineteenth century an annual holiday in the modern sense was a pressing social necessity for the ordinary wage-earner. The country was still predominantly rural. In 1801 London with 865,000 people was the only town with more than a hundred thousand inhabitants. Manchester with 84,000, Liverpool with 78,000, Birmingham with 74,000, and Bristol with 64,000, all smaller than modern Oxford, came next to London, while in Wales the largest town was Swansea, with a population only slightly exceeding 6,000. Just under half

[1] Royal Commission on the State of Large Towns, *Second Report* (1845).

of the population were engaged in agriculture, and of the remainder most lived in the country. Except in the new industries the rhythm of life was slow, and sufficient respites from work were normally afforded by periods when trade was slack and by the traditional holidays at the great religious feasts and during the local fairs.

The industrialization of the country was, however, proceeding rapidly. One consequence was the concentration of the population in the large industrial centres under conditions which were to make adequate holidays essential to health and efficiency. At the same time, the speed of industry accelerated, the scale of industrial organization grew, and the personal element in industrial relations diminished. The need for holidays increased; the opportunities decreased. Under the old system the traditional holidays were accepted by both employers and employed, and it was possible to allow individual absences from work without serious detriment to efficiency. Under the new system, the efficiency of the factory depended more and more upon each unit, and the welfare of the workpeople was subordinated to the profit of the owner in the supposed interests of all.

The holidays mentioned in the various reports on factory conditions in the early nineteenth century fall into three groups: those enforced by the employers owing to the state of industry and contrary to the wishes of the workpeople, those taken by the workpeople contrary to the wishes of the employers, and those which were recognized by both. To apply the word 'holidays' to the first group now seems a misuse of the term, and it is revealing of the change in the conception of a holiday which has taken place that casual unemployment should have been so regarded. To some extent it served the same purpose, and by the better paid such periods might be used for holiday excursions; but for the majority, as was stated in connection with the mining industry, such 'holidays' were 'far more than is agreeable. Holidays with pay going on are very pleasant, but when the rule is, no work no pay, holidays are a subject of complaint if many in number.'[1]

[1] Royal Commission on Employment of Children (1842), 2. 141. An account of the official reports which have been drawn upon will be

The unauthorized holiday presented a major industrial problem. The practice of taking a holiday on the day after the week-end when wages were paid was so general in some industries, not only the coal mines, that employers accepted it as inevitable. The number of absentees on the Monday after pay day often necessitated the total suspension of work, and the full complement might not be back until Wednesday or Thursday. The absentees were then faced with the need to make up for the time they had lost, to the special detriment of the children who worked with them. In an extreme case, that of the lead-smelting mills of Durham, Northumberland and Cumberland, some of the men worked very long shifts from Thursday to Saturday and from Monday to Wednesday, and took the whole of the following week as a holiday. A system under which spasms of intensive effort alternated with spasms of ill-spent idleness was in every respect vicious, but in different forms it was widespread throughout industry. The cotton industry seems to have been the one important exception, and a spinner told the Select Committee on the Factories Bill in 1832 that, in contrast with the position in other trades, cotton workers were bound to attend as regularly on Mondays as on other days.

As for recognized holidays, the workers clung hard but with only slight success to the holidays to which they had been accustomed. A mine at Levant in Cornwall where an old custom of giving six holidays a year was observed was mentioned as exceptional in 1842, and of another mine in the same district it was stated that whereas formerly there were many holidays in the year, there were now only two recognized holidays, Christmas Day and Good Friday. The lugubrious practice of the London journeymen of taking the eight hanging days at Tyburn as holidays died out in the early years of the nineteenth century, and Bartholomew Fair, May Fair and Southwark Fair ceased to be occasions of popular

found in the Bibliography. By far the most useful for information about holidays are the various reports of the Royal Commission on the Employment of Children, from which a substantial proportion of the material given below is derived. The Subcommissioners were specifically instructed to inquire about the number of holidays and half-holidays allowed the children.

merrymaking. Of a silk mill at Hull, the Select Committee on the Factories Bill were told in 1832 that there were few holidays and they were being cut shorter and shorter. The Bank of England closed on 47 holidays in 1761, on 44 in 1808, on 40 in 1825, on 18 in 1830, and on only four in 1834—Good Friday, Christmas Day, the 1st May and the 1st November.[1]

The masters on the whole were unsympathetic to holidays. They argued that more than enough leisure was given by enforced and unauthorized holidays, and that in any event leisure was abused by the working classes. To take into account periods of unemployment was logical up to a point, but it failed to recognize the distinction between voluntary leisure and involuntary idleness, often accompanied by privation. The argument from the existence of absenteeism was superficially fair, but it was disingenuous to infer from the frequent misuse of leisure that it was not in the interests of the workers that they should be granted holidays. Both views ignored the responsibility of the employers for the conditions which led to the taking of unauthorized holidays and the evils associated with them, and overlooked the connection between the latter and the curtailment of the workers' leisure.

The lack of recognized holidays bred the unauthorized holiday: barbarous industrial and social conditions bred drunkenness, sexual immorality, gambling and the other evils of which the employers complained. 'As a manufacturer,' a Staffordshire china manufacturer told the Child Employment Commission in 1843, 'I have not the least doubt but that I should prosper greatly if I could depend upon the working hours of men. They often come about the premises, but will not buckle to. If I give them a day or two at Easter they take a week, if at Christmas they take another week; indeed they are not to be depended on.' An extreme statement of the view that holidays were harmful to the recipients came from the manager of a Monmouthshire ironworks who was opposing a holiday on Sunday. 'So far from their deriving any comfort or moral improvement from suspension of Sunday

[1] *Report* of the Departmental Committee on Holidays with Pay (1938), 11.

labour, the contrary in the majority of cases will be the result; instead of attending a place of worship, a beer shop, the great curse of the country, would be their resort: the Government would be conferring a much greater boon on the lower classes, and improving their morals to a much greater extent, were they to close the "kidley winks" [beer shops] than to suspend the furnaces.'

Adult males could expect no relief from Parliament, but they benefited indirectly from the measures which were taken to protect children and young persons. The Factory Act of 1833 modestly provided that persons under eighteen years of age should be entitled to eight half days each year, and to Christmas Day and Good Friday in addition. Where adults and children were employed upon the same processes it was impracticable to deny the benefits of the Act to the adults, and where part of the activities of a factory had to be suspended it was an easy step to the suspension of all. The modesty of the Act of 1833 is evidence of the curtailment which had already occurred, and it is illustrative of the attitude of many employers that they took advantage of loopholes in the Act to deprive the children of the meagre rights which it conferred. The use of the words 'shall be entitled' in relation to Good Friday and Christmas Day was ambiguous: and the Law Officers held that: 'The master of a factory is not subject to a penalty for employing children and young persons on the above days, with their free consent. At the same time the *onus* would lie upon the master to prove that the children and young persons found working on those days preferred work to play.' Proof was the main difficulty; dishonest employers intimidated workpeople to swear that they had been consulted, and suspicion that there had been no consultation did not constitute legal proof. Further difficulties were that proceedings had to be instituted within fourteen days of the offence, and that since the eight half-holidays could be taken together or spread out at the option of the factory owner, it was necessary to wait until the 27th December before proceedings could be considered in respect of the year.

The factory inspectors found that on the whole these provisions were observed; but there were many factories in which the holidays granted to adults fell below the standards prescribed for the young. They seem chiefly to have been in industries and trades where the work had to go on continuously all the year round. At *The Times* printing press the only holidays were half days at Christmas and on Good Friday. In the blast furnaces and ironworks there was sometimes only one recognized holiday, Christmas Day. Practice varied considerably according to locality, trade, and employer, and generalization is difficult. Christmas Day was almost invariably a holiday, Good Friday, or Easter Monday as an alternative, was commonly given, there was usually a Whitsuntide holiday of a day upwards, and in most districts work ceased for periods ranging from a few hours to several days during the local wakes, fairs or 'pranks', which were widely observed and of which there might be more than one a year.[1] Some employers organized annual outings for their workpeople; in some cases 'club days' were observed as holidays; and time was taken off for prize fights and similar occasions. In the North New Year's Day was commonly a holiday, in a few areas a half or whole day was taken on Shrove Tuesday, in others fast days were holidays, and apart from wakes and fairs there were a number of local holidays of the same character such as 'Christening Day' (Sidmouth), and 'Offering Day' (Norwich). Sometimes holidays were not taken when trade was brisk; and sometimes the time lost was made up. In Birmingham the larger factories commonly closed for a week or two at Christmas for stocktaking.

The practice of granting holidays at the fairs and wakes was firmly established in the North. In Manchester the traditional Whitsuntide holiday when the races were held on Kersal Moor lasted for four or five days, and it is notable that the wakes were

[1] Interesting evidence of their importance is provided by the number of cases where the 1841 Census Report referred to temporary increases in population due to the annual feast or fair, and occasionally friendly or benevolent society anniversaries. A few examples out of many are: Drayton Parslow (Bucks) 52 visitors, Coton (Cambs) 43, Haddenham (Cambs) 143, Barrow upon Soar (Leics) 70, Messingham (Lincs) 283, Finningley (Notts) 143, Kirtlington (Oxon) 157, Cleobury Mortimer (Salop) 10, Southam (Warwick) 50. The visitors will doubtless mainly have been dealers, fairmen and similar folk. This was not of course a new development; it went back to much earlier times.

most prolonged in the centres of the cotton industry, in which the unauthorized holiday was not tolerated. Exceptionally enlightened employers were even prepared to allow their men a summer holiday of a week or fortnight. One such employer, Henry Ashworth, whose firm owned two cotton mills at Bolton, told the Select Committee on the Factories Bill in 1840 that he was 'partial to holidays; . . . in our own concern, we give permission to our workpeople to take a week or more if they choose every year for an excursion, or to go and see their friends, or to consider themselves at liberty to spend the time as they like, and they may either go in groups or they may go singly, and we undertake to find others to fill their places, and to see that the work is done properly; in fact, we allow them permission to leave work, but we do not allow that work to stand idle'.

In the wakes holidays and in the practice of the few employers like Ashworth who shared Southey's singular view that 'the want of holidays breaks down and brutalizes the labouring class', and that where they occur seldom they are uniformly abused, may be seen the glimmerings of the paid annual holiday for the manual worker. But as yet there was no question of holidays with pay except for the salaried and a few special classes such as domestic servants and dressmaking apprentices whose emoluments included free board and lodging. Some of the latter had as many as five or six weeks holiday during the slack season at the end of the summer, but no general conclusions can be drawn from this: they were under training and the employers saved the cost of their keep.

The fact was that neither masters nor men thought that manual workers should receive the same treatment as the salaried. One reason may have been purely practical. Industrial wages were directly related to output either in terms of time or of piecework, whereas salaries were usually calculated by periods of upwards of a month and did not vary directly with productivity. The issue was also obscured by the superior social status of the salaried and by the closer personal relationship between them and their employers when office staffs were almost universally small. But there were secondary considerations. The conception of pay without work was foreign to the economic thought of the time, under which the worker sold his labour in the open market as he might have sold any other commodity. The grant of paid holidays to the salaried was the aberration. 'There is no instance in the whole kingdom of rest from colliery labour for a single day or even half a day, the wages going on during the cessation of the work,' reported the Royal Commission on Mines in 1842—not, however, it is only right to point out, without a certain note of surprise. Labour organization was rudimentary, and if the dream of annual holidays with pay had occurred to the men, there were many more urgent questions to engage their attention, including the curtailment of existing holidays.

Some of Ashworth's men took advantage of the opportunity of a summer holiday to go 'to Ireland or London or Scotland, wherever the coach or the steamboat will carry them, and spend their time rationally'. The use of the word 'rationally' in this context is characteristic and revealing. A familiar lament of employers, moralists and officials was that the working classes failed to employ their leisure in a 'rational' manner. Hence the argument that to add to it would add to their opportunities for degradation. It was said that instead of using their leisure hours in 'rational' pursuits they filled the beer shops and the gin parlours, and that their favourite holiday pastimes, prize fights, betting, bearbaiting, dog and cock fighting, were brutal and demoralizing. Of the Whitsuntide fair on Kersal Moor one writer used language which evidently seemed the ultimate condemnation when he said: 'Pleasure reigns with almost Parisian despotism.'[1]

These criticisms, as it is easy to see now, were misconceived. From medieval times the Englishman had been accustomed to take his pleasures in Falstaffian manner and to relish a brutal strain in his sports. To condemn the working man for extravagances which could still be paralleled amongst the aristocracy showed a narrowness of outlook on the part of his mentors, most of whom belonged neither to the aristocracy nor to the working classes. It ignored the degrading effect of industrial and social conditions. It was not the fault of the factory worker that when his work was over he was 'utterly unfit, except in extraordinary cases, for any-

[1] Joseph Aston, *Manchester* (1816), 190.

thing like mental improvement, and not very fit for much social enjoyment with his family', as one of the factory inspectors, Leonard Horner, told the Select Committee on the Factories Bill in 1840. It was not his fault that he was seldom literate, that he thought 'of little else than eating, drinking, sleeping, and working' (as a Leeds doctor told the Royal Commission on the Employment of Children with reference to the colliers), and that when opportunity offered he indulged often to excess in the pleasures of the flesh. It was not the workers who were to blame for the limited facilities for 'rational' enjoyment.

The Government tolerated the enclosure of the common fields on which had formerly been played the traditional games of football, quoits, bandy, bowls, and cricket whose decline the critics regretted, and many of the critics came from the classes to whom the enclosers themselves belonged. Until irreparable damage had been done Parliament did not intervene to preserve the open spaces 'calculated for public walks', which the Select Committee on the Health of Towns (1840) thought 'essential to the health and comfort of the poorer classes'.[1] It was regrettable, and partly due to Government policy, that the licensed houses developed not as places of family entertainment like the Continental café but as establishments for perpendicular drinking to which respectable women could not accompany their husbands. It was unfortunate, but not the fault of the working man, that dancing was associated with immorality. 'Dancing (and very often music), which in many countries is enjoyed with open hearts and in the open air, and considered a laudable and creditable recreation,' observed one of the Sub-Commissioners of the Child Employment Commission, 'is too generally looked upon by our labouring people, and many of those who influence them, as a kind of dissipation, and resorted to only at doubtful and disreputable places, and often with a kind of mystery and concealment, as if it were a questionable or improper indulgence.'

[1] Tennyson's remedy for the problem of open spaces deserves to be recalled: *Why should not these great Sirs*
Give up their parks some dozen times a year
To let the people breathe?

It would also be wrong to assume that in the country as a whole the picture was as black as it was painted. There was a large God-fearing, sober and industrious element, especially among the chapel-going sections of the working classes, upon whom the drab rigours of their everyday life, the restricted opportunities for rational enjoyment and their enforced immobility must have borne more hardly than on their fellows. But, admitting that large sections of the population misused their leisure, the remedy was not still further to reduce working-class leisure. The evils arose in part from insufficiency of leisure, in part from inadequate provision for the utilization of leisure, and ultimately from a low wage level. The remedy was not to close the public houses or to suppress the other social evils by direct action. These were merely symptoms, and suppression was at best a palliative. It lay in improved social conditions, in education, in reduced working hours, in the provision of alternative means of amusement. In the short run no factor was more important than the improvements in transport which increased the mobility of the working classes and enabled them at holiday times to leave the confined and enervating environment of the towns.

'Of all inventions, the alphabet and the printing press alone excepted', said Macaulay, 'those inventions which abridge distance have done most for the civilization of our species.' 'I rejoice to see it,' wrote Dr. Arnold of a railway train, 'and think that feudality is gone for ever. It is so great a blessing to think that any one evil is really extinct.' The remark was apt. It was of the essence of feudalism that the poor man was bound to the land on which he lived. This had ceased to be the position in law; it was largely due to the railway that it ceased to be the position in fact. The growth in the mobility of the population which the railway brought about is shown by the passenger statistics. Between 1842 and 1847, the number of passengers a year in the United Kingdom rose from twenty-three to fifty-one millions. By 1851 it had nearly reached 79 millions: it was 160 millions in 1860, 604 millions in 1880, 817 millions in 1890 and 1,455 millions in 1913.

At first, however, the potentialities of the railway were not fully appreciated. Like generals planning for the next war in terms of the last the railway promoters thought in terms of the old system and of the coach-using classes. Just as the early motor-car was designed as a horse carriage with a petrol engine, so the railway train was conceived as a steam-drawn coach. 'The system generally adopted on the introduction of railways', said the Select Committee on Railways (1844), 'was to provide a description of accommodation, and establish a scale of fares, analogous to those of the conveyances which were superseded. Thus each train had a first class, corresponding to the inside of the old stage coach; and a second class, in the absence of cushions, stuffing, and other comforts and in the exposure, or partial exposure to the weather, corresponding to the outside.' Fares were fixed 'just low enough to preclude the possibility of competition, and to give the railway the advantages of what may be called the latent coach traffic, developed by a slight advantage in economy', and 'an immense advantage in point of time and facility, but not so low as to call into play an entirely new description of traffic'.

As long as the 'high-fare system' was maintained the advantage enjoyed by the railway over the coach from the point of view of pleasure travel amongst the poorer classes was slight, except as regards short journeys. One 'great advantage' to the poorer classes from the establishment of railway communications, reported the Select Committee on Railways in 1840, was stated to be 'to convey the labourer cheaply and rapidly to that spot where his labour might be most highly remunerated'. A secondary advantage would be that 'the health and enjoyment of the mechanics, artizans, and poor inhabitants of the large towns would be promoted, by the facility with which they would be enabled to remove themselves and their families into healthier districts and less crowded habitations'. Both these points were somewhat theoretical, while of travel for pleasure there was no mention at all.

Third-class travel was not only dear. Such trains as carried third-class passengers were intolerably slow, uncomfortable and inconvenient. A Poor Law official, hardly likely to be unduly sentimental, told the Select Committee on Railways in 1844 that 'the risk and exposure of the poor people in the open stand-up carriages, particularly in the winter time, is so severe, that I would sooner pay the difference out of my own pocket than subject the poor under my charge to the danger of that conveyance'. The institution of the 'Parliamentary train' in 1844, on the recommendation of this Committee, under an Act which compelled the companies to run such trains at a penny-a-mile fare and laid down a minimum standard of comfort for them, was a notable advance, but the statutory requirements were low and the companies as a whole were unwilling to exceed them. There were some, indeed, who thought that far from having gained by the introduction of the railway the poor in some cases lost, because the stage wagons, vans, carts and other methods of conveyance which they had formerly used were driven out. The Select Committee on Railways Acts Enactments in 1846 reported that 'it appeared as if it had been determined to exclude the great body of the nation, unable of course to pay first and second class fares, from the benefit communicated to the more wealthy order'.

The public also were conservative. There was at first a good deal of suspicion of the railway. Though the dangers were exaggerated, there were many accidents; trains were not always to be relied upon; the comfort was uncertain even in the first and second classes; and railway travel was thought to be injurious to health. It was believed, said Granville, that a speed of twenty or thirty miles an hour must 'affect delicate lungs; that to such as are of a sanguineous constitution, and labour under fullness of blood in the head, the movement of rail-trains will produce apoplexy'; that the sudden plunging into darkness in tunnels and the equally sudden emergence were bad for the eyes; that the air in the tunnels 'is of a vitiated kind and must give rise to the worst effects', and at the bottom of cuttings, 'being necessarily damp, will occasion catarrhs, and multiply agues'. The best answer to such fears was experience, which confirmed Granville's sage conclusion that railway travelling '*per se*' as a mode of conveyance was 'not more likely to do mischief to people's health than any other hitherto adopted', but none the less they tended to discourage travel for pleasure. On the whole, too, though under the system of independent companies development was unco-ordinated and haphazard, the first stage was the building of arterial lines between the main centres of industry and population. With few exceptions, the extension of the railway to the holiday resorts came later.

Yet from the earliest days many working people made use of the railway for short pleasure trips. In 1839, for example, the ordinary fifteen-minute service between London and Greenwich had to be trebled at Easter and Whitsun.[1] It was not, however, until the development of the railway excursion that pleasure travel on a large scale began.

Sir Rowland Hill, who became Chairman of the Brighton Railway Company in 1843, claimed to have been the originator of excursion trains, which 'by their extension to other lines, and by increase in the scope of their operation, have obtained an importance far beyond any expectation that I could then have formed'.[2] But there were certainly railway excursions before 1843, though their origin is obscure and probably cannot be attributed to a single individual. There are a number of disconnected instances of reduced fares. Thus in 1839 the organizers of a church bazaar at Grosmont persuaded the local railway company to issue cheap tickets for their horse-drawn trains from Whitby and Pickering on two days in August. In 1840 the clergy and teachers of a number of Manchester charity schools applied to the Manchester and Leeds Railway Company for cheap excursions to take upwards of 40,000 schoolchildren into the country. The *per capita* railway tax made it difficult to comply with this request, but the company discovered a way out by taking three children out of four free of charge, ten thousand tickets thus being sold in all.[3] On the newly opened Midland line in the same year the success of excursions at half price organized by the local Mechanics' Institutes in connection with exhibitions in Nottingham and Leicester led the company in August to organize the first excursion train of its own. This left Leicester at 9 a.m. and returned from Nottingham at 6 p.m. Tickets, which cost 6s. first class, 4s. 6d. second class and 2s. third, had to be obtained beforehand. It was so popular that a second excursion was run later in the month. This consisted of

[1] Select Committee on Railways, *Second Report* (1839), 78.
[2] *Life* (1880 ed.) II, 21.
[3] Select Committee on Railways, *Fifth Report* (1840).

65 coaches, 49 of them second class, and 8 third class, and carried more than 2,000 passengers. A large crowd, including 'elegantly dressed females', welcomed it at Nottingham, and the band of the Duke of Rutland was in attendance to enliven them. This was fortunate, because the train was considerably late. It had been overloaded, and a second engine had to be sent to its assistance.[1]

The railway excursion is, however, especially associated with the name of Thomas Cook.[2] Cook, a young wood turner and—a point to be noted—secretary of the South Midland Temperance Association, began the career which was to make him famous when he organized an excursion from Leicester to a temperance demonstration at Loughborough on 5th July 1841. The fare was one shilling return, and 570 travellers took part. Similar excursions followed, and in 1845 Cook started to arrange them commercially. His method was to hire a special train at his own risk and to sell the tickets at greatly reduced prices.

By 1844, reported the Railway Department, 'pleasure trips prevailed extensively'. The *Railway Chronicle* said that in the first three days of Easter week hundreds of thousands were transported to 'the green fields, the smokeless heavens, and the fresh free beauties of Nature', and the railways boasted 'a new and nobler characteristic in their almost universal adaptation to the wants and recreations of the million'. One train on the Brighton line consisted of four engines and forty carriages, and carried 1,100 passengers, and altogether nearly 15,000 passengers travelled from London to Brighton on the three Easter holidays.

Thus, as the *Railway Chronicle* also said in the same year, 'the degree in which railways are everywhere contributing to the recreation and health of all classes, by removing them in the intervals of labour from the confinement of streets and lanes to the fresh air and verdure of the country, furnishes a most valuable proof of their utility'.

The attitude of the authorities was at the same time becoming

[1] C. E. Stretton, *The History of the Midland Railway* (1901), 42–5.

[2] The information here and later about Thomas Cook is largely derived from W. Fraser Rae, *The Business of Travel* (1891), a competent and interesting record of Cook and his firm.

more sympathetic. In a circular about safety precautions on excursion trains the Board of Trade desired that it should be clearly understood that 'they by no means wish to suppress excursions of this character; their Lordships are aware of their useful influence on the portions of the community who profit by them'. Yet they took 'the opportunity of stating also, that the primary object of each company is to carry passengers generally, according to the published time tables: and their Lordships conceive that, in no case should the trains so published be postponed or delayed, or otherwise interfered with, by casual trains, however beneficial to a particular section of the public, or profitable to the Railway Company'.[1] In the next year, the Report of the Board of Trade on

[1] This circular (*Report* of Railway Department of Board of Trade, 1844–5) is worth reproducing for the light which it throws on the conditions of excursion travel and the attitude of the authorities. (It may also be of interest to the connoisseur of official English.)

'The attention of the Lords of the Committee of the Privy Council for Trade having been called to the extent and character of trains for excursions for pleasure, and eminent engineers and managers of railways having represented, in reply to their Lordships' inquiries, that much danger to the passengers is incurred on these occasions, from the unmanageable size of the trains, travelling at a high rate of speed, and without guards in proportion to the number of carriages and passengers, I am directed to request that you will be so good as to bring under the notice of the Board of Directors of the
Company, the great importance of conducting these excursions in a manner which shall diminish the chances of accidents.

'Their Lordships do not propose to advise your Company to adopt any particular arrangement; but they direct me to inform you, that the professional gentlemen above-mentioned, whose opinions on the above subject are worthy of the gravest consideration, have stated their conviction, in which their Lordships entirely concur, that danger is to be apprehended, unless the size of the trains be considerably diminished, or their rate of speed lessened.

'Some of these gentlemen recommend that the excursion trains should be divided into sections of a size suitable to the powers of one locomotive engine only. Others are of opinion that two locomotive engines, coupled with a proportional number of carriages, are not objectionable.

'In these instances the usual speed may be kept up, provided great precautions are taken to prevent collision.

Schemes for extending Railway Communications in Lancashire and the Adjoining Districts, mentioned amongst 'the benefits to the operative class, from the general introduction of Railways' the opportunities afforded not only 'for keeping up family ties by visits to parents and relatives', and 'for moving in search of employment' but also 'for excursions for innocent and healthy recreation on holidays'. By 1850 such arguments were part of the stock in trade of the railway companies themselves and brought out for use whenever it suited them.

The success of the excursion trains was a witness both to the need of facilities for cheap pleasure travel and to the demand for them. They only met part of the need and part of the demand; for they were far from general and they only ran on special occasions. Soon, however, they were supplemented by other cheap facilities, reduced fares for return journeys and for half-day, day, week-end and longer trips, not confined to one train though not as yet available on all, and the Parliamentary trains at a penny a mile

'Again, there are others who do not object to the use of a greater number of engines, but who strongly insist on the necessity of restricting the speed to 15 miles per hour. These gentlemen, however, admit that, on such occasions, it is difficult to regulate the speed, and bring it within due limits. All of them agree that the carriages for this purpose should be provided with bearings and drawing-springs; that a number of guards, adequate to enforce the Company's regulations, and preserve order, should be attached to the trains; and that arrangements should be made for preventing the platforms at the stations being crowded to excess.

'In conveying these sentiments, my Lords desire that it may be clearly understood, that they by no means wish to suppress excursions of this character; their Lordships are aware of their useful influence on the portions of the community who profit by them; but my Lords are most anxious that their very utility and consequent magnitude should not lead to the disastrous results, which must ensue, if the practice of conveying great multitudes along railways be not accompanied by a better system than that which has hitherto prevailed.

'My Lords take this opportunity of stating also, that the primary object of each company is to carry passengers generally, according to the published time tables; and their Lordships conceive that, in no case should the trains so published be postponed or delayed, or otherwise interfered with, by casual trains, however beneficial to a particular section of the public, or profitable to the Railway Company.'

which ran at all times. Special facilities were given for Sunday School treats and other outings. Benevolent employers chartered trains to take their employees to the country or the seaside, and the occasion was often celebrated with pomp and ceremony. In 1844, for example, when a Lancashire manufacturer took 650 of his workpeople and about seventy of their friends on a pleasure trip to Fleetwood, the Church of England band accompanied them to the station, and the procession was adorned with two royal standards and a number of other flags.[1]

The factory inspectors in 1845 commended the example of such employers to their fellows, and pointed out that 'railway carriages may be as easily hired as steamboats may be chartered for summer excursions'. 'It is difficult to say', they observed of one firm, 'whether we should most admire the benevolence, the confiding practical good sense, or the enlarged views of their own happiness and interests evinced by the proprietors . . . in these arrangements.' They mentioned one case (1845) where tickets were given on proof of good conduct, as evidenced by attendance at some place of instruction or of public worship.

At holiday times, ignoring the congestion and the discomfort, the people poured out of the great cities. They cared little where they went, and excursions to other inland towns to see exhibitions, zoos, museums, monuments, even factories, seem to have been as popular as excursions to the coast. The novelty of railway travel was sufficient for many; for most merely to exchange one city for another was an adventure and an exploration.

Some of the consequences were foreseen by the *Manchester Guardian* in 1845: 'The most remarkable feature of this Whitsuntide was the larger numbers leaving Manchester rather than spending the holidays in the traditional way at the Kersal Moor races.' It was estimated that 150,000 had left by the railways. Most of them returned on the same or the following day and many made several excursions. The writer thought that as it was the first year with fares at a penny a mile this was but a glimpse of greater things to come. 'This is, socially speaking, one of the greatest advantages of this annual week's holiday to a population like that of Man-

[1] *Railway Chronicle*, 7th September 1844.

chester. The birth of this new and cheap means of transit is as if the wings of the wind had been given for a week to the closely confined operative, the hard-working mechanic, and the counter-riveted shopkeeper. They enjoy the needful relaxation from the toil or care or confinement of business; they see new scenes and acquire new tastes for the beautiful in nature as, whirled along by the steam-car, they rush, "Forth to fresh fields, and pastures new".

'The advantages of these railway excursions are many; but amongst their principal social benefits, on such occasions as the present week, we may notice that they are greatly conducive to health, by combining pure air with the active exercise of field sports; that they are not less productive of cheerful, sober, and innocent enjoyment; and that they are eminently social and domestic in their character—and in all these respects are infinitely preferable to the tumultuous, disorderly, and intemperate scenes of the racecourse—scenes in which wives and children cannot and ought not to participate.'

Already then the popular response to the provision of cheap railway facilities was a striking demonstration of the readiness of the public to avail themselves of opportunities for 'rational' enjoyment if they existed. And it was only a foretaste of the revolution in social habits which it portended. The excursion ticket, 'that boon', as it was described in a guide book in 1849,[1] 'to those, whose duties confine them during the greater part of the year, to the close atmosphere of our overgrown city', was a great civilizing instrument, which may not unfairly be compared in importance with the penny post, whose contemporaneous introduction was also a consequence of the invention of the railway.

[1] *Handbook of Travel round the Southern Coast of England*, iii.

VI

THE NEW WATERING PLACES

The Census Report for 1851 analysed the rates at which towns of different types had grown during the previous fifty years. Of the categories into which it divided them—London, manufacturing towns, seaports, mining and hardware towns, county towns, and watering places—it might have been expected that in a period of unprecedented industrial development the manufacturing group would show the highest rate of growth, and that the seaports and the mining and hardware towns would run them close. It is somewhat of a surprise to find the watering places separately distinguished at all. In fact the watering places came first, with an average annual rate of growth of 2·561 per cent as compared with 2·380 for the manufacturing towns, 2·336 for the mining and hardware towns, 2·191 for the seaports, 1·820 for London, and 1·609 for the county towns.[1]

Too much must not be read into these figures. They included not only places such as Bath and Cheltenham, which by 1851 were

[1] The sources chiefly used for this chapter have been guide books and histories of particular resorts, general topographies, and the census returns. Special mention should be made of A. B. Granville, *The Spas of England and Principal Sea-Bathing Places* (1841), which has been invaluable, particularly as regards the spas.

primarily residential in character,[1] but Dover, which was also a seaport. On the other hand, the fifteen watering places taken for the purpose of the comparison by no means comprised all the important holiday resorts. The four spas were Bath, Tunbridge Wells, Leamington and Cheltenham; the eleven seaside resorts were Brighton, Ramsgate, Margate, Worthing, Weymouth, Scarborough, Ryde, Cowes, Ilfracombe, Dover and Torquay. The list was thus far from complete. Important omissions included Harrogate and Buxton amongst the spas, and Hastings, Folkestone, Teignmouth and Aberystwyth amongst the seaside resorts. If these and the many lesser resorts had been taken into account, the rate of growth would have been found to be considerably greater.

But the position as shown by the Census Report was sufficiently remarkable. The population of the selected watering places had risen from 78,766 in 1801 to 278,930 in 1851; the population of England and Wales had increased during the same period from 9,000,000 to just over 18,000,000. In 1801 less than 1 per cent of the whole population lived in the fifteen resorts; by 1851 the proportion had nearly doubled.

So what Macaulay called 'the towns in which wealth, created and accumulated elsewhere, is expended for the purposes of health and recreation' now by official admission ranked in the national economy besides those where wealth was produced and the wheels of commerce turned. Ten resorts were considerable towns of more than 10,000 inhabitants. The biggest of them all, Brighton, with a population of 65,569, was nearly ten times as large as in 1801. The next in size, Bath (54,240) and Cheltenham (35,051), had changed in character, but they owed their growth to the same initial cause. Of the others Hastings (16,966—but not in the Census list), Scarborough (12,915), Ramsgate (11,838) and Margate (10,099) were, like Brighton, first and foremost holiday

[1] It would be interesting to trace the history of the practice of retiring from work on pension or savings to enjoy what is in effect an indefinite holiday. It may be surmised that it was connected with the growth of life assurance, and that our overseas expansion, necessitating residence in the tropics by officials and merchants and hence provision for their support on their return home, was also a contributory factor.

resorts; Leamington (15,692) and Tunbridge Wells (10,587), like Bath and Cheltenham, were chiefly residential. Dover had a population of 22,244.

If the seaside resorts are taken separately, the advance which had been made is seen to be still more astonishing. The population of the eleven selected seaside resorts had been 39,447 in 1801, and at 163,360 was more than four times greater in 1851. The four spas had not quite trebled in size. These figures are an indication of how rapidly the inland watering places had been outstripped by their rivals. By 1851 it was clear that the unequal struggle, the outcome of which had still seemed open as recently as the 'thirties, was at an end.

The story of the gradual disappearance of the old splendour and of the attempts of the spas to avert the inevitable is not without pathos, the more so because the end of the great days came so suddenly. It was postponed by the Napoleonic Wars, which had arrested the development of Continental travel, it was preceded by subtle changes in the character of the spa visitors, and its advent was obscured by the rise of the new spas which enjoyed a transient popularity while the older ones were declining.

To outward appearances the spas continued to flourish during the first quarter of the century, even if they no longer held the middle of the stage. Brighton might have succeeded Bath as the holiday centre *par excellence* of the younger and smarter sections of fashionable society, but who was to deny that the prosperity of the latter rested on more solid foundations than the patronage of a dissolute Prince and his butterfly associates? If royal visits were the test—and what better?—Bath was never more prosperous than between 1817 and 1830, when the number of royal visitors was unprecedented. Certainly, there seemed on a superficial view little need for the Bath of Jane Austen's day to fear the future, and for all her fun at its expense, Jane Austen took it for granted as an established and permanent feature in the social life of the upper classes. And, if there might be doubts whether Bath was holding its own, conclusive proof of the vitality of the inland watering place as an institution might seem to have been provided by the extraordinary rise to fame first of Cheltenham and then of Leamington.

Cheltenham owed its popularity to the visit by George III in 1788, and by 1841 it had a population of 30,000. Exclusively a pleasure and health resort, for a time it outstripped Bath. Its fine squares and dignified buildings remain as evidence of the great popularity which it so rapidly attained and so rapidly lost. This reached its zenith in the eighteen-twenties, and it is noteworthy that for the prototype of the inland watering place Macaulay chose Cheltenham and not Bath or Tunbridge Wells.

In the 'twenties, however, Leamington was taking the place of Cheltenham and becoming, as Granville later called it, the fashionable retreat for 'dukes and their duchesses, marquesses, earls, and barons, with their coroneted partners—not to mention the Lady Augustas and Louisas, baronets and their spouses, besides military knights and their ladies'. The rise of Leamington was still more spectacular than that of Cheltenham. It had been little known until the publication in 1794 of a paper about its waters by a Dr. Lambe, and in 1816 it had only two hotels. Ten years later, said a foreign visitor, it was 'a rich and elegant town, containing ten or twelve palace-like inns, four large bath-houses with colonnades and gardens, several libraries, with which are connected card, billiard, concert and ballrooms (one for six hundred persons), and a host of private houses, which are almost entirely occupied by visitors and spring out of the earth like mushrooms'.[1] It grew from about 2,000 to 6,000 in the 'twenties and more than doubled in size in the 'thirties.

As for the other spas, Tunbridge Wells, though the magnificence of the days of Nash was no more than a memory, continued at first to be quietly prosperous. An increase in the population by 3,000—or nearly half—during the 'twenties was attributed in the Census Report of 1831 partly to the influx of fashionable visitors. 'Though later fashion has diverted the stream to other channels,' said a topographical writer, just over a decade earlier,[2] 'yet these wells still draw a respectable conflux of summer visitants.' Clifton had become a suburb of Bristol and the Hotwells were falling into

[1] Pückler-Muskau, quoted by M. Letts, *As the Foreigner Saw Us* (1935), 114.

[2] John Aikin, *England Described* (1818), 371.

disuse. Epsom Wells were for all practical purposes forgotten, though the author of a history of Epsom expressed the hope in 1825 that the waters would be given a fair trial by the medical profession and would be found worthy of the high repute of which fashion had deprived them.[1] On the other hand, Harrogate, Buxton, Matlock, Malvern and Llandrindod Wells, while none of them more than large villages, had not ceased to flourish, and new spas were still being developed. Ashby de la Zouch dated as a resort from 1805 and the famous Ivanhoe Baths were built in 1826; an iodine spa was discovered at Gloucester in 1814, and another in 1819 at Woodhall, which, according to Granville, was chiefly frequented by farmers, shopkeepers and others of the 'industrious classes'; and the Royal Brine Baths were opened at Droitwich in 1836.

But there were already signs of decadence beneath the seeming prosperity. The transience of the popularity of Cheltenham, the increasingly residential character not only of Bath and Tunbridge Wells, but of Cheltenham itself while it was at the height of its fame as a watering place, the rise in the average age of the visitors and the consequent change in the social atmosphere, all pointed down hill. The spread of the practice of private entertaining, on which Nash had frowned with good reason, boded ill. It threatened the homogeneous social life upon which the maintenance of the distinctive character of the spas so largely depended. The closing of the Lower Assembly Rooms at Bath in 1807 which was symptomatic of the trend away from public entertainments was a bad omen. The change in the company had also become noticeable. Bath, said a French traveller in 1811, was 'a sort of great convent . . . peopled by superannuated celibates of both sexes, but especially women', and the author of a pamphlet with the significant title *The Decline and Fall of Bath* accused the clergy of ruining the town. 'Nothing thrives in Bath nowadays but preaching and praying . . . the parsons have completely got the whip hand of the good people of Bath.' And, in the light of the future, there was irony in Lady Jerningham's account of Tunbridge Wells in

[1] Henry Pownall, *Some Particulars relating to the History of Epsom* (1825), 86–7.

1806. 'The Hours are delightful: Dinner at 4, meeting a Little after seven, and parting before eleven, so that Tunbridge is like a Large Convent, everyone asleep in their beds before 12.'

When a resort has reached the stage at which it is congratulated on being monastic, it is fairly obvious that whatever its future may hold it is drawing to the end of its days as a pleasure resort. The dead hand was upon Bath and Tunbridge Wells, and it is only surprising that it took so long for this to become apparent. When, however, obvious decline began, it was the more catastrophic because of the delay. With the one exception of Leamington, whose turn was soon to come, the leading spas entered a period of depression in the 'thirties. At Bath the pumprooms were run at a loss, and the once famous orchestra, said Granville, was reduced to scraping 'upon a few sorry cremonas the same eternal bars of Corelli and Handel every day at two o'clock' for the entertainment of a score or two of idlers. The arrival of the end at Tunbridge Wells was symbolized by the suppression of the post of Master of the Ceremonies in 1836, just a hundred years after Nash had been appointed. Granville was told that Cheltenham contained a large proportion of 'spinsters and old maids . . ., widows and half-pay yellows from the Indus and the Ganges, together with lots of methodists and teetotallers'. As for Leamington, in 1855 Nathaniel Hawthorne found from the visitors' book at the Clarendon Hotel, by far the most splendid hotel he had seen in England, that only about 350 guests had stayed there during the previous two years.

'No one can deny', wrote Granville in 1840, 'that mineral waters have, for the last thirty years, been growing out of fashion; that those, even, which were most in repute have become nearly forgotten; and that if one or two mineral watering-places of recent formation have, during that period, started into existence, their temporary elevation has been due to causes alien to the intrinsic and legitimate object of mineral waters; while their continuing or not in the enviable position they occupy is becoming every day more and more problematical. Need I quote Bath and Tunbridge to illustrate the first, and Cheltenham and Leamington to illustrate the second part of my proposition?'

For a picture of the spas on the point of decline Dickens's caricature of Bath in *Pickwick Papers* may be recommended. Written only twenty years after Jane Austen's death, it makes an interesting contrast to the picture given in her novels. The accustomed motions are gone through, the established traditions are observed, the old pretensions remain, but life is ebbing away.

The keynote is struck by the manner of the welcome given to Pickwick and his party when they came to sign the register of distinguished visitors.

'Welcome to Ba-ath, Sir,' said Angelo Cyrus Bantam, Esq., Master of the Ceremonies. 'This is indeed an acquisition. Most welcome to Ba-ath, Sir. It is long—very long, Mr. Pickwick, since you drank the waters. It appears an age, Mr. Pickwick. Remarkable!'

'It is a very long time since I drank the waters, certainly,' replied Mr. Pickwick, 'for to the best of my knowledge, I was never here before.'

The daily routine is little changed.

'Every morning, the regular water drinkers, Mr. Pickwick among the number, met each other in the Pump Room, took their quarter of a pint, and walked constitutionally. At the afternoon's promenade . . . all the great people, and all the morning water drinkers, met in grand assemblage. After this they walked out, or drove out, or were pushed out in bath chairs. . . . After this, the gentlemen went to the reading-rooms and met divisions of the mass. After this, they went home. If it were theatre night, perhaps they met at the theatre; if it were assembly night, they met at the rooms; and if it were neither, they met the next day.'

As for the assemblies, according to the Master of the Ceremonies, they had lost nothing of their former splendour. Ball nights at the Assembly Rooms, he explained, were 'moments snatched from Paradise; rendered bewitching by music, beauty, elegance, fashion, etiquette, and—and—above all, by the absence of tradespeople'.

All this was typical. The spas continued to make a brave show. Bath was full, and the 'company and the sixpences for tea, poured in, in shoals', but when it was analysed the company—for all the 'gaiety, glitter, and show'—consisted of three or four 'match-making mammas', a vast number of queer old ladies and decrepit old gentlemen, flirtatious girls, 'various knots of silly young men, displaying various varieties of puppyism and stupidity', and 'divers unmarried ladies past their grand climacteric'.

There is exaggeration in the pictures of decay no less than in those which had been painted during the ascendancy of the spas. But the fact of decay was incontestable. Granville, looking at the problem with the eyes of a doctor who was professionally interested in mineral waters, yet not without a certain detachment, since he was also interested in the seaside resorts, attributed the plight of the spas in large part to their own errors. The charges were exorbitant in comparison with those on the Continent. Many spa doctors ill-advisedly interfered with the natural action of the waters. It was a mistake to send Bath and Tunbridge water to other parts of the country; the natural heat of the Bath water could not be restored artificially. Intrigues and electioneering in the choice of the Master of the Ceremonies often led to violence, acrimony and disturbance. Bath itself was overgrown: its unnatural growth and extension had converted a spa with a town into a town with a spa.

In so far as the spas can be spoken of as corporate entities, it was no doubt true that they had been wanting in foresight. They should have abandoned or moderated their pretensions as centres of pleasure and concentrated on their development as health resorts. As it was, they were ill-prepared for the débâcle. While they were never deserted and never entirely lost their former fame, they found it difficult to adjust themselves to the new conditions. It was not until the later years of the century that revival began. The visit to Bath of Princess Mary of Teck in 1877, the first royal visit for nearly fifty years, was a sign that 'that grass-grown city of the ancients', as Dickens had called it in *Bleak House*, was emerging from the depression.

Not all of the spas were to come through as well as Bath. The wheel had turned full circle. It was primarily as health resorts that they would be judged in the future. As such they were subjected not only to the competition of the great watering places of the

Continent, now in the steam age so much easier of access, but also, with the progress of medicine, to more exacting scientific tests, which some of them failed to pass successfully. Granville himself had expressed scepticism about the medicinal value of the Tunbridge waters, and had fallen foul of the inhabitants in consequence. Significantly enough, the three inland resorts which were pre-eminent when, at the end of the century, this transitional stage was over, were the three which had been earliest frequented, Bath, Buxton and Harrogate.

Meanwhile the seaside resorts consolidated their supremacy. At the beginning of the century, still novel, imitative of their inland precursors, not fully assured of permanent favour, by 1851 they were without important competitors. Whereas the spas had become anachronistic as a result of the Industrial Revolution and the social changes to which it led, the seaside resorts, despite their kinship with the spas, flourished under the new conditions.

It may not be self-evident why they did so and why an entirely new type of resort did not come into being. The explanation lies partly in the fact that the seaside resorts were already established. In the absence of any obvious alternative it was natural that the new holiday-makers should choose to go to them. They had the great advantage that they were associated in the public mind with the Royal Family and the upper classes. Hence to visit them was prima facie desirable to inferior sections of society. 'One of the fashionable pleasures of the day', had written William Hutton in 1788, 'is to visit a watering place. . . . Wherever the people in high life take the lead, the next class eagerly follow.' This was true not only of the middle classes: it applied throughout society.

More important still, the seaside resorts, unlike the spas, were sufficiently adaptable and almost infinitely capacious. Taking them as a whole there could be no question of an excess of visitors within any foreseeable period, and it mattered little whether the visitors were of the same social type, important though this might be in individual cases. They were aided, too, by the form taken by the revolution in communications brought about by the railway. Easy access by railway was of the greatest possible advantage to a holiday resort, but the extent of the holiday traffic was not such that the promotion of lines to watering places could command priority. The railway promoters naturally preferred to route their lines through places which were already populous, and for good practical reasons they chose routes through the low-lying country along the coast rather than through the hills and mountains in which rivals to the established holiday resorts were most likely to develop. The Lake District, the Highlands of Scotland, the Killarney area, and the Welsh mountains were favourite centres for tourists, but for this amongst other reasons they were never serious competitors of the seaside places.

There were also more positive reasons for the direction of the flow from the cities. One was the belief in the recuperative qualities of a seaside holiday. Doctors even continued to send their patients to drink the sea water. Granville, in language which recalls that of Russell, recommended its use both externally and internally, and a medical handbook published in 1860 stated that the usual dose was half a pint, and that to make it more palatable it could be mixed with port wine, milk or beef tea.[1] Its 'active principles', Granville explained, included iodine, bromine, common salt, muriate of magnesia, muriate of potash, Epsom salts, and, according to a German professor whom he quoted, 'a quantity of subtile and volatile animal particles of which chemistry knows nothing, but which extraordinarily increase (its) stimulating power'. The beneficial results which might be expected from its use, provided that it were judiciously recommended, might be as much as those to be attained from the employment of other mineral waters 'proportionate to and in accordance with their respective chemical composition'. 'In cases of languor and debility, hysterical affections, epilepsy, St. Vitus's dance, convulsions in children, etc., etc.,' said a guide book to Margate in 1820, 'bathing, at proper times, has been found remarkably efficacious.'[2] In 1828 cold and warm sea baths were recommended in a medical pamphlet (which was thinly disguised propaganda for Hastings) as effective in the following amongst other conditions: acute and

[1] Spencer Thomson, M.D., *Health Resorts of Britain; and How to Profit by Them.* (1860), 29–30.

[2] Oulton, 54.

chronic rheumatism, gout, consumption, asthma, indigestion and hypochondriasis, diseases of the liver, haemoptysis, scrofula, rickets, measles and whooping cough.[2]

As the century went on, the drinking of sea water dropped out of medical practice, and it was recognized that the uses of sea-bathing as a specific remedy were limited. The emphasis changed to the value of the sea air, in which, Granville's German professor had said, 'even the muriatic acid in sea water is volatized', and in which the ozone came to be regarded as one of the chief health-giving elements. The seaside—in winter and summer—was particularly recommended for convalescence, and the milder resorts, notably Torquay and Bournemouth, for pulmonary complaints. Granville noted as illustrations of the number of tubercular patients at Torquay the spittoons in the hotel bedrooms and the frequent tolling of the funeral bell, and in 1867, when it was asked in connection with a proposal to give Torquay a seat in Parliament, what interest it would represent, the answer given was 'the pulmonary interest'.

The faith which the medical profession placed in the sea water and the sea air for specific complaints reinforced the belief in the value of a holiday by the sea to the health generally, and this was one of the main factors in the development of seaside holidays. 'One of the best physicians our City has ever known,' said Thackeray in *The Newcomes*, 'is kind, cheerful, merry Doctor Brighton.' Sharing his opinion, the professional man and the black-coated worker came to think that there were peculiar virtues in a seaside holiday.

There was another reason for the popularity of the seaside which fundamentally may have been the most important of all. In the discovery of nature, the sea and the mountains, amongst the grandest and at the same time the most mysterious phenomena of nature, had a special fascination. Both play an important part in the history of holidays, and it was only to be expected that as far as England was concerned, the sea should have been the more important of the two. The sea has not lost its capacity for stirring the emotions, but its power is now so diluted by familiarity that

[2] Harwood, op. cit.

some exceptional stimulus is required before it becomes effective. It is easy, therefore, to forget that a hundred years ago, when large sections of the population had never seen the sea, there were romance and magic in aspects of the seaside scene which would now be merely commonplace. The enthusiasm which was shown was in many respects childlike.

The visitor, said Charles Lamb, by way of explaining the disappointment felt by so many people at the sight of the sea for the first time, 'thinks of the great deep, and of those who go down unto it; of its thousand isles, and of the vast continents it washes; of its receiving the mighty Plata, or Orellana, into its bosom, without disturbance, or sense of augmentation; of Biscay swells, and the mariner

> *For many a day, and many a dreadful night,*
> *Incessant labouring round the stormy Cape;*

of fatal rocks, and the "still-vex'd Bermoothes"; of great whirlpools, and the water-spout; of sunken ships and sunless treasures swallowed up in the unrestoring depths; of fishes and quaint monsters, to which all that is terrible on earth—

> *Be but as buggs to frighten babes withal,*
> *Compared with the creatures in the sea's entral;*

of naked savages, and Juan Fernandez; of pearls and shells; of coral beds, and of enchanted isles; of mermaids' grots.'

To some, like Cowper, the sea was a symbol of divine power.

> *Ocean exhibits, fathomless and broad,*
> *Much of the power and majesty of God.*
>
> (*Retirement*, 1782)

To others it stood for the terrible mystery of nature. Sir Edward Denham in Jane Austen's *Sanditon* spoke 'in a tone of a great Taste & Feeling . . . of the Sea and the Sea shore—& ran with Energy through all the usual Phrases employed in praise of their Sublimity, & descriptive of the *undescribable* Emotions they excite in the Mind of Sensibility.—The terrific Grandeur of the Ocean in a Storm, its glassy surface in a calm, its Gulls & its Samphire, & the deep fathoms of its Abysses, its quick vicissitudes, its direful Deceptions, its Mariners tempting it in Sunshine & overwhelmed by the sudden Tempest'. William Hutton wrote in 1788 of 'that vast element, the sea, which comprehends more than half the globe, and which, at some times, wears an aspect supremely beautiful, and at others terribly grand. The history of man, and his unbounded connections, arise from this fluid.' 'The majestic and swelling ocean, presents at once an outline infinitely diversified, and unceasingly interesting,' said a guide book to Blackpool in the 'thirties; and the scene when it was rough formed 'a singular but yet awful combination of the pleasing and sublime.' As Hazlitt had observed, it was a 'strange, ponderous riddle, that we can neither penetrate nor grasp in our comprehension'. 'There is something in being near the sea, like the confines of eternity. It is a new element, a pure abstraction.'

These were rationalizations of an emotion which in a greater or less degree must have affected most of the visitors to the seaside. It took a mild form with the old gentlemen who were content to watch the rise and fall of the tide or to spend hours with a telescope, examining, as it seemed, nothing but the wide expanse of the horizon. With the more susceptible it was almost uncontrollable. Charlotte Brontë's reactions when she saw the sea for the first time at Bridlington in 1839 differed in degree rather than kind from those of thousands of less articulate and less sensitive young women. 'The idea of seeing the SEA—of being near it—watching its changes by sunrise, sunset—moonlight—and noonday—in calm—perhaps in storm—fills and satisfies my mind.' When at last she saw it, 'in its expanse, she was quite overpowered, she could not speak till she had shed some tears—she signed to her friend to leave her and walk on; this she did for a few steps, knowing full well what Charlotte was passing through, and the stern efforts she was making to subdue her emotions—her friend joined her as soon as she thought she might without inflicting pain; her eyes were red and swollen, she was still trembling, but submitted to be led towards where the view was less impressive; for the remainder of the day she was very quiet, subdued and exhausted.' And the realization of enjoyment was 'as intense as anticipation had depicted'. Though she could only afford to stay a week, her 'impressions of the sea never wore off; she would often recall her views of it, and wonder what its aspect would be just at the time she was speaking of it'.

So much for the reasons why the majority of the new holiday-makers made for the sea instead of—as a minority did—spending their holidays in the mountains or the country or in touring or at home. They do not explain, however, why the visitors went to particular sections of the coast in preference to others, or the vicissitudes in the popularity of particular resorts, why Brighton prospered while Weymouth stagnated, why Blackpool outgrew Scarborough, and Southend took the place of Gravesend as the favourite resort of the London populace.

While all the seaside towns selected for the Census Report of 1851 are still important, a number of the most popular modern resorts were absent from the list; and some of them were not mentioned in the Census returns. Southend was not given separately until 1871. Bournemouth, described in 1830 as used for a breeding place by bustard and hen-harriers, consisted of 695 people in 1851, but was not recorded separately until 1871. Skegness was mentioned in 1841 (when a population of 316 included, as already stated, 44 visitors for the seabathing), but not in 1851. In the latter year Blackpool had a population of 2,180, Eastbourne 3,433, Bognor 1,913. In 1836 Fleetwood was a rabbit warren. A generation was to pass before the remote Essex village of Great Clacton became Clacton-on-Sea.

On the other hand, there were many resorts then more or less well known, but now obscure or forgotten. Instances include Topsham (where there was bathing at high tide), Appledore (to which visitors came from 'distant parts' in 1821), Instow (with

61 visitors at the time of the 1841 Census), and Barnstaple, all in Devonshire; Allonby in Cumberland, 'much frequented' in 1818 but already in decline by the 'thirties; Alnmouth and Cullercoats in Northumberland (with respectively 28 and 50 visitors in June 1841), Benfieldside (81 visitors) in Durham, and Alderton (13 visitors) in Suffolk. Resorts of a different kind whose destiny lay in other directions included Hartlepool, Runcorn and Swansea, where the holiday trade was killed by the progress of industry, and Southampton, where, said Granville, 'the all-devouring railway company, and its still more grasping twin sister the dock company, swept clean away the bath-buildings and the bathing-shores'.

In the rise of some resorts and in the decline of others nature, fashion, accident, communications, local enterprise, all played their part. 'The situation of the place', Russell had said, 'should be clean and neat, at some distance from the opening of a river; that the water may be as highly loaded with sea salt, and the other riches of the ocean as possible, and not weakened by the mixing of fresh water, with its waves. In the next place one would choose the shore to be sandy and flat; for the conveniency of going into the sea in a bathing chariot; and lastly that the sea shore should be bounded by lively cliffs and downs; to add to the chearfulness of the place, and give the person that has bathed an opportunity of mounting on horseback dry and clean; to pursue such exercises as may be advised by his physician, after he comes out of the bath.'[1] Russell was thinking primarily of the sea water cure, but, though his schedule of requirements may not have been conclusive or all-embracing, it covered the ground pretty well. A resort which satisfied his standards was doubly fortunate: the attributes for which he looked were good in themselves, and they were also the attributes for which others looked on the strength of his authority. It was natural that the resorts should do their best to fit themselves into Russell's formula. Jane Austen's *Sanditon*, according to its promoters, had 'the finest, purest Sea Breeze on the Coast—acknowledged to be so—Excellent Bathing—fine hard sand—

[1] Quoted by Gilbert, 25, from a translation of Russell's work published in 1753. It does not appear in the 1752 and 1760 editions.

Deep Water 10 yards from the Shore—no Mud—no weeds—no shiney rocks'. 'Never was a place more palpably designed by Nature for the Resort of invalids—the very Spot which Thousands seemed in need of.'

A sandy shore was probably the most valuable natural asset, both from the point of view of bathing and increasingly as time went on because it was suited to children. Climate was of growing importance as the emphasis changed from sea water to sea air and later to sunshine. The mild weather enjoyed by the south coast of Devonshire explains its popularity for winter residence and for consumptives: the pines at Bournemouth were thought to impart to the atmosphere qualities which were particularly valuable for lung patients. On the other hand, at Margate and Scarborough, where the climate was bracing, stress was laid on its invigorating qualities. It continued to be an asset to possess a spa, as at Scarborough; Granville thought that the 'Royal German Spa', where artificial waters of dubious value were supplied by a self-styled German professor, was the only reason for sending 'real patients' to Brighton, and the chalybeate spring which Russell had exploited long continued to be used.

Nature predisposed: man disposed. The public were capricious, particularly in the earlier days when the number of visitors was small. This was due partly to the desire for novelty: partly to the rapidity with which the less fashionable pressed upon the heels of the fashionable, and drove the latter to seek new haunts. 'They', said Southey, in *Letters from England* (1807), of the visitors to the seaside, 'frequent a coast some seasons in succession, like herrings, and then desert it for some other, with as little apparent motive as the fish have for varying their track. It is fashion which influences them, not the beauty of the place, not the desirableness of the accommodation, not the convenience of the shore for their ostensible purpose, bathing. Wherever one of the queen bees of fashion alights, a whole swarm follows her.'

The importance of good communications and of easy access from the main centres of population has already been emphasized. It was one of the main reasons for the pre-eminence of Brighton. The rapid development of Southport and Blackpool dated from the opening of direct railway communications. Eastbourne suffered for a time from an inferior railway service; a branch to Hailsham on the main London line was opened in 1849, but was at first served by only one engine. The growth of Bournemouth was retarded by the delay in extending the railway from Poole until 1870. In 1871 the population was 5,896: ten years later it was 16,859. The Select Committee on the Devon and Dorset Railway Bill were told in 1853 that whereas rents at Sidmouth had pre-

TORQUAY, 1832

viously been about the same as at Teignmouth, they were now little more than half, and property had depreciated a quarter in ten years, because the journey by coach from Exeter deterred many possible visitors to Sidmouth.

That the resorts were alive to the value of good railway communications is shown by the efforts which they made to promote them and the welcome which they gave the railway when it came. At Brighton there was a popular demonstration when the station was opened in 1841, and in 1848 the people of Torquay received the first train with three cheers and a public holiday. There were a few diehards, like the writer of a pamphlet opposing the projected York–Scarborough railroad in 1840 who had 'no wish for a greater influx of vagrants, and those who have no money to spend', and predicted that in a few years the novelty of having no railroad would be Scarborough's greatest recommendation. As a rule the difficulty was not want of enthusiasm at the resorts. It lay in persuading the railway companies and Parliament to give priority to their wishes.

Thus the destiny of the aspiring seaside resort was shaped largely by factors over which its inhabitants had little control. There was nothing which the fisher folk of Topsham, several miles up the estuary of the Exe, could do to make their village a Southend or a Blackpool. The millions were never likely to come to Cornwall or to the west coast of Wales. Geography set limits to the growth of Dawlish and Budleigh Salterton, which lay in narrow hollows between the cliffs. On the other hand, a minimum of natural advantages and a minimum of effort were sufficient to assure the growth of the resorts which were situated near the large cities. As the Directors of the Eastern Counties Junction and Southend Railway foresaw in 1845, 'cheap and expeditious travelling to and from Southend' would inevitably 'establish it as a place of recreation and resort to a portion of the population of the Metropolis' and would form 'a large source of revenue'.[1]

There always remained, however, plenty of scope for local enterprise. The time had passed when visitors were content to lodge in fishermen's cottages and were satisfied with half a dozen bathing machines for their entertainment. Competition was keen, and the equipment of a successful holiday resort involved heavy capital expenditure. Much of this came from the pockets of the private speculators who built boarding houses and hotels, bathing establishments and piers, shops and private residences, theatres, concert halls and other places of entertainment. But communal action was also necessary. A good promenade was indispensable:

[1] *Railway Register*, I (Railway Advertising Sheet, Prospectus of Eastern Counties Junction and Southend Railway, 1845).

a good water supply and modern sanitation[1] were becoming essential: roads and lighting were important: and when these elementary needs had been supplied, rising standards necessitated refinements such as ornamental gardens and bandstands, the provision of which could not always be left to private enterprise.

In the nineteenth century private enterprise was naturally more important than communal action, and some of the leading seaside resorts owed their existence or their distinctive characteristics to speculators or groups of speculators. St. Leonards, Eastbourne and Bournemouth are outstanding examples. St. Leonards was designed by Sir James Burton as a resort for the *élite*, and the opulence of its architecture—a favourite theme for admiration at the time—reflected the intentions of its author.[2] The planned development of Eastbourne was due to the Dukes of Devonshire, who owned the land on which it stood. Bournemouth was planned as a high-class resort, especially for invalids, by three men, an enterprising landlord, Sir George William Tapps-Gervis, a far-seeing architect and estate agent, Decimus Burton, and an influential doctor and publicist, Granville. The last saw in it 'a perfect discovery among the sea-nooks one longs to have for a real invalid', and, given 'great judgment, discrimination, knowledge of the laws of climate, and, finally, taste', an opportunity for creating 'a real Montpellier' in England.[3] Other examples of speculative enterprise included New Brighton, which was developed—the conception is shown by the name—as a watering place for the wealthier inhabitants of Merseyside, and Torquay, the foundations of the prosperity of which were laid by a progressive Lord of the Manor, Sir Lawrence Palk. Instances of speculations which did not at first realize the hopes of their promoters were Bognor, in which in the previous century the London hatter, Sir John

[1] Cf. Mrs. Carlyle on Ramsgate in 1861. 'The smells are nasty! (Spoiled shrimps complicated with cesspool!)'

[2] *The Architectural Review* of September 1941 had an interesting article on this subject.

[3] The claim to be an English Montpellier was a favourite one. Clifton, said *The Bristol Guide* in 1815, 'had been long ago so styled'. Cheltenham was called the 'Montpellier of Britain' in 1821 (Evans). Southport was making a similar claim in 1880 (Murray's *Handbook*).

Hotham, had sunk £60,000, and Herne Bay, where a group of speculators invested £50,000 in the erection of an enormous wooden pier in 1831.

These were a few of the more conspicuous of the thousands of private individuals who in their different ways played their part in the prodigious expansion of the seaside resorts. Landlords, tradesmen, builders and architects, town councillors and local government officials, hotel and boarding house keepers, all had their contribution to make, and imperceptible though it may ordinarily be now, all have left their mark for good or ill on the seaside resorts of to-day. Most of them were practical men, who did not look beyond the possibilities of personal profit, and men of education and vision were exceptional among them, though no more so than in the great industrial and commercial centres. What they made of their opportunities is discussed in the next chapter. Here it is enough to say that they were most of them good business men who set out to give the public what they thought it wanted. In so doing they in their turn stimulated the movement to the seaside.

VII

BY THE SEASIDE

The most extravagant expression of the first great period in the history of the English seaside resorts culminated in Regency Brighton. The growing pains were over: Brighton had succeeded Bath as the metropolis of fashion: aristocracy enjoyed a last wild fling before it was compelled to re-orient itself to the new world created by the silent revolution which was bringing the rising middle classes to the top. The Regent's bizarre Pavilion, the architectural embodiment of this extraordinary episode in social history, still stands as the monument of its eccentricity, profligacy and splendour.

George IV's Brighton is the extreme example of the aristocratic tradition as it expressed itself at the seaside resorts. A more sober tone was set by his father at Weymouth: there was always a tinge of Cockney about Margate and of Northern austerity about Scarborough. Brighton stood out for gaiety and lack of restraint: yet there was more in common between the Regent's Brighton and George III's Weymouth than between them and the typical seaside resort of the next generation. They enjoyed a common heritage of exclusiveness, urbanity, wealth and fashion, which whether the form it took was sober or extravagant could not withstand the invasion of the newcomers brought in the train of the industrial revolution, whose numbers made exclusiveness impossible, who had no tradition of culture, whose purses were tighter, whose wealth had been hard earned, and who moved in circles far removed from the centres of fashion in London and on the Continent. It made no difference that many of the invaders were anxious for nothing more than to be absorbed in the aristocratic social round. The new element was basically incompatible with the old, and there could in the long run be neither absorption nor compromise.

The classes which predominated amongst the earlier visitors may be represented by the Darcys and the Bennets. The classes which predominated by 1850 had been comprehensively summed up by Cobbett as 'stock-jobbers'—'mostly stockbrokers', Charles Lamb had said—businessmen and industrialists, Dombeys and Forsytes, born of the new industrial and commercial prosperity. But inferior sections of the community were already joining them, the classes represented by Dickens in *The Tuggses at Ramsgate*, and these in their turn were to preponderate before another fifty years had passed.

The social changes were gradual. A visitor to Scarborough in 1806 referred to a decline in the quality and an increase in the quantity of the visitors. The additions were 'chiefly cloth makers and merchants from the West Riding; a set of honest, hearty fellows, who undermine the best constitutions in the world and die, by eating and drinking.'[1] On the other hand, Granville in 1839 remarked on the extent to which Scarborough still attracted those of superior rank. The clothmakers' brethren from the cotton mills and warehouses of Lancashire preferred Blackpool and Southport. At first diffident in their unfamiliar surroundings they soon acquired confidence and, from choosing the more modest hotels, before long they were to be found reclining on the red damask sofas of the very best. Granville described an advanced stage in their infiltration of Harrogate. 'At one time your opulent Leeds, and Sheffield, and Manchester factors, whose ideas of supreme happiness at a Spa were limited to a moderately dear hotel or boarding house, no more dreamt of stopping at the gates of the

[1] *Catherine Hutton's Letters* (ed. C. Hutton Beale, 1891), 150.

Dragon, still less at those of the Granby, for admission, than they would at the palace of my Lord Harewood, by the way, for that purpose. . . . The Dragon and the Granby were sacred places. Now . . . cutlers and cotton spinners aspire to great assembly rooms and gigantic banqueting-saloons; and nothing pleases the wealthy townsman of Bradford and Huddersfield, Halifax and Rochdale, but the *lambris dorés*, the well-stuffed sofas of red damask, and the *cuisine par excellence* of those two crack hotels.' Still, however, the parvenus did not contest the supremacy of the fashionable during the high season: they came to Harrogate in June and July, and left before this began in August.

By 1850 the tables had been turned. The aristocracy had yielded place to the middle classes. Royalty no longer patronized Brighton, Weymouth and Southend. William IV and his Queen had been faithful to Brighton. Victoria found its inhabitants 'very indiscreet and troublesome' and never went again after 1843. 'Persons of distinction and fashion' were deserting Blackpool for other watering places, for Scotland, Ireland, the Lakes and the Continent;[1] the highest in rank at Granville's hotel at Blackpool were, he thought, a Yorkshire ironfounder and a retired Liverpool wine merchant. It was in vain that in order to maintain the exclusiveness of Brighton the high season was changed first to September and then to October. The railway had brought it to the doorstep of London, and it was impossible to keep out London's thousands, 'those swarms . . . daily and weekly disgorged on its Steyne from the cancer-like arms of the railroad'.[2] The City men who as early as 1823 had 'skipped to and fro' by coach between London and Brighton every day were the nucleus of a growing dormitory population.

Not that the doors were opened wide at once. In the second half of 1844, which included most of the holiday months, the passengers of all kinds on the Brighton Railway numbered only 360,000, and in 1859 it was considered remarkable that 73,000 passengers were carried to Brighton by rail in one week. Its size helped it to assimilate new elements, and it lost its fashionable

[1] *New Description of Blackpool*, 10.

[2] Stone, II, 294.

patrons more slowly than most of its rivals. It was a microcosm of London society. Brighton in the season, said Thackeray, was 'London *plus* prawns for breakfast and the sea air'. It was 'a portion of the West End of London *maritimized*', said Granville. Thackeray recorded in *Punch* that, surveying the crowds on the cliffs in 1845, he had picked out forty-nine railroad directors, thirteen barristers, including the Solicitor-General, and at least twelve well-known actors or actresses; and claimed in the course of a stroll in 1847 to have counted at least three hundred acquaintances within a quarter of an hour, including dandies, City men, and Members of Parliament. Brighton society was nothing if not varied. In addition to the directors and the Members of Parliament there were tight-laced dragoons, 'trotting up and down with solemn, handsome, stupid faces, and huge yellow mustachios; myriads of flies, laden with happy cockneys; pathetic invalid chairs. . . .'

There were still many survivors of the old aristocratic days; there were a few precursors of the democratic days of the future; but the upper middle classes were in the ascendant. Working people already came in their thousands on day trips to the seaside places within easy distance of the large centres of population, but few of them stayed longer. The only important exceptions to the general rule were Gravesend, Margate and Ramsgate. Though, as Granville found, factors and artisans, the rich and the 'middling comfortable' mixed at Blackpool and Southport 'either for a week or two's residence, or for a mere frolic', both were still small, and neither was specifically popular.

Gravesend was a riverside version of Peckham Rye and Hampstead Heath, and there were subtle distinctions of social standing between it and Margate and Ramsgate. When Mr. Joseph Tuggs in Dickens's *Tuggses at Ramsgate* (1836) suggested that the Tuggs family should celebrate its accession to wealth by going to Gravesend 'the idea was unanimously scouted. Gravesend was *low.*' After Brighton—which was evidently within the possibilities—had been discussed, the family decided on Ramsgate. Yet, from *Bleak House*, it would appear that the distinction was unimportant. In the long vacation 'all the young clerks are madly in love, and . . . pine for bliss with the beloved object, at Margate, Ramsgate, or Gravesend'.

At Margate all classes were represented. 'Few places present a more singular mixture of society,' said a guide book to the South Coast in 1849. The popular element was represented by the 'host of merry mermaids, happy, no doubt, to exchange the dirty alleys of Whitechapel and the Minories, for a week's dip in the blue sea'. Its amusements were 'chiefly adapted for the Million'.[1] With 'the bustle of a great inn, and the motley look of a fair day',[2] it was no place for the lover of quiet. The number of visitors was growing rapidly. In 1860 it was estimated at 100,000 a year, and Margate was recommended as a 'cheery, bright, life-loving, and a not too constrained seaside resort, with all the materials for healthy enjoyment and *abandon*', but voted by some 'low, *bourgeois*' because of 'its outside amusements, its lotteries and, perhaps, its yellow slippers'.[3] If Brighton was the West End of London by the sea, it was at Gravesend, Margate and Ramsgate that the Cockney spirit found expression. This may have been vulgar, but at least it was spontaneous, vital and cheerful. Margate was as essentially a product of Cockney London as Blackpool was later of industrial Lancashire.

Despite the increase in numbers and the changes in the social composition of the visitors, the superficial resemblance between life at the seaside and life at the eighteenth-century spa was slow to disappear. Tradition was strong; the inhabitants were conservative, and the newcomers were anxious to live up to the old standards. The indoor bathing establishments were the most obvious link with the past. There were reading rooms and circulating libraries. There was music. On the promenade (or esplanade as it was often called), the company took the air and exchanged their daily greetings as on the public walks at Bath and Tunbridge. The pleasure-seeker mingled with the seeker after health, and 'the consequent assemblage of invalids, and of the healthy, who make it a pleasure, frequently produces many whimsical scenes'.[4] There

[1] *A Handbook of Travel round the Southern Coast of England*, 12.
[2] M. Walcott, *Guide to the South Coast of England* (1859), 120.
[3] Thomson, 70–1.
[4] Oulton, 54.

were regular public assemblies, though but poor imitations of their predecessors.

But in the long run snobbishness and conservatism pulled in vain against the forces which made for change. Lady Jerningham in 1806 had contrasted the 'quiet, pleasant, sociable intercourse' of Tunbridge Wells with 'this great Staring, Bustling, Unsocial Brighton'. At the spa the baths were a focal point at which every visitor met; at the seaside there was no such centralization. The lack of a social or cultural common denominator and the lack of a focal point round which the visitors could circulate assisted in the disintegration of the company into small units, and in the development of the characteristic Victorian family holiday. This was possibly the most important change of all. The spas and the early seaside resorts were essentially resorts for adults. There was no place for children in Nash's Bath, and its patrons could make other provision for their children when they went away from home. The seaside, on the other hand, was admirably adapted for children's holidays, and most of its patrons were compelled by economic necessity to take their families with them. One of the earliest references to children at the seaside occurs in Schofield's *Guide to Scarborough*, which was published in 1787. The ailing and infirm, the gay, the opulent and the juvenile, it said, held festive summer residence there. In 1803 William Hutton described the children at play on the beach at the same resort. 'To observe the little animals, in the greatest degree of health and spirits, fabricating their pies and their castles in the sand, is a treat for the philosopher.' Fifteen years earlier he had only mentioned 'ricketty and puny' children at Blackpool.

Thus, within the framework of the eighteenth-century tradition, there grew up a new tradition in correspondence with the spirit and the social stratification of the age. 'Watering places may be divided into two classes,' wrote a social historian in 1856, '(1) those in which is a circle of visiting, to which presentable people find access; (2) those without any general circle of visiting or society whatever. This is an important distinction, and great effects result from the operation of either condition. . . . Some desire to be private, some are inadmissible. Both these classes choose a town without a circle: to others, visiting and morning calls, added to a sojourn by the seaside, render the place very desirable.'[1] The classification was too simple, but it is a useful illustration of the transitional stage through which the resorts were passing. The second category were coming to prevail, and the suppression of the post of Master of the Ceremonies at Brighton in the previous year may appropriately be taken as marking the dividing line between the old and the new.

The new tradition was essentially middle class in character. The visitors to the eighteenth-century resorts had been drawn from the wealthiest and most cultivated classes in the community. The visitors to the nineteenth-century resorts were some of them wealthy, but few of them could pretend to be cultured. Margate, said Matthew Arnold, was a 'brick-and-mortar image of English Protestantism, representing it in all its prose, all its uncomeliness —let me add, all its salubrity'. His remark was true not only of Margate; it applied to all the newer resorts, and it not unfairly summed up the spirit of the middle-class family holiday.

There was little to take the place of the old tradition. Nineteenth-century Protestantism and nineteenth-century economics provided an excellent philosophy for work. They had little to contribute to the organization of leisure. At least their contribution was negative. This is not to say that the Victorian family did not enjoy itself on holiday. But the disintegration of the social life, the presence of children, the lowering of the level of manners and education of the visitors, and the increase in numbers meant that seaside life was no longer London social life on another stage, and that the social arts no longer flourished.

One of the most obvious signs of degeneration was in the physical appearance of the resorts. Except in the rare instances of planning, this reflected the unco-ordinated efforts of individual enterprise; and when in a period of low aesthetic standards lack of taste was added to lack of planning the results were often unfortunate. They are still with us, and the reader can judge them for himself. They are amusingly described and illustrated in Mr. Osbert Lancaster's satire on the imaginary resort which he called

[1] G. Roberts, *Social History of the Southern Counties* (1856), 559.

Pelvis Bay, and how they came about in one part of the country is told, though with some exaggeration, by Mr. Edmund Vale: 'In 1850 the Chester and Holyhead Railway opened up an absolutely virgin coastline. . . . It was like a gold-rush. The scum of the building trade got there first, and staked their claims. The pioneers were Englishmen or Scotchmen. They ran up apartment houses at competitive speeds and sooner or later a scratch town council fitted out an esplanade in front of them. Meanwhile, the Welshman who was sufficiently interested to watch what was going on, found that it was neither fashionable nor profitable to build small solid houses as his forefathers had done. He quickly learned the trick of jerry-building, and added a few tricks of his own to it. Thus was established the Welsh local contractor, and the Welsh town councillor, whose combined essays in the creation of "accommodation" for visitors have done more to ruin the beauty and romance of Wales than the destructive forces of all the belligerents engaged in a world war could have done.'[1]

There were not lacking at the time, as is sometimes supposed, those who lamented the damage which was being done, but there was no means of controlling the 'brick-and-mortar speculators' who, as Granville said, ran up 'interminable terraces, parades, paragons, and parabolas of houses of every sort and size and description'. Granville warned the inhabitants of Bournemouth not to line their coast 'with a whole mile of monotonously uniform houses, or spread whole streets and squares in the plain, and convert a present garden into a future huddled town': Murray's Guide to Devon and Cornwall complained in 1856 of the speculators whose ugly houses were spoiling the romantic seclusion of Babbacombe. Complaints were to little purpose, and the inevitability of what was happening was well conveyed by *The Times*, when it said (30th August 1860) that 'Marine Terraces, Sea Villas, "Prospect Lodges", "Bellevues", hotels, baths, libraries and churches soon accumulate.'

If there was chaos in the background, there was anarchy in the foreground. The scene was one of immense but apparently aim-

[1] Quoted by Howard Marshall in *Britain and the Beast*, ed. Clough Williams-Ellis (1937), 166.

less activity, the antithesis of the disciplined routine imposed by Nash.[1]

An impression of disorder was conveyed by the unceasing procession along the promenade; the crowds on the sands and in the water, bathing, paddling, shrimping, reclining in deck chairs; the harassed parents watching their offspring build 'impossible fortifications' and the elderly gentlemen 'looking at nothing through powerful telescopes for hours, and when at last they saw a cloud of smoke, fancying a steamer behind it, and going home comfortable and happy',[2] the bright young things as 'busy as bees' and attended by their 'mothers, and aunts, and sisters, and cousins, and friends', braving the water with the conventional squawks and squeals, 'squeaking, giggling, kicking, splashing and wincing' as they were lifted into the sea by the bathing machine attendant,[3] or decorously flirting with whiskered beaux.

The sands of a popular seaside resort appeared 'one indiscriminate moving mass of cabs, cars, carts and carriages; horses, ponies, dogs, donkies, and boys; men, women, children, and nurses; and, the least and the biggest—babies and bathing-machines . . . little boys with spades; nurses with babies; mammas with sewing; young ladies with novels; young gentlemen with Byron, canes, and eye-glasses; older ones with newspapers, sticks and spectacles.'[4]

The promenade was always crowded, and apart from those who perambulated it on foot there was a colourful variety of carriages—'the cabs, the flys, the shandry-dans, the sedan-chairs with the poor invalids inside; the old maids', the dowagers' chariots, out of which you see countenances scarcely less deathlike; the stupendous cabs, out of which the whiskered heroes of the gallant Onety-oneth look down on us people on foot; the hacks mounted by young ladies from the equestrian schools, by whose sides the riding-masters canter confidentially. . . .'

[1] One excellent source for the details of seaside life is *Punch*. Leech's numerous drawings on seaside subjects may in particular be mentioned.

[2] Dickens, in letters from Broadstairs.

[3] Head, *Home Tour* (1836), 47-8.

[4] Stone, II, 299-300.

SEASIDE SCENE, 1856 ('*Phiz*')

So Thackeray described the scene at Brighton in 1847, and this constant perambulation was a feature of all the resorts. The evening parade on the pier at Bridlington struck Charlotte Brontë 'as the greatest absurdity. It was an old pier in those days, and of short dimensions, but thither all the visitors seemed to assemble in such numbers, it was like a packed ballroom: people had to march round and round in regular file to secure any movement whatever.' Southport, said Nathaniel Hawthorne in 1857, was the same as ever, 'the visitors perambulate to and fro without any imaginable object'.

There was at any rate exuberance and vivacity in this activity. The accommodation in which the visitors stayed, on the other hand, was often as drab as the stock jokes about seaside lodgings made out. The practice of staying in hotels and boarding houses was growing, but, as in the previous century, most of the visitors took furnished apartments. Whatever the kind of accommodation, the quality tended to be inferior. The service was unsatisfactory. The food was bad. The standard of comfort was low, and in the season there was deplorable congestion.

'They used to be content, so long as they were at Blackpool, if they were crammed a dozen in a bed,' said an old Blackpool man, later in the century, 'but now they grumble if there's only five.'[1] Thackeray wrote of apartments at Brighton in which a bedstead in the drawing-room was disguised as a chest of drawers. Referring to a hotel at Ryde which she was told was the dearest in Europe, Mrs. Carlyle said in 1843: 'The cream was blue milk, the butter tasted of straw, and the "cold fowl" was a lukewarm one, and as tough as leather.' She moved to lodgings and found that she had fallen among bugs.[2] It was of a meal at one of the best hotels in Brighton, also in 1843, that Macaulay made the famous remark that it was 'a dinner on yesterday's pease-soup, and the day before yesterday's cutlets; not an ounce of ice, and all beverages, wine, water, and beer, in exactly the state of the Church of Laodicea'. Another visitor to Brighton was still more unkind. 'The

[1] Article in *Manchester Guardian*, 10th June 1938.

[2] Jane Welsh Carlyle, *Letters and Memorials* (ed. J. A. Froude, 1883), I, 219, 226.

dinner was very bad; a sprawling bit of bacon upon a bed of greens; two gigantic antediluvian fowls, bedaubed with parsley and butter; a brace of soles that perished from original inability to flounder into the ark, and the fossil remains of a dead sirloin of beef.'[1]

Other complaints were those made of the best hotels by Nathaniel Hawthorne in 1855. The menu consisted of 'joints, joints, joints, sometimes, perhaps, a meat pie, which weighs upon your conscience, with the idea that you have eaten the scraps of other people's dinners'. 'We pay like nabobs, and are expected to be content with plain mutton.' What is more you felt as if everybody from the landlord downward was 'united in a joint and individual purpose to fleece' the traveller. The tipping system was also a subject of criticism. If the tip was too small, said Hawthorne, 'a look of profound surprise, a gaze at the offered coin (which he nevertheless pockets) as if he either did not see it, or did not know it, or could not believe his eyesight', came over the face of the servant. 'The tendency to impose upon travellers at almost all these establishments', said Granville, 'is evinced from the very first onset.'

The two institutions which, perhaps, most typified life at the nineteenth-century seaside resort were the bathing machine and the pier. The bathing machine was a reminder of the continuity with the spas, and its passing in the early years of the next century was symbolical of the revolution in morals and manners since the time when the popularity of seaside places could be measured by the number and quality of their bathing machines and they vied with one another in the modesty of their bathing arrangements. The bathing machine was the outdoor department of the bathing establishments which were the descendants of the pumprooms at the spas. In these establishments newspapers, books, telescopes and pianos were available for the entertainment of those who were waiting to use the machines; there was provision for warm sea water and other mineral baths; sometimes there were swimming baths; and in the evening the amusements included dancing and concerts.

[1] James Smith, quoted by Sitwell and Barton, 313 Granville, however, said that the gourmand need not despair at Brighton.

The bathing machines survived the bathing establishments. This may seem strange. They were uncomely; they were inconvenient and cumbersome; with their horses and attendants they were expensive to maintain; and the charges for using them (ordinarily a shilling) were high. In all these respects, the bathing cabin and tent, which began to take their place towards the end of the century,[1] were superior. They were inferior in the protection which they gave to modesty, and this was the main reason for the survival of the machine.

The concern with modesty went to such extremes that it stressed what it was desired to minimize. Ample protection from too inquisitive eyes should have been given by the voluminous bathing costumes worn by the ladies. As the attendant of the ladies' department at Bath told Granville in 1841, 'what harm did it ever do, or could it do, to see the nice dear creatures go down the steps out of their private undressing-rooms, and enter the bath with their bathing-wrappers, made of rich stuff and fashionably cut, down to the feet and hands, and fastened to the waist,—their hair gathered up under a very elegant coiffe—walk up through the water to shake hands and exchange morning salutations with the gentlemen of their acquaintance already in the bath, attired in the very pink of fashion? One might as well object to their walking together, or meeting and greeting each other in the Grove, in dresses not very far different. There they are immersed in air—and here they are immersed in water. Of the two, the latter is the most decent element, as it is not quite so transparent.

Oh! 'twas a glorious sight to behold the fair sex
All wading with gentlemen up to their necks.'

The generosity of the bathing attire was the first line of defence.

[1] The bathing machine was an established *Punch* joke, and its history can be traced in the volumes of *Punch*, which show, for example, how it was gradually going out in the years before the war of 1914–18.

'A MERMAID', 1854 (*John Leech*)

The second was the machine itself, though it was inconsistent that the ladies submitted themselves without embarrassment to the arms of the lusty male attendants who lifted them into the water. Yet a third, as we have already mentioned, was provided by regulations ensuring the complete segregation of the sexes, such as the rules at Southport prohibiting pleasure boats under a penalty of five shillings from approaching within thirty yards of the area where the ladies bathed, and requiring the gentlemen's and ladies' machines to be at least a hundred yards apart. These precautions defeated their own object, and a favourite theme of writers of the time was the assiduity with which the gentlemen tried to circumvent the restrictions upon their freedom of view. It might be worth while to incur the fine. 'The gentleman fined, provided his eyes be tolerably good, has no cause to complain of the draft on his purse.'[1] If his eyesight was inadequate he could make use of artificial aids. The complaint was made of Ramsgate and other places in 1860 that the visitors left both manners and modesty in their lodgings, so that 'bathers on the one hand, and the line of lookers-on on the other, some with opera-glasses or telescopes, seem to have no more sense of decency than so many South Sea islanders'.[2]

It continued, on the other hand, to be usual for men to bathe naked. This was one of the reasons for the ban on mixed bathing, which did not begin to be lifted until the end of the century. It was because he was naked that Mr. Jorrocks was so embarrassed when he was rescued from the sea after a bathe at Margate. Granville described it as a stain upon the gentility of Brighton that owing to the absence of hoods over the steps the persons of gentlemen bathers were wholly exposed when they came out of the machines. Certain ladies at Brighton turned the practice to good account. As a method of protesting against the desecration of the Sabbath by those who bathed on Sundays, they took their camp stools to the beach, and, prayer books in their hands, sat where they blocked the return of the delinquents from the sea.[3] In short, an 'almost heathen indecency' prevailed, 'which makes one think that much of our boasted refinement is but surface deep. In most places but Britain, male bathers are compelled to wear some sort of decent covering, such as short drawers, which do not in the least impede the movements of the body; it should be imperative in this country also, and one might give a hint that the present

[1] Head, 47.
[2] Thomson, 73.
[3] Valerie Pirie, *A Frenchman Sees the English* (1935), 296–9.

indecency is not diminished by the blushing intrusiveness of some of the fair sex.'[1]

The piers, straddling 'out on their iron legs, where the seas were not too abruptly deep or too stormy', were, said Professor Clapham, 'as symbolic of what archaeologists call a culture, as are axeheads and beakers and other durable products of man's handiwork'.

The building of a pier was a sign that a seaside resort was of age, and the resorts rivalled one another in the elaboration of their piers. In origin a landing stage, the pier became a meeting place, a promenade, an amusement centre. To some extent it corresponded to the assembly room at the spa. The standard type was an 'iron promenade pier not made for trade',[2] which usually expanded at the end to carry a pavilion, where entertainments and refreshments were provided. But large sums were spent at the bigger resorts on the erection of more imposing structures. The rebuilding of the pier at Margate after it was damaged by storm in 1808 cost in all £100,000. It was a 'magnificent piece of architecture, which must ever reflect credit upon Mr. Rennie, under whose plan and directions it has been executed'. In the centre was a gallery where a band played on fine days, and there was a promenade, admission to which cost a penny. The imposition of this charge was the occasion of a demonstration by several hundred people in 1812. The crowd broke through the barrier, and on the following day, in spite of the presence of additional constables, there were scenes of violence in which one of the toll gatherers was nearly thrown over the pier and some arrests were made. The building of a second pier in 1856 was a sign of the progress made by the town in the meantime, and further progress was marked by the addition of a pavilion in 1871. At Brighton the celebrated chain pier was built in 1823 for the purposes of the cross-Channel service, and a second pier was added in 1866. From the beginning excellent provision was made on the former for mental and physical refreshment; in 1824 it boasted a camera obscura, a sundial, two small cannon, several green benches, and

[1] Thomson, 33.

[2] J. H. Clapham, *Economic History of Great Britain*, II, 518.

some mineral water booths, and on special occasions was illuminated in the evening. In 1839 a weighing machine was mentioned, the name and weight of every person using it being recorded, an early example of what has become a popular feature of the modern holiday resort.

Another link between the old resorts and the new was the popularity of music. But the musical standards of the eighteenth century were not maintained. The place of the stringed orchestra was taken by the brass band, which was especially popular in the North, where the brass-band movement was a flourishing expression of the musical tastes of the people.[1] Military and German bands became established institutions. Lady Jerningham mentioned a band of German musicians at Brighton in 1806, and the Prince Regent had arranged for the Gloucestershire Militia to be permanently stationed there because of the excellence of its band. 'The usual delights of watering places', it was said in 1863, were 'reading rooms, shrimps and German bands.'[2] That any form of musical expression should flourish was healthy, but the nineteenth century was not a great period in English musical history and the standard of seaside music was low. Yet music was ubiquitous, in the streets, on the piers and the beaches, in the bandstands, concert halls, bathing establishments and hotels. Of the popular resorts in general it might be said, as Mrs. Carlyle said of Ramsgate in 1861; 'Indeed, noise seems to be the grand joy of life.'

Dickens suffered at Broadstairs from the innumerable itinerant musicians with their 'most excruciating' organs, fiddles, bells, violins, music boxes and voices. Eastbourne was recommended in 1849 to those to whom 'raffling, bazaars, military bands, and forced merriment are unnecessary to happiness'.[3] Hawthorne described 'the constant succession of organ grinders and other itinerant musicians' at Southport, and Thackeray complained of the brass bands at Dover, whom stupid listeners stimulated with beer. Mrs. Carlyle found the noise at Ramsgate continuous:

[1] J. F. Russell and J. H. Elliot, *The Brass Band Movement* (1936), gives a full account of this interesting movement.

[2] Murray, *Kent and Sussex* (1863), 99.

[3] *Handbook of Travel round the Southern Coast of England*, 148.

'A brass band plays all through our breakfast, and repeats the performance often during the day, and the brass band is succeeded by a band of Ethiopians, and that again by a band of female fiddlers! and interspersed with these are individual barrel-organs, individual Scotch bagpipes, individual French horns!'

Lectures and scientific demonstrations were another link with the past. On the other hand, except in connection with horse-racing, gambling was for practical purposes non-existent, and dancing in public was suspect. There was drama of a kind, at Brighton given by London performers, 'blazing Macreadys, resplendent Miss Cushmans, fiery Wallacks, and the like', to quote Thackeray (1845), and at lesser resorts presented by amateurs and by troupes of itinerant barnstormers. Fairs and circuses paid visits during the season. Firework displays delighted and amazed both young and old, while balloon ascents by celebrated aeronauts occasionally provided even more sensational diversions.

Sport was taken in a light-hearted spirit. Bathing, 'that luxury to the healthful, and restorative to the sick',[1] was for some a medicine, for others a social occasion, but many did not bathe at all, and there are few references to swimming, which was hardly as yet considered a branch of athletics. Fishing and boating were, of course, favourite pursuits, and many were the stories of adventures and accidents, often amorous in character, which arose on boating expeditions. Riding was popular, but was a social institution rather than a sport. Golf was almost unknown outside Scotland, lawn tennis was an invention of the 'seventies, the popularity of cricket as a spectacle dates from about the same period, and until late in the century all were subordinate to the more sedate and ancient pastimes of bowls, croquet and archery. Amusement, not athletic achievement, was the main object of the sports contests which were a favourite entertainment. Sir George Head described the events at Southport in 1835. Men hopped in sacks, trundled wheelbarrows blindfold, chased a pig with a soaped tail. Boys were set to climb a greased pole for a gold-laced hat, and with their hands tied behind their backs dipped with their mouths for coins drowned in a bowl of treacle.

[1] Barber's *Isle of Wight* (1845), 16.

By the Seaside

'Every year a month or so by the sea, sands and donkey rides, sea anemones, bathing, blackberries and cream.' Thus Lowes Dickinson summed up his holidays as a child in the 'sixties. 'Sea shells and sea anemones being my chief objectives in life at that period, thanks to Philip Gosse's *Aquarium* and a native predilection, they were Paradise enow to me,' wrote Julian Hawthorne

DIVING BELLES, 1862 (*John Leech*)

of the previous decade, 'and donkeys and donkey boys, with their thwacking cudgels, taught me patience both vicarious and personal.'

Donkeys and sea anemones. No account of the Victorian seaside holiday would be complete without a reference to them both. In different ways each is symbolical—donkey riding of the more democratic social life in which children were important and the pence had to be counted,[1] and the passion for collecting—sea anemones, sea shells, sea weeds, pebbles—of the acquisitiveness and love of detail of the age. In fact both were part of the inheritance from the past. In the latter years of the eighteenth century donkeys were on hire at Brighton and Tunbridge Wells. As for collecting seaside objects, in the seventeen-sixties visitors to Margate went on the sands at low tide to collect 'pebbles, shells, seaweeds, etc.'[2] 'The pursuit of picking up shells and weeds every day', it was said of Hoylake in 1813, 'is something to help on existence between breakfast and dinner.'[3] At Scarborough, recorded Granville, it was an intellectual treat to visit Mr. Bean's unparalleled collection of shells both recent and fossil. Kidd's *Picturesque Companion to the Isle of Thanet* (c. 1840) devoted a separate section to the pursuit—more grandiosely called 'conchology'—and stated that 'with the visitors and their children, the search after shells is a fashionable and daily amusement'. 'Much taste was displayed in the arrangement of shells, pebbles, and seaweed', it was said in 1856, 'much energy in the search after them.'[4]

Something of the romance and mystery of the ocean attached to the simplest objects connected with it.

> *Oh call us not weeds, but flowers of the sea,*
> *For lovely, and gay, and bright-tinted are we;*
> *Our blush is as deep as the rose of thy bowers,*
> *Then call us not weeds—we are ocean's gay flow'rs,*
> *Not nurs'd like the plants of the summer parterre,*
> *Whose gales are but sighs of an evening air;*
> *Our exquisite, fragile, and delicate forms*
> *Are the prey of the ocean when vex'd with his storms.*[5]

[1] Sage advice was given in a guide book of 1860 (Thomson, 32). 'If you want a quick ride, take your donkeys by the distance, but if you want a slow one, by time.'

[2] Beaumont and Disney, 54.

[3] Richard Ayrton, *Voyage round Britain*, 78.

[4] Roberts, 556.

[5] Roberts, 556-7.

Then there were shrimps. What pleasure they gave in the catching and the consumption! An interesting essay might be written on their rise and decline in esteem; their history was to be the opposite of that of the oyster. Brighton was early famous for its shrimps. As James and Horace Smith wrote in 1828,

> *Here with choice food earth smiles and ocean yawns,*
> *Intent alike to please the London glutton,*
> *This, for our breakfast, proffers shrimps and prawns,*
> *That, for our dinner, Southdown lamb and mutton.*

'Hail, then, purveyor of shrimps, and honest prescriber of South Down mutton,' said Thackeray in *The Newcomes*. And it is strange to read now Disraeli's statement in a letter about a visit to Brighton in 1840: 'I have eaten a great many shrimps.'

Such, then, was life at the seaside, a confused medley, in which shrimps and donkey rides, military bands and song recitals, sand castles and sea anemones, refuse to sort themselves out. No Nash appeared to dominate the scene and to impose order upon it. As the grand tradition slowly dissolved, and royalty and aristocracy ceased to set the tone, it was set instead by Cobbett's stockjobbers and Granville's textile manufacturers, by the Tuggses and the clerks madly in love, by the day trippers of the North country wakes weeks and the Cockney mermaids from the Minories. There was no sharp break in continuity, and the new was inseparably interwoven with the old. It is, therefore, difficult to define the change, unmistakable though it was. The stage was the same but the cast was transformed. It was like the difference between Ascot and Epsom, Goodwood and Aintree, an intangible difference of spirit and atmosphere. It was the difference between Jane Austen's Bath and Thackeray's Brighton on the one hand, and the England of Jerome K. Jerome and Ally Sloper on the other. But, whatever it may have lacked, at least the Victorian seaside resort did not lack what G. K. Chesterton called the 'great gusto' of the age.

By the Seaside

NOTE

The spirit of the seaside in middle and late Victorian England is so well conveyed by the following extracts from Richard Jefferies and F. Anstey (the author of *Vice Versa*) that they may serve to round off this chapter.

'Mamma goes down to bathe with her daughters and the little ones; they take two machines at least; the pater comes to smoke

ALLY SLOPER'S HALF HOLIDAY

his cigar; the young fellows of the family-party come to look at "the women", as they irreverently speak of the sex. So the story runs on *ad infinitum*, down to the shoeless ones that turn up everywhere. Every seat is occupied; the boats and small yachts are filled; some of the children pour pebbles into the boats, some carefully throw them out; wooden spades are busy, sometimes they knock each other on the head with them, sometimes they empty pails of sea water on a sister's frock. There is a squealing, squalling, screaming, shouting, singing, bawling, howling, whistling, tin-trumpeting, and every luxury of noise. Two or three bands work away; niggers clatter their bones; a conjurer in red throws his heels in the air; several harps strum merrily different strains; fruit-sellers push baskets into folk's faces; sellers of wretched needle-work and singular baskets coated with shells thrust their rubbish into people's laps. These shell baskets date from George IV. The gingerbeer men and the newsboys cease not from troubling. Such a volume of uproar, such a complete organ of discord—I mean a whole organful—cannot be found anywhere else on the face of the earth in so comparatively small a space. It is a sort of triangular plot of beach crammed with everything that ordinarily annoys the ears and offends the sight.

'Yet you hear nothing and see nothing; it is perfectly comfortable, perfectly jolly and exhilarating, a preferable spot to any other. A sparkle of sunshine on the breakers, a dazzling gleam from the white foam, a warm sweet air, light and brightness and champagniness; altogether lovely. The way in which people lie about on the beach, their legs this way, and their arms that, their hats over their eyes, their utter give-themselves-up expression of attitude is enough in itself to make a reasonable being contented. Nobody cares for anybody; they drowned Mrs. Grundy long ago.'

(Richard Jefferies, *The Open Air* (1885). Essay on the Bathing Season. The extract describes a scene near the West Pier at Brighton.)

THE JOYS OF THE SEASIDE

Oh, I love to sit a-gyzing on the boundless blue horizing,
When the scorching sun is blyzing down on sands, and ships, and sea!
And to watch the busy figgers of the happy little diggers,
Or to listen to the niggers, when they choose to come to me!

Chorus

For I'm offully fond of the Sea-*side!*
If I'd only my w'y I would de-*cide*

By the Seaside

To dwell evermore,
By the murmuring shore,
With the billows a-blustering be-*side!*

Then how pleasant of a morning, to be up before the dorning!
And to sally forth a-prorning—e'en if nothing back you bring!
Some young men who like fatigue'll go and try to pot a sea-gull,
What's the odds if it's illegal, or the bird they only wing?

Chorus

For it's one of the Sports of the Sea-*side! etc.*

Then what j'y to go a-bything—though you'll swim, if you're a sly thing,
Like a mermaid nimbly writhing, with a foot upon the sand!
When you're tired of old Poseidon, there's the pier to promenade on,
Strauss, and Sullivan, and Haydn form the programme of the band.

Chorus

For there's always a band at the Sea-*side! etc.*

And, with boatmen so beguiling, sev'ral parties go out siling!
Sitting all together smiling, handing sandwiches about,
To the sound of concertiner—till they're gradually greener,
And they wish the ham was leaner, as they sip their bottled stout.

Chorus

And they cry, 'Put us back on the Sea-*side! etc.'*

There is pleasure unalloyed in hiring hacks and going roiding!
(If you stick on tight, avoiding any cropper or mishap),
Or about the rocks you ramble; over boulders slip and scramble;
Or sit down and do a gamble, playing 'Loo' or 'Penny Nap'.

Chorus

'Penny Nap' is the gyme for the Sea-*side! etc.*

By the Seaside

Then it's lovely to be spewning, all the glamour of the mewn in,
With your love his banjo tewning, ere flirtation can begin!
As along the sands you're strowling, till the hour of ten is towling,
And your Ma, severely scowling, asks 'Wherever have you bin?'

Chorus
Then you answer, 'I've been by the Sea-*side! etc.'*

Should the sky be dark and frowning, and the restless wind be mowning,
With the breakers' thunder drowning all the laughter and the glee;
And the day should prove a drencher out of doors you will not ventcher,
But you'll read the volumes lent yer by the Local Libraree!

Chorus
For there's sure to be one at the Sea-*side! etc.*

If the weather gets no calmer, you can patronize the drammer,
Where the leading lady charmer is a chit of forty-four,
And a duty none would shirk is to attend the strolling circus,
For they'd all be in the workhouse, should their antics cease to dror!

Chorus
And they're part of the joys of the Sea-*side! etc.*

(F. Anstey, *The Young Reciter and Model Music Hall* (1888). Encore verse and final chorus omitted.)

VIII

TOWARDS HOLIDAYS WITH PAY

The Census of 1861 recorded for the first time an excess of urban over rural population. The English nation, said the Census report, had 'assumed the character of a predominating city population'. There were seventy-two towns with more than 20,000 people in England and Wales; London with a population of 2,803,989 was the largest city in the world; Liverpool with 443,938, Manchester with 357,979, and Birmingham with 296,076 exceeded the quarter million; Leeds, Sheffield and Bristol exceeded 150,000. The unparalleled concentration of the population in great cities without easy access to the open air and the countryside was part of the price paid for industrial and commercial prosperity, and as the cities enlarged the need for opportunities of escape also grew.

The railway had removed the chief technical obstacle to the satisfaction of this need. What may be called the social obstacles were slower to disappear. The advance which was most important —because it was the essential preliminary to any general advance —was the gradual dissolution, almost complete by the end of the century, of the prejudice amongst employers against holidays even for themselves. What they denied to themselves they were unlikely to yield to others.

Towards Holidays with Pay

The idea that a holiday was a waste of time meant by God or natural law to be devoted to the increase of wealth died hard; but, as *The Times* said in 1871, with reference to the Bank Holiday Act, there had been 'an increasing tendency of late years among all classes to find excuses for Holydays. Among those who are well-to-do the annual trip to the seaside has become a necessity of which their fathers, or at least their grandfathers, never dreamt. A merchant or a tradesman in those days was quite contented with his Sundays, and, like John Gilpin, would patiently work without intermission "for twice ten tedious years" and even then would only be decoyed into a day's disasters by the importunities of his wife.' It was pleaded in justification of the demand for holidays that we worked harder and faster than previous generations, an excuse which, said *The Times*, it would be ungracious as well as vain to question. But there were still many exceptions to the general rule amongst the middle classes, and it will be observed that *The Times* referred to the well-to-do when it spoke of the seaside holiday as a necessity.

The second half of the century was marked by three other important developments. The weekly half holiday became widespread in industry, though not in shops and agriculture; the Bank Holiday Act not only gave statutory sanction to some of the traditional holidays but added to them; the practice of granting an annual holiday to manual workers was growing, and there were the beginnings of holidays with pay.

Inquiries made by the Royal Commission on Labour in the 'nineties showed that most workpeople had a weekly half holiday, and that, where there was no half holiday, work ordinarily stopped earlier than usual on Saturdays. Yet even the weekly half holiday was of comparatively recent origin. It had not been common until the Factory Act of 1850 prohibited the employment of young persons and women in any factory after two o'clock on Saturday afternoon. This provision had the usual consequence that the men tended to benefit as well. There was opposition on familiar lines. The Select Committee on Bleaching and Dyeworks were told, for example, in 1857 that the weekly half holiday had led to dissipation and folly instead of mental or moral improvement, and in some cases to fraud and misappropriation by young men whose expenses exceeded their wages. But the general opinion was favourable to the system, and it was eloquently defended by the Inspectors of Factories (1859).

'The possession of the Saturday afternoon for themselves is an immense boon conferred upon the people in relation to their social state; for now, the wages can be carried home in ample time for the market, and the husband and wife can spend their money together. And a still greater boon is, the distinction at last made clear between the worker's own time and his master's. The worker knows now when that which he sells is ended, and when his own begins; and, by possessing a sure foreknowledge of this, is enabled to prearrange his own minutes for his own purposes.

'This it is which has given the impetus to so many institutions for mutual improvement that have sprung up so rapidly of late years, in almost every hamlet of our industrial districts. This it is, which has enabled so many operatives from time to time to visit our national exhibitions, and thus to acquire enlarged views, not only of the commercial greatness of their country, but of the important part which they are called upon to play in its promotion. It was by this indeed, that they were enabled to realize the Exhibition of 1851 as a fact which they have never forgotten, and never will; for it lighted up a flame of observation in the minds of many, which has never yet dwindled; and it stirred up a spirit of inquiry, which has been of lasting benefit to the people as well as to the country at large.'

This was to take a rosy view of the desire and capacity of the workers for self-improvement, but there was no doubt about the social value of the weekly half holiday, nor about the high store which was soon set on it. It was, 'as it were, a part of our religion in Bradford', the Child Employment Commissioners were told in 1866. In the Nottingham hosiery trade the Saturday half-day was given instead of certain irregular holidays at times such as the races and the fair, and its introduction was said not to have diminished the amount of work done. Employers in other industries mostly came to the same conclusion, and in some cases productivity was actually found to increase. There remained, however, some who, though they were friendly to the principle of holidays for the poorer classes, genuinely doubted whether the grant of more holidays, including the weekly half holiday, was in their real interests. A sympathetic expression of this point of view was given in 1863 in a leading article in the *Illustrated London News* on 'People's Parks and People's Holidays', which was favourable in principle to an increase in the holidays enjoyed by the millions who 'must toil six days in every week in every month of the year . . . and if they are prudent enough to eschew the worship of St. Monday, know of no real holiday but Christmas Day, and Easter and Whit Mondays'.

'There is, perhaps, no social problem more difficult of solution than that which involves the affording of more holidays to the working classes without at the same time diminishing their means of subsistence. The Saturday half holiday, if it has not exactly become an institution in this country, has been established to a considerable extent; but we have never yet been able to ascertain whether even this has not been achieved solely at the expense of the worker. . . . The relations between employer and employed are so peculiar and so delicate that it is hardly possible to interfere with them without affecting, in a degree, the material interests of the latter; and we confess to a hopelessness of any arrangement which will, without any pecuniary sacrifice on his part, guarantee to the working man any increase to his holidays proper.' (19th September 1863.)

Practical experience provided one answer to this plausible argument, but it was not without substance.

The weekly half holiday was a modest step towards the annual holiday with pay. The Bank Holiday Act of 1871 was a leap forward. Its passage into law illustrates a change of attitude which was revolutionary in its implications. The work largely of one man, Sir John Lubbock (later Lord Avebury), but for his pertinacity it might not have reached the statute book for a generation. Yet it went through both Houses of Parliament with remarkable ease.

In its actual terms it was not a radical measure. It made statutory the enjoyment by a limited class of four holidays three of which had long been widely, though far from universally, observed. But it was revolutionary in two respects. It treated these holidays no longer as part of the great religious festivals but as secular days of leisure, and it added a new and entirely secular holiday in the principal holiday month. There was thus a certain irony in the nickname which the *Daily Telegraph* suggested for the August Bank Holiday—'Saint Lubbock's Day'.

Lubbock's success in carrying through this reform was partly due to the skill with which his Bill was drafted. The public at large benefited by a side wind. Possible opponents were misled by its carefully restricted title and did not realize its full significance. Lubbock's own view was that its easy passage was 'partly the result of an accident. On the old holidays, Bills of Exchange are payable the day previously, i.e. Sunday Bills on Saturday. We felt that it would be difficult to extend this to the new holidays, and after some consideration we determined to propose that they should be payable the day after instead of before. Hence we had to devise some special name for the new holidays, and we called them "Bank Holidays". If we had called our Bill the "General Holiday Bill", or the "National Holiday Bill", I doubt not it would have been opposed; but the modest name of "Bank Holiday" attracted no attention and roused no opposition.'[1]

The formal purpose of the Bill was 'to amend the law relating to the Payment of Bills of Exchange and Promissory Notes falling due on Bank Holidays'. The fate of a similar Bill which Lubbock had introduced in 1868 was not encouraging. This had passed its Second Reading, but when referred to a Select Committee it was emasculated of one of its principal provisions, namely that Boxing Day should be a bank holiday, and it made no further progress. This proposal was rejected because of the inconvenience which might be caused to business, and the Select Committee were not persuaded by the argument that the bank clerks had fewer holidays

[1] The account of the bank holiday legislation and the first bank holidays which is given here is based mainly on H. G. Hutchinson, *Life of John Lubbock, Lord Avebury* (1914), *The Life Work of Lord Avebury* (ed. the Hon. Mrs. Adrian Grant Duff, 1924), the Parliamentary Reports, *The Annual Register*, and *The Times* and other newspapers.

than other similar classes. Merchants, lawyers, all other trades and professions, had their slack periods. Not so the banks, though it was true that they gave their employees an annual holiday, which varied in different firms from a week to a fortnight, and sometimes rose to three weeks in the senior grades, in comparison, as was pointed out by a member of the Committee, with the customary fortnight in other business offices.

Under the 1868 Bill the bank holidays would have been Sundays, already holidays by common law; Christmas Day, which was similarly observed by common usage; Good Friday, a statutory bank holiday under an Act of 1800; any day appointed by Royal Proclamation for a solemn Fast or Thanksgiving, as provided by an Act of 1827; the day after Christmas Day, or, when Christmas Day fell on a Saturday, the following Monday; and any day appointed specially by Royal Proclamation as a bank holiday in any part of the United Kingdom or in any city or borough thereof.

The 1871 Bill was more radical in that it added to the existing holidays not only Boxing Day but Easter Monday, Whit Monday and the first Monday in August. It is not surprising in view of the experience of 1868 that opposition was expected. Sir D. Salmon, M.P., Chairman of the London and Westminster Bank, told Lubbock that the Bill did not stand a chance. Another banker asked Disraeli to support it, but after some delay was informed that the difficulties were so great that the Government could not take the responsibility.

Yet it received the royal assent within little more than three months after its introduction, and without opposition in either House. This was remarkable enough. It was still more remarkable that the House of Lords extended its scope. It is clear from the Debates that Lubbock's intention that it should not apply only to banks was fully comprehended. Lord Overstone in fact suggested the omission of the word 'bank' as likely to lead to confusion, and the substitution of the word 'general'. He saw no reason why the opportunities of relaxation which it provided should be confined to banks. They should be open to everybody in this hard-working country.

This proposal was rejected, but not because of opposition to the principle. Speaking against Overstone's proposal, Lord Salisbury supported the view that the scope of the Bill should be extended but argued that it was not necessary to construct its language anew. It was in the main a Bank Holiday Bill and there was no reason why the title should not be used. It would be a Bank Holiday Bill because of the compulsory duties to which the banks were subject. To alter the terminology would cause delay, and it would be better to secure the same object by a new provision.

In consequence the House of Lords added a clause enacting that no person was to be 'compellable to make any payment or to do any act upon any such bank holidays which he would not be compellable to do or make on Christmas Day and Good Friday, and that such obligation shall be transferred to the following day'. This clause was permissive, and it was ambiguous, but its importance was that it was not limited to the bank clerks. It applied generally, and both in letter and spirit it helped to transform the Bill from a sectional into a national measure.

The interest of the Debates in the Lords lies mainly, however, in the attitude towards the question of holidays which they exemplified. Evidently, as Lord Overstone said, the Bill was in harmony with the social tendencies of the times. Such suggestions as were made were in the direction of extending its scope. Lord Redesdale thought that six holidays a year would not be too much to give to persons closely confined to business and that they should be equally distributed over the year. He suggested the addition of the first Mondays in February and November. Another proposal was the addition of Ascension Day. This was rejected partly on the ground that it was too close to Whit Monday, and the Bishop of Winchester made the interesting point that it was inadvisable to confound State and ecclesiastical holidays. It is of interest, too, that *The Times* still referred to 'holydays'.

Opinion in Parliament reflected opinion outside. With a simple faith in the popular memory the *Daily Telegraph* wrote that 'the people may forget a great many deeds of glory and names of renown; but they will never forget him who has given them a new and universal day of repose and recreation'. There was a practical demonstration of public appreciation on the first August Bank Holiday, when especially in London there were amazing scenes at the railway stations and the steamboat piers. Neither the railways, the steamers, nor the public houses were able to accommodate the enormous crowds. At Cannon Street, Charing Cross and Fenchurch Street (the terminus for Southend and Margate) there was an unprecedented scramble. The Margate boats arrived after they were scheduled to return. One of the vessels was eaten out of food within ten minutes, and along the upper reaches of the Thames the public houses ran out of tobacco.

Yet the observance of the early bank holidays was far from complete. On Whit Monday, 1871, the first bank holiday under the Act, most of the offices in the City closed, others shut early, and four-fifths of the shops kept open. This was at a traditional holiday period, and the observance of the first August Bank Holiday was still less complete. Though it was observed in Liverpool almost as strictly as Good Friday or Christmas Day, in London, as on Whit Monday, business went on as usual except in the City. As required by law the Customs and other public offices were open. In Regent Street only twelve shops shut, and afterward *The Times* gave a gentle hint to West-End shoppers to be more considerate. In Manchester most of the warehouses were closed but the mills were at work, and the mass of the people did not seem to be aware that the day was a holiday. The crowds who went from London to the seaside for the week-end and filled the excursion trains, of which three or four times the usual number ran to Margate and other popular resorts, were City workers and other members of the middle class, and on Hampstead Heath there were none of the popular celebrations associated with Easter and Whitsun.

It took some time for the public to realize the full meaning of the Act, but not long. Within a year August Bank Holiday, said *The Times* in 1872, had already acquired 'at least as decisive a popular acceptance as the old traditional Holydays. Last year . . . people scarcely realized their opportunity. But yesterday was all but universally observed. Business was suspended, not merely in the City, but throughout the busy part of the Metropolis'; and the *Daily News* remarked 'how much such a day of relaxation was needed, its universal acceptance proves'. There were inevitably a few who doubted whether the bank holidays were in the true interest of the working classes, but the passage of the Holidays Extension Act in 1875 was a further proof of its acceptance. This extended the Act of 1871 to docks, customs houses, inland revenue offices and bonding warehouses, and incidentally made it easier for many business houses to observe the bank holidays: it further provided that when the 26th December was a Sunday, the 27th should be a bank holiday. Here the extension of bank holidays has stopped, and though various Bills have been introduced for the addition of new holidays, such as Empire Day and the first Monday in July (which it was suggested should be called Victoria Day), the prediction of *The Times* in 1872 (6th August) that a bank holiday would be instituted between August and December has not been realized.

As wages rose and industrial conditions improved it was an easy stage from the weekly half holiday and the bank holiday to longer annual holidays, though it took time. From the material collected by the Royal Commission on Labour and from other sources it is clear that, while it was still far from general at the end of the century for working people to take a summer holiday, the practice was growing. Of London Charles Booth said in his *Life and Labour of the People in London* that, where the workpeople did not themselves take irregular holidays, 'the granting of a week's holiday by the employer is not unusual', while full advantage was taken by almost every one of bank holidays and other established holidays. It was common for employers to shut down in the slack season in the summer, sometimes ostensibly to give the work-people a holiday; and comparatively few employments were 'so constant as not to yield vacation enough, and in some cases when the slack season falls at a convenient time of year, advantage is taken by those who can afford it, to arrange a week at the sea-side'. But, Booth added, 'otherwise, and more generally, enforced idleness is a poor substitute for a holiday'. At York, which was not typical because of the large number of railway workers—they not only had better holidays than the average, but enjoyed special rail facilities—Seebohm Rowntree found in 1901 that it was becoming common for a few days' summer holiday out of the city to be taken by his class 'D', which included families with an income of 30s. a week or over and comprised 52.6 per cent of the working-class population.

Amongst large sections, however, the level of wages left little or no margin for holiday expenditure. These included not only the aged, the infirm, and the unemployed, but the mass of the rural population and a high proportion of the industrial workers. The average annual earnings of adult male manual workers in 1885 were estimated at £60; under 2 per cent earned 40s. a week or upwards, and 82 per cent earned 30s. or less.[1] Agricultural earnings were still lower, averaging 15s. 11d. a week in the 'nineties; and in the towns many thousands were living near the starvation level. Thirty-five per cent of some nine hundred thousand residents of East London were by Charles Booth's standards either 'poor' and having a struggle to obtain the bare necessities of life, or were 'very poor' and in a state of chronic want. William Booth wrote less scientifically but with force of the 'submerged tenth' as a disgrace to a wealthy community which complacently assumed that it was Christian and civilized.

On the other hand the economic position of the average man was not static. It fluctuated with trade conditions, and, more important, at different stages in his life. His bachelor days were comparatively affluent: whilst his children were young he sank into poverty: when they began to earn he was more prosperous: and he relapsed into poverty when they left home and he declined in years. There were ways and means, too, by which even the

[1] Estimates given by Sir R. Giffen to the Royal Commission on Labour (*Final Report*, 1894). These figures were for Great Britain and Ireland. The number of persons receiving more than £400 a year cannot have much exceeded 100,000 in the early eighties: the Royal Commission on the Depression in Trade and Industry (*First Report*, 1886) were informed that the number of assessments to income tax of £400 or over in England under Schedule D (Trades and professions) and Schedule E (excluding Government employees) was 59,026 in 1870, 78,409 in 1875, 81,129 in 1880, and 87,591 in 1883. The number of assessments under £400 was 467,248 in 1883, when the exemption limit was £150.

poorest could contrive to take holidays, though they were by no means universally available. Single men joined the militia for the sake of a few weeks under canvas in the summer; poor families made holiday at the same time as they picked fruit or hops to cover the cost of keeping themselves; there were some, though not many, agencies for helping the poorest people to have holidays. Those who were fortunate enough to have relatives and friends in the country or at the seaside could stay with them, while working people could save for their holidays through the 'going off' clubs and similar institutions which flourished especially in the North.

Still it is no matter for surprise that holidays without pay were not always welcome. 'If at all it must be with payment,' the Lancashire Branch of the Gasworkers' and General Labourers' Union told the Royal Commission on Labour, 'as at present the pay is not sufficient to keep wife and family.' The Sheffield Table Blade Grinders who had to pay rent for their wheels during holidays found them particularly irksome; the Warrington Painters' Society not only objected to too many enforced holidays but said they could also spare bank holidays very well; and the experience of a firm of Leeds machine toolmakers who gave foremen and well-conducted men on application from four days to a week to go away to the seaside—which they considered improved the men's health—was that most of those who were eligible did not take advantage of the privilege.

As regards the part which holidays played in the lives of working people there is valuable evidence in a study of industrial conditions by the German sociologist, G. von Schulze-Gävernitz (1892).[1] According to him a great part of the cotton operatives and engineers spent some of their savings on excursions during the wakes weeks which occurred in most of the Lancashire industrial towns in the months of July, August and September. They went, he said, to Derbyshire and the Lakes, many of them to see the sights of London, some even to the Continent, but the sea was beloved over all else, and the favourite resorts were the Isle of

[1] *Der Groszbetrieb, ein wirtschaftlicher und sozialer Fortschritt. Eine Studie auf dem Gebiete der Baumwoll-industrie.*

Man and Blackpool. In six out of seven working-class budgets which he analysed there was expenditure of some kind on holidays. The exception was naturally the poorest family, that of a Darwen weaver, who had three children to support on a total income from his own earnings and those of his wife of £100 a year. Though he had ten days' holiday in the year he spent nothing on them. At the other economic extreme was a fustian cutter at Hebden Bridge who, with six children all earning, had a surplus of nearly £70 out of a family income of £244 and had spent an unspecified part of this surplus on holidays, of which he had in all about twenty days: the children had about fourteen days' holiday each. The family of a Bacup weaver, with all seven children earning and £168 coming in, saved about £50, part of which went on holidays. Out of the income of £206 of an Oldham mule spinner, £15 was allocated to 'other expenses', 'especially holiday during factory holidays for self and family'. In the three other cases the holiday expenditure was £5 or less. A Hyde cotton spinner, with two children, both earning, and two weeks' holiday himself, spent £5 out of a family income of £132 on 'other expenses' including holidays; a London engineer, with six children, two of them earning, a family income of £145, and nine days' holiday a year, spent £3 18s. on excursions and recreation; and an affluent Northumberland mining family in which there were three wage-earners and five small children spent £3 10s. on the same purposes out of a total income of £234. Beatrice Webb, when visiting her poor relatives at Bacup in 1883, had found that the young men and women often spent a week at Blackpool in the summer, and sometimes went on excursions to London. Booth said (1902) that holiday-making was spoken of as 'one of the most remarkable changes in the habits in the last ten years', and that the statement applied to all classes. But he was thinking primarily of public holidays. Very rarely, he observed in the same context, did one hear a good word for the bank holidays, and the more common view was that they were a curse.

The inability to afford longer holidays was one of the reasons for the survival of the unauthorized holiday—in other words, absenteeism—particularly in the industries and trades in which conditions were worst. For the contrary reason it was tending to disappear where conditions were better. The representatives of the colliery managers before the Royal Commission on Labour estimated the time lost by the coal hewers, including unavoidable absences, at 20 to 25 per cent; and absence on the Monday after the monthly pay day continued to be common and even recognized by the masters. In South Wales 'Mabon's Day', or 'Mr. Abraham's Day', as it was variously called, so often extended in practice over the greater part of the week that the owners preferred to speak of 'Mabon's Week' or 'Mr. Abraham's week'. According to one mineowner, giving evidence before the Commission, it resulted in an average increase of fivepence halfpenny in the cost of raising each ton of coal during the week in which it occurred, and over the whole year threepence three farthings a ton. On the other hand, a trade union representative said that in the view of the chief managers of the mines in the Rhondda Valley the men were losing less time than formerly on the days following Mabon's Day.

In London Booth found examples of unauthorized holidays amongst both the best paid and the poorest classes of worker. Amongst the small but highly organized and comparatively affluent body of saddletree makers it was 'not a very uncommon thing for men to remain "on the booze" for weeks together'. Some of the best pianoforte workers did not want to work every week in the year: 'hard work and large earnings succeeded by idleness and hard drinking make exactly the life that suits them.' At the other end of the scale a similar lack of regularity was prevalent amongst the casual labourers, who often sought 'some compensation for the precariousness of their existence in spurious independence'. The same was true of some women workers. About 60 per cent of the girls in the Victoria Match Factory were voluntarily absent for from a half to two days a week, and this unreliability was general amongst the 8s. to 10s. girls, as Booth called them. The girls were content with this income and preferred taking a holiday to earning more. A complaint made to the Royal Commission on Labour was that in the textile industry men would strike to get a holiday.

There was no indication in the evidence before the Royal Commission on Labour that the trade unions were interested in holidays with pay, which continued to be confined almost entirely to the blackcoated classes. As regards these the Civil Service Inquiry Commission in 1875 collected information about holidays in business houses and public utility corporations where conditions were analogous to those in the Civil Service; this covered representative banks, insurance companies and stores, the Mersey Docks and Harbour Board, the Railway Clearing House, and the London and North Western Railway. It showed a considerable uniformity of practice. The usual allowance for office workers was a fortnight, often rising to three weeks or a month amongst the higher grades or after long service.[1] The offices about which the Civil Service Inquiry Commission collected information were all of a sheltered character; but Booth's *Survey* and other evidence suggest that in the 'nineties a fortnight's holiday with pay was general amongst clerical employees in commerce and industry, certainly in the larger firms, though there must still have been many exceptions in small offices. It is interesting that a firm of solicitors mentioned by Booth gave gratuities of from £2 to £25 before the holiday was taken, probably by way of an annual bonus or commission.

From Booth it appears that paid holidays were also common amongst other blackcoated workers such as shop assistants. Amongst grocers in London the custom was universal in large businesses; though on the ground that the assistants could not be spared on Saturday the holiday ordinarily lasted from Sunday or Monday to Friday. The draper's assistant was more fortunate and could expect a fortnight after twelve months' service. The period

[1] The changes which had occurred during the century would provide an interesting subject for research. Cf. Charles Lamb's *The Superannuated Man* (1825): 'Besides Sundays, I had a day at Easter, and a day at Christmas, with a full week in the summer. . . . This last was a great indulgence; and the prospect of its recurrence, I believe, alone kept me up through the year. . . . Without it . . . I could scarcely have sustained my thraldom. . . .' This referred to Lamb's youth in the eighteenth century. On the other hand J. S. Mill in his *Autobiography* stated that at India House there were holidays not exceeding a month in the year.

I (a). RICHARD NASH

I (b). RICHARD RUSSELL

PIONEERS

2. 'CHARACTERS AT TUNBRIDGE WELLS' 1748

3. 'COMFORTS OF BATH'—THE KING'S BATH

4. SCARBOROUGH 1735

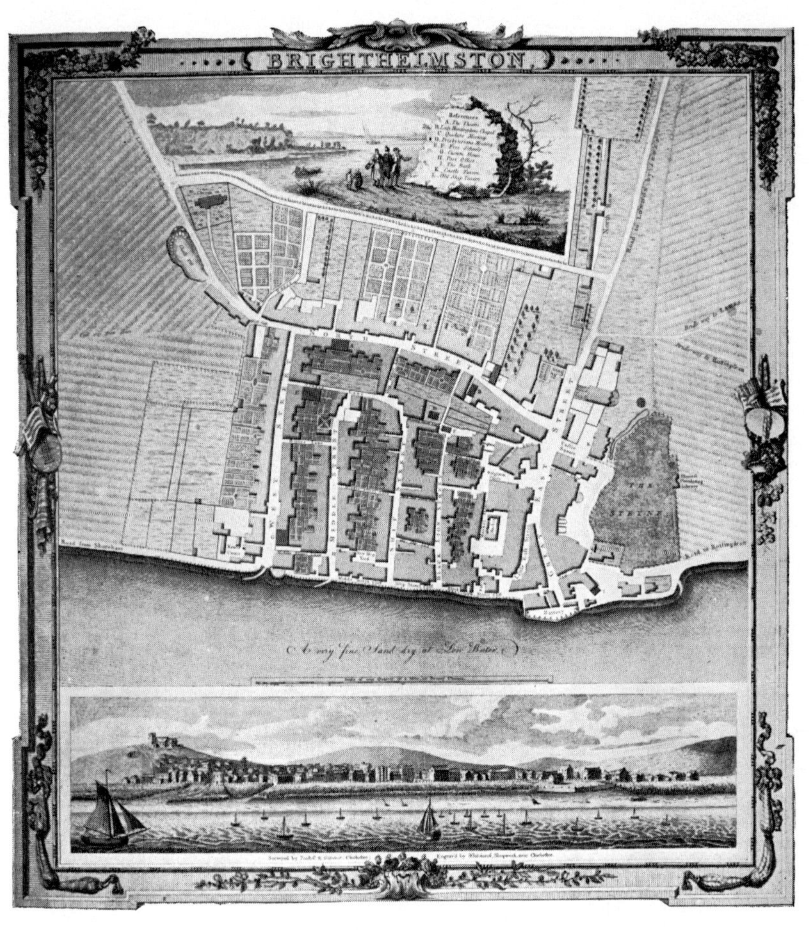

5. BRIGHTON 1779

6. RETURN FROM THE GRAND TOUR
'Well a day! Is this my son Tom?'

7 (a). THE ENGLISHMAN IN PARIS 1767

7 (b). THE ENGLISHMAN ARRIVES AT A FRENCH INN

THE ENGLISHMAN IN PRE-REVOLUTIONARY FRANCE

8. TO CALAIS 1824

9 (a). MORNING PROMENADE UPON THE CLIFF 1806

9 (b). THE PRINCE REGENT ENTERING A BATHING MACHINE 1818

REGENCY BRIGHTON

10. SUMMER AMUSEMENTS AT MARGATE 1813

11 (a). BATHING MACHINES AT BRIGHTON—EARLY NINETEENTH CENTURY

11 (b). RYDE 1845

12 (a). BLACKPOOL *c.* 1836

12 (b). BOURNEMOUTH 1855

13. TO BRIGHTON AND BACK FOR 3s. 6d. 1859

THE EXCURSION TRAIN GALOP

THIRD - CLASS

S. E. R.

CONCANEN & LEE LITH.

STANNARD & DIXON ...

BY

Ent. Sta. Hall **FRANK MUSGRAVE.**

LONDON BOOSEY & SONS 24 & 28 HOLLES STREET

14. 'THE EXCURSION TRAIN GALOP' 1862

15. TOURISTS ON THE TRAMP 1874

16 (a). CRUISING IN THE NINETIES. THE POTATO RACE ON AN EARLY CRUISE TO NORWAY

16 (b). CO-OPERATIVE HOLIDAYS ASSOCIATION OUTING 1901

COMMUNAL HOLIDAYMAKING

17 (a). ON THE SANDS

17 (b). PIERROTS

AT THE TURN OF THE CENTURY

18. PIONEERS

Top left: THOMAS COOK
Top right: T. A. LEONARD
Opposite: W. E. BUTLIN

19. MEDITERRANEAN CRUISE 1930
(*Frontispiece of Evelyn Waugh's 'Labels'*)

20 (a). ASCENT FROM GSTAAD

20 (b). DESCENT TO WENGERNALP

WINTER HOLIDAYS

21 (a). BLACK SAIL HUT

21 (b). HOUGHTON MILL

YOUTH HOSTELS

22 (a). FILEY HOLIDAY CAMP

22 (b). START OF AN ORGANIZED HIKE, LED BY A RED COAT

'BUTLINISM'

23. HOLIDAY ADVERTISING 1946

24 (a). DESIGN FOR A TRAVCO HOLIDAY CENTRE

24 (b). DESIGN FOR A NEW PIERHEAD AT BOURNEMOUTH

TOWARDS THE FUTURE

allowed was usually short, but the principle was well established.

The Departmental Committee on Holidays with Pay (1938) referred to no instance of paid holidays for manual workers earlier than 1884, when a large chemical firm gave a week. The Industrial Welfare Society has traced an instance as early as 1875, and research if sufficiently diligent would no doubt find much earlier cases. Exact dates are unimportant, and it was in the 'eighties that the practice began slowly to spread. The Royal Commission on Labour found a few examples of its adoption. In some firms paid holidays were limited to apprentices and foremen, but in others all were eligible. A large London bakery gave a week to all employees with service of a year or more, and a fortnight to foremen; a London crucible company allowed three days to a week according to length of service, or the equivalent in wages if the holiday could not be taken; and a firm of newspaper proprietors, publishers and printers at Bristol granted a week to printers, as compared with a fortnight to literary men and clerks. Booth recorded that men in the traffic departments of the principal railways had three or four days with pay, while those in the locomotive departments were as a rule allowed to take a short holiday without pay. On the London and North Western Railway in 1890 'a great proportion' of the men received a week with pay, but it was emphasized that this was not a matter of right but rather of reward for good conduct and depended upon the discretion of the superintendent.[1] Amongst municipalities and other public and semi-public bodies practice varied greatly. Of thirty-four vestries and other bodies in the London area about which Booth had information only one gave no paid holidays. The practice of the others ranged from two days —Good Friday and Christmas Day—in one case and three to six days in seven cases, to twelve days in sixteen cases. Members of the London County Council fire brigade were entitled to at least one week's annual holiday in addition to twenty-six days' ordinary leave, but were otherwise always on duty; the police were entitled to one day in fourteen, and after twelve months in the Metropolitan Police Force or eighteen months in the City Police

[1] Select Committee on Railway Servants (Hours of Labour) Bill, 1890–1.

constables and sergeants had a week or ten days', inspectors two or three weeks' leave a year. The Gas Workers' and General Labourers' Union, representing employees of a partly municipalized industry, reported to the Royal Commission that signed hands had a week's holiday with pay, provided that they had not lost more than seven days work in the previous twelve months. Some of the permanent staff of the Mersey Docks and Harbour Board had a week every year or alternate year. Shipwrights and riggers in the Royal Dockyards were entitled respectively to four and a half and four days a year, and the riggers at least to not more than fourteen days without pay in addition.

What is important, however, is less the number of persons affected than the acceptance of the principle. It is at first sight curious that the initiative seems to have come from the employers, and it is notable that the lead was taken by public and semi-public concerns. There is no evidence that the preferential treatment of the salaried was resented by the manual workers. They appear to have regarded pay without work as a contradiction in terms, though Booth mentioned that the programme of the National Municipal Labour Union included an annual summer holiday of not less than a week with pay. 'A man should be paid well for the time he is at work and lose time for holidays,' the Royal Commission on Labour were told by the Sheffield Engine Drivers and Stokers Society. 'A man that wants paying without working is a drone to his fellow men.' A representative opinion was that expressed to the Select Committee on the Sale of Liquors on Sunday Bill more than twenty years earlier (1868) by George Potter, President of the London Working Men's Association. He thought that there should be less work on weekdays, and that instead of Sundays being spent in recreation there should be some national holidays on which working people could enjoy a change of air. Decidedly, however, the holidays should not be holidays with pay. 'But then I should anticipate that before those things are adopted a man will have more money for his labour, in order that he may be able to afford to lose his time. It would not do under our present system.'

What was the reason then for the seeming generosity of the

employers who granted paid holidays in advance of the expressed wishes of their employees and of orthodox economic thought? This is not a question which it is easy to answer. One factor was undoubtedly that experience showed the value of holidays in terms of industrial efficiency. But the explanation is partly to be found in the more benevolent social philosophy of the last quarter of the century which took such practical forms as the Settlement movement. The head of a Bristol firm, announcing the grant of a week's holiday with pay in 1889, expressed the hope on behalf of the firm that it would materially contribute to the health and happiness of the workpeople,[1] and there is no reason to doubt that there was an element of genuine philanthropy in the new attitude.

The dawning appreciation of the importance of holidays as one of the conditions requisite for decent living in the great cities was illustrated by the rise of charitable agencies the object of which was to enable persons otherwise unable to take holidays to do so. It was characteristic of the time that the chief of these should have been the Children's Country Holiday Fund, which was set up in the 'eighties with the purpose of arranging for poor London children to spend a holiday of a week or a fortnight in the country. The organization of summer camps was one of the earliest activities of the boys' clubs which emerged as separate entities in the course of the 'eighties; the Hulme Club at Manchester, which is sometimes said to have been the first boys' club in the modern sense, was founded in 1886 and held its first summer camp in 1887. But the movement was not confined to children. The columns of *The Times* in the 'eighties contained many appeals from churches, missions and similar bodies for subscriptions to the cost of excursions and outings for both adults and children from poor districts. The Polytechnic's 'Holiday by Proxy Fund', which provided holidays entirely without charge, extended to adults, and in its first year (1890) 370 of the poorest inhabitants of Marylebone were sent to Brighton under its auspices. A more specialized agency of the same kind was the London Poor Clergy Holiday Fund, which had been started in 1876.

It will be evident from what has been said that economic cir-

[1] Departmental Committee on Holidays with Pay (1938), 8.

cumstances were of primary importance in determining who had holidays and how they were spent, and the duration and the nature of the holidays taken by an individual were a fairly reliable indication of his economic position. 'Amongst the upper classes', said Booth, 'holidaymaking has been raised to the level of a fine art and invested almost with the character of a religious observance', and 'the amount of holiday taken and the way in which it is spent, from a fortnight at the seaside to a winter in Algeria or Egypt, serves very fairly to distinguish the various social grades'. Amongst working people there was every shade of distinction between the fortunate minority who spent a week or fortnight by the sea and the many thousands who could hope for nothing better than a factory outing to Blackpool, an excursion to the races on Kersal Moor or a bank holiday jaunt to Hampstead Heath, while there were still many amongst the most depressed classes—the farm labourers and the 'submerged tenth' of the cities—who never had a day's outing.

NOTE

As a footnote to this chapter it may be of interest to mention the findings of the Royal Commission on Public Schools as regards school holidays (1864). Except in two London schools (St. Paul's and Merchant Taylors'), holidays, whether taken twice or three times a year, varied from fourteen to sixteen weeks, which the Commission did not think excessive. The precise dates, however, varied, and as it was desirable that boys of the same family should be at home together, it was suggested that the Governors should try to make them coincide; but the Commission did not wish to interfere with schools which had holidays only twice a year. Thus, for very good reasons, they advocated the reverse of what is now called 'staggering'.

The following are examples of the holidays at different public schools:

Eton: 3 weeks and 4 days at Easter. 6 weeks and 4 days at Election. 4 weeks and 4 days at Christmas.

Westminster: 3 weeks at Whitsun. 7 weeks in August and September. 4 weeks at Christmas.

Charterhouse: 4 weeks from 2nd week in May to the 1st or 2nd week in June. 12th or 13th August to 23rd or 24th September. 12th December to 16th January.

St. Paul's: 6 weeks from the Tuesday following the third Thursday in July. 4 weeks from the Tuesday following the third Thursday in December. A week at Whitsun with Whit Monday and Tuesday.

Merchant Taylors': A fortnight at Easter. About 6 weeks in August and September. 4 weeks at Christmas.

Harrow: 3 weeks at Easter. 6 weeks from the last Tuesday in July or the first Tuesday in August. 5 weeks at Christmas.

Rugby: 7 weeks at Christmas. 8 weeks just after Midsummer.

Shrewsbury: 8 weeks in June and July. 8 weeks in December and January.

Winchester: 6 weeks and a day or two in July and August. 5 weeks and day or two in December. 16 days at Easter. (Commoners had nearly a week more.)

E's an Excursionist dreaming of Beer.

T for our Tourists—at home anywhere.

IX

WAYS AND MEANS

Parallel with the developments described in the last chapter went advances in communications which were in part their consequence and in part their cause.[1] By the 'seventies the railway network was essentially complete, and by the end of the century Britain, always famous for its express services, also stood out for the excellence though not the cheapness of the facilities which were provided for third-class passengers. Yet as recently as 1867 the railway companies had been rebuked by a Royal Commission for their neglect of the needs of the masses. With the important exception of excursion trains, their contribution to the development of popular travel had been inadvertent rather than deliberate, and slight by comparison with the immensity of the opportunities which they so largely missed. Even the enormous growth in the number of excursion trains which marked the 'fifties was due mainly to savage competition, though when it was convenient the companies did not hesitate to claim that they were

[1] The chief primary sources used for the early part of this chapter have been the official reports relating to railways; the various reports on liquor licensing contain much useful material about railway excursions. The histories of the railway companies have also been valuable, despite a surprising inadequacy on the development of excursions.

social benefactors, who had provided a great boon to the industrial population, and, as one company submitted, had afforded 'health and recreation to large masses of women and children'.[1]

The 'fifties were the heyday of the excursion train. The system, said the Railway Department in 1852, had principally developed in the previous two years, and it was characteristic of the age that the Railway Commissioners put pressure on the companies to provide exceptional facilities in connection with the Great Exhibitions of 1851 and 1862.[2] By a happy accident the former coincided with a decline in fares below the economic level. The return excursion fare from Leeds to London, for example, fell to 5s. and the appetite of the public was almost insatiable. The railway system was strained nearly to breaking point. Between June and 27th October 1851, the London and North Western alone carried 774,910 passengers to and from London by excursion train, in addition to greatly increased numbers by ordinary train. In connection with an inquiry into an accident in September the Railway Department was told that 'the excursion traffic of the present season has heavily taxed the locomotive power at the disposal of the Company, and both engines and men are doing an amount of work which, when kept up continuously, must materially diminish their efficiency'. Competition had gone to such lengths by 1858 that, as a railway shareholder protested, excursionists enjoyed '15-inch seats, stuffed cushions and backs to lean against'. The strain was also heavy in 1862. There were more than 6,200,000 visitors to the 1862 Exhibition, including large numbers of work-

[1] *Report* of the Railway Commissioners for 1850.

[2] In 1851 the Railway Commissioners with some inconsistency criticized the Great Western Railway Company for failure to take the necessary safety precautions and urged them to check rather than to stimulate excursion traffic 'unless their staff have time, and are able, to make ample arrangements for their proper and safe conduct'. The Company pointed out in reply that before the opening of the Exhibition they had been much pressed by the Commissioners for greatly reduced fares 'to afford all classes of the community an opportunity of participating in an enjoyment which could not be expected to recur; and they felt bound to meet a demand so popular in its character, and urged from such a quarter'. In the face of this argument the Commissioners modified their criticisms.

ing people, and it was thought that there would have been many more if the times had been more prosperous in the North, which was suffering the effects of the American Civil War. For hundreds of thousands these excursions were an introduction to travel for pleasure.

When conditions became more normal the number of excursion trains was reduced and fares were increased. The poor and rowdy elements who in the 'fifties offended the inhabitants of Brighton by their rags and tatters and their ill-shod feet had to stay at home, and the bulk of the excursionists seem to have been middle-class folk and respectable artisans. One railway company made the doleful complaint to the Royal Commission on Railways in 1867 that they had run an excursion train whose only passengers were six county families and their servants.

In the later 'sixties excursion trains were chiefly confined to Sundays, fixed holidays and special occasions such as race meetings, but they continued to be comparatively numerous and cheap. In 1867 the average cost per mile third class ranged from less than ¼d. to ⅗d. as compared with about 1d. for ordinary trains.[1] Most of the travel covered a short range, and the majority of the excursionists went to the open spaces on the outskirts of the cities, from London to Kew, Richmond, Blackheath, Epping Forest, from Manchester to Eccles and Kersal Moor, from Liverpool by steamer across the Mersey. The number of travellers was great: in Whitweek of 1865 the Lancashire and Yorkshire Railway carried 653,000 passengers, of whom a large proportion were excursionists, and between June and October of the same year there were 582 excursions on the North Eastern and 867 on the Midland.

Sabbatarian opposition contributed to the reduction in the number of excursions trains, but the reaction which it provoked was probably in the long run favourable to their development.

[1] Royal Commission on Railways, 1867. The excursion fare from London to Margate, Hastings and Dover was in each case 3s. 6d. return. Even in the 'eighties, when there had been a further rise in fares, typical return excursion fares were 5s. to Margate as compared with 10s. ordinary return, 5s. to Portsmouth as compared with 11s. 6d., 10s. to Great Yarmouth as compared with £1 1s. 6d.

For the time being, however, it had its effect both on the policy of the railway companies and on the attitude of the public. Excursionists to Brighton on a summer Sunday fell from six or seven thousand in the 'fifties to not more than two thousand. In many parts of the country there were no Sunday trains at all, as Dickens found to his disgust when he wanted to travel from York to Scarborough in 1858. But thanks partly to the extravagance of the wilder Sabbatarians, who went to the length of opposing the Sunday opening of public libraries, museums and picture galleries, the advocates of the 'rational Sunday' gradually began to prevail.

'I believe it to be absolutely necessary', said Cardinal Manning, a leading spokesman of this school of thought (1868), 'that we should provide for the people some occupations and some recreations on the Sunday, which are rational and innocent. There is nothing I should like to see more than a man and his family going out of London on the only day he can leave it, which brings to my recollection what I used to see in my youth in country villages.' The National Sunday eague, which had been formed in 1855 by a young working man, R. M. Morell, to press for the Sunday opening of art galleries and similar institutions, soon, by organizing its own excursions, carried into practice the principles of which Cardinal Manning was so vigorous an exponent, and in 1868 its Secretary estimated that every Sunday about a quarter of a million people left London for Hampton Court, the seaside and the country.[1] Henceforward Sabbatarianism in this as in other respects was slowly on the wane, though it was stubbornly rooted especially in the provinces.

The indifference with which the railway companies regarded excursion trains and the scant consideration which was accorded to the passengers also restricted their spread. Excursion trains 'meant all that was horrible: long and unearthly hours, packed

[1] The expression 'excursionist' had, it will be noted, a wider sense than to-day. Cf., for example, George Potter's sage remarks in evidence before the Select Committee on the Sale of Liquors on Sunday Bill (1868). 'I consider that excursionists do the hardest work that can possibly be imagined, whether it is seeing pictures, or whether it is seeing fields, or whether it is going through galleries.'

carriages, queer company, continual shunting aside and waiting for regular trains to go by, and worst of all the contempt of decent travellers. We had a little rhyme about them, which ended:

> "*Grown old and rusted, the boiler busted,*
> *And smashed the excursion train.*" '[1]

Yet such was the popular demand for cheap holiday travel that despite everything the excursion trains prepared the way for the revolutionary advance represented by the decision of the Midland Company in 1872 to provide third-class accommodation at a penny a mile on all trains, and in 1874 to abolish the second class and reduce first-class fares to the former second-class level. Enlightenment was coming at last. This was no leap in the dark but a well-considered change of policy, based on the realization that the three-class system was uneconomical and that larger returns were to be derived from stimulating than from discouraging third-class travel. Though unconvinced and indignant, the other companies had no alternative but to follow the example set by the Midland. There was no reduction in fares except to those who exchanged from the superior classes to the third, yet speedy and comfortable travel was made generally available. Soon third-class accommodation equalled the old second; soon it was much better. Seats were upholstered; dining and breakfast cars, lavatory compartments, electric light and other amenities were provided. Before long critics were lamenting that the railways were pampering the working classes, and in contrast with the Royal Commission of 1867 the Select Committee on Railway Rates and Fares in 1882 far from finding fault said that the complaints received in respect to passenger traffic were unimportant, and local rather than general.

These advances in third-class railway travel were a major cause of the accelerated growth of the popular seaside resorts in the 'seventies and 'eighties. Though at first they added little to the

[1] M. Vivian Hughes, *A London Child of the 'Seventies* (1934), 26.

opportunities for travel of the poorer sections of the community, they were a great boon to the middle classes and the more prosperous working people. Potentially they were of the greatest importance for all: railway policy as regards passenger traffic was no longer determined primarily by the interests of the wealthier passengers, and since the 'eighties, despite many improvements in detail, has not fundamentally changed.

'A MALVERN MOUNTAINEER', 1856

Of the other methods of locomotion which had a share in the growth of holiday travel amongst the poorer classes little need be said. Their role was similar to that of the railway, though their importance was secondary. The steamer was used for pleasure trips from the great cities and the seaside resorts themselves. Buses, trams, brakes, chars-a-bancs and other forms of horse-drawn transport were used for short excursions to the outskirts of the cities at week-ends and on holidays, including factory, club, Sunday school and other outings. In London, said Booth, excursions in brakes were without end. Rambling—or pedestrianism, to use the ugly contemporary term—was less popular than might perhaps have been expected. In some parts, especially in the North, it was a favourite pastime of young working men, but on the whole it was confined to the sedentary and the intellectual. One reason was no doubt that in his short leisure periods the manual worker sought rest rather than exercise; another was that he rarely possessed the education or the sophistication to appreciate the delights of the countryside. Public opinion regarded with disfavour the association of unmarried members of both sexes in the intimacy of a walking tour, and rambling is not a pastime well suited to a family. Like mountaineering, it was specially associated with students, and, as is shown by the guide books, it was assumed as a matter of course that the pedestrian's equipment would include interest in the botany, geology, archaeology, and history of the districts which he visited.

The amazing popularity of the cycling tour in the latter years of the century is not as inconsistent as might appear with what has been said about rambling. Like the early railway excursionists, many of the cyclists seem to have cycled rather for the sake of getting about than to see the countryside or to visit particular places. The appeal of the bicycle lay partly in its novelty, partly in the freedom and the scope for individual enterprise which it gave as compared with the railway. It was cheaper than any other method of travel (not excluding rambling, which ordinarily necessitated expenditure on travel at the beginning and the end of a tour), and it was important not least because of its contribution to the rediscovery of the countryside. Thus, as the steamer had anticipated the railway, the bicycle prepared the way for the motor-car. Dr. Arnold had welcomed the railway as the solvent of 'feudality'. The contribution of the bicycle was summed up by Lord Balfour: 'There has not been a more civilizing invention in the memory of the present generation . . . open to all classes, enjoyed by both sexes and by all ages.'

Introduced into England in the 'sixties as the 'velocipede', the safety bicycle remained a toy until the 'eighties. Its development as a means of transport was hindered by the decay of the country roads and inns which had followed the coaching age. Road surfaces were bad, signposts were neglected, maps were inferior, and innkeepers were unprepared for and often unfriendly to their new guests, whose sometimes strange attire and frequently dusty or muddy condition did not add to their welcome. But the hazards and uncertainties of the road stimulated rather than deterred the pioneers, and the cycling boom of the 'nineties could not have taken place but for the work of pioneer organizations such as the Cyclists' Touring Club (which was founded in 1878)[1] and the National Cyclists' Union in persuading local authorities to improve the roads, in setting up signposts, and in negotiating fixed and moderate tariffs for cyclists at hotels and boarding houses.[2]

Cycling clubs on the model of the Cyclists' Touring Club sprang up all over the country, and the progress of the boom was reflected in the membership of the Club itself. This rose from 142 in 1878, 3,356 in 1880 and 6,705 in 1882, to a steady level of about 20,000 between 1885 and 1890, and after falling off for a year or two soared to the record figure of 60,449 in 1899. That it then declined (to 35,786 in 1905 and 18,227 in 1910) was a sign not that cycling was waning in popularity but that from being a craze it had become an institution.

The members of the Cyclists' Touring Club formed only a small proportion of the vast army of cyclists who filled the roads at week-ends and during the holiday seasons. As yet not seriously challenged by the motor-car, the bicycle was popular with all classes, but it meant most to the young men and women of the factories, the shops and the offices. For them it was a liberating

[1] The first cycling tourists are said to have been two members of the Liverpool Velocipede Club, who set off to Chester and thence to London in 1869.

[2] The list of recommended hotels published by the Cyclists' Touring Club was the precursor of the lists since published by the great motoring organizations.

agency to be compared only to the railway in the previous generation.

The development of communications provided the machinery which made pleasure travel possible on a large scale. A role which was ancillary to this was performed by the tourist agencies, of which Thomas Cook's was the prototype. Cook was one of the first to appreciate the significance of the railway in widening the horizon and raising the cultural level of the masses. His belief in travel as a medium of education coloured all his own activities and influenced those of his competitors and successors. Though a highly profitable undertaking, his agency was not directed solely by financial considerations.

Appropriately the Great Exhibition of 1851 marked the turning point in Cook's career. Taking full advantage of the low fares which prevailed, he brought 165,000 excursionists to the Exhibition from Yorkshire alone. Every party was accompanied, all trains except the day express were made available for excursionists, and the night mail was often run in two to six parts. The popular excitement was described by his son, J. M. Cook: 'At the call of a band of music I saw workpeople come out of factories in Bradford, pay five shillings for a ticket, and with a very few shillings in their pockets start off on Saturday night to spend Sunday and Monday in London, returning to work on Tuesday morning.' 'The people of Yorkshire were thus educated to travel,' and one of Thomas Cook's schemes was the organization of clubs of working men to save the cost of their trip.

In 1854 Cook gave up other work, and with his first Continental tour on the occasion of the Paris Exhibition of 1855 there began what was to prove the most important chapter in his whole career; for it is with foreign travel that Cook's name is especially associated.[1] Aided by a fertile imagination and considerable business acumen he went from success to success. Instances of his inventiveness are his children's excursions, and his moonlight trips, the object of which was to enable the journey to be done by night so as to give a full day by the sea. When in 1865 he somewhat diffidently established an office in London, the final stage in the

[1] See Chapter XI.

growth of his agency into a national and soon an international organization had begun. More than a million passengers had passed through his hands by 1864, and, after a slow start, the establishment of the London office led to further increases in the volume of his business.

Cook's patrons came from all classes. There were, according to Edmund Yates in *All the Year Round* (1864), 'tradesmen and their wives, merchants, clerks away for a week's holiday, roughing it with a knapsack, and getting over an immense number of miles before they return; swart mechanics, who seem never to be able entirely to free themselves from traces of their life-long labour, but who . . . are by no means the worst informed, and are generally the most interested about the places they visit'. To the sophisticated the enthusiasm of the Cook's tourist seemed crude and ignorant, their earnestness ridiculous. But it was part of the growing-up process of the English middle and working classes. For the fathers and grandfathers of these adventurous spirits the world had been bounded by the market town or the industrial city, and a Cook's tour meant release from the drab drudgery of everyday life and an introduction to experiences and excitements of which a previous generation was able only to dream. In this great achievement lies Cook's claim to be one of the foremost civilizers of the English people.[1]

To a greater or lesser degree all the other travel agencies were modelled on Cook's. Their contribution to the growth of popular travel was similar, and a feature common to most of them was that they were not purely commercial in character or origin. Thus, John Frame, who is chiefly noteworthy for his share in popularizing the Highlands, was, like Cook, a fervent teetotaller; his first tour was in connection with a temperance demonstration in 1881, and he imposed strict temperance rules on his clients. Dean and Dawson's originated in a privately arranged excursion to Paris from a Stockport factory in 1871. Sir Henry Lunn's entry into the tourist business was an unexpected offshoot of the Grindelwald Conference on Reunion of 1892: some of his fellow-delegates

[1] The foregoing account of the work of Thomas Cook is mainly based on W. Fraser Rae, *The Business of Travel* (1891).

asked him to organize a tour to Rome, and for a time he catered especially for ministers of religion and their families. The Polytechnic Touring Association had begun with the establishment at Brighton in 1872 of a holiday home for poor members of the Polytechnic, and it was not formally separated from the Polytechnic itself until 1911. Organizations such as the Children's Country Holiday Fund were wholly charitable. Some such as the Toynbee Travellers' Club, which was composed of students at Toynbee Hall (whose first Warden, Samuel Barnett, was a firm believer in the educative value of popular travel), and the Arlington Travel Club, which was connected with the City Literary Institute, were, like the Polytechnic Touring Association, derivatives of social and educational institutions.

Amongst the non-commercial agencies the most interesting was the Co-operative Holidays Association, which began in 1891 in informal excursions by members of the Social Guild of the Rev. T. A. Leonard, a Congregational Minister at Colne, and became a non-profit making company in 1897. Its purposes were set out in its articles as 'to provide recreative and educational holidays by purchasing or renting and furnishing houses and rooms in selected centres, by catering in such houses for parties of members and guests, and by securing helpers who will promote the intellectual and social interests of the party with which they are associated'. They were explained more fully in the annual report for 1902. 'We are making an honest attempt towards the better use of the people's holidays. We offer them the healthful ways of an out-of-door life among the hills, instead of the rowdy pleasures of popular holiday resorts. We provide a simple, homely life in our guest-houses, and whilst discouraging extravagance in both food and dress, help people to find joy in music, literature, nature-study, and that best of all exercises, walking, with all that it brings to mind and body. And, most potent of all, during those holiday weeks we establish the unwritten law of unselfishness, and find pleasure in serving each other's needs.'

The interest of this experiment lies less in its immediate practical results, which were not spectacular, than in its forward-looking character. On a number of points it anticipated and influenced the future. The object was not so much to promote holidays for working people as to improve the quality of popular holidays. It was already possible to take the former for granted and to concentrate upon their better use.

fond of mountains.

X

THE TURN OF THE CENTURY

By the end of the nineteenth century, the practice of going away from home for an annual holiday was widely established throughout the middle classes, and was extending to the better-paid manual workers, though far from universal amongst them. What this meant in a community, one of the features of which was the high proportion of its members who belonged to the middle classes, is in nothing better exemplified than in the advances made by the holiday resorts in the second half of the century, and particularly its latter years.

There were 163,360 people in the eleven seaside resorts specially mentioned by the Report of the Census of 1851. In 1871 the analysis was extended to forty-eight towns.[1] The population of these amounted to 430,118 in 1861, 522,444 in 1871, and exceeded 900,000 in 1901. If all the seaside resorts—excluding towns such as Portsmouth and Plymouth not primarily dependent on holiday-makers—are taken into account the total for England and Wales in 1901 must have been of the order of 1,200,000; and this is apart from the spas, favourite holiday districts such as the Lakes, and the towns of historic interest and touring centres which also attracted holiday visitors. In other words, more than one person

[1] See Appendix I.

in twenty-five was living in a holiday resort, as compared with about one in a hundred in 1801.

These figures do not provide an exact gauge of the expansion which had taken place. To assess their full significance would require a thorough investigation into such matters as the extent to which the inhabitants of the resorts, directly or indirectly, derived their livelihood from holidaymakers, the average duration of visits, the length of the season at the respective resorts, and the ratio between the number of visitors and the number of hotel, boarding house and apartment house keepers, domestic workers and tradespeople. Without such an investigation it is in particular difficult to draw conclusions about the actual number of visitors. Recent estimates suggest that at the more popular resorts before the war there were as many as fifteen or twenty visitors each season for every resident, and broadly speaking the more fashionable the resort the lower the proportion will be. The scope for variation is great, and it would not be wise to say more than that a million residents must have meant that the visitors, excluding day excursionists, numbered several times more.

The seaside resorts were growing not only in size—there were seventeen with over 20,000 inhabitants in 1901—but also in number; a handbook of the 'nineties listed over two hundred.[1] At the same time the ascendancy so long enjoyed by the South was coming to an end. In 1851 all the important resorts except Scarborough were on the South Coast, and in language which for an official document is commendably picturesque but unusually vague the Report on the 1871 Census described the movement of holidaymakers in terms which suggested that the other areas could be disregarded: 'London throws its weight into Margate, Ramsgate, Hastings, Brighton, and other towns on the south coast which has the attractions of the sea in all its varieties of mood; farther west is Torquay and Torbay with the charms of an Italian Lake; to the west lie Ilfracombe and the Welsh towns of the sea and mountains; to the north-east Scarborough, the fair mistress of that coast.' This was already somewhat behind the times, but even in 1871 Southport (18,000 inhabitants) was the only Lanca-

[1] See Appendix I.

shire resort with more than 10,000 people; Blackpool had 6,000, and St. Anne's and Morecambe were neither of them separately recorded. Less than 3,000 people lived in Southend, and there was no East Coast holiday resort except Scarborough with more than 5,000, if ports such as Yarmouth are excluded.

By 1900 the situation had been transformed. The Lancashire coast, North Wales and the Isle of Man were the playground of industrial Lancashire and to a lesser extent of the West Riding and the Midlands. From the Midlands as from London visitors flowed in all directions. On the doorstep of Bristol was Weston-super-Mare; Tyneside was served by Tynemouth and Roker; and the South Wales industrial area by Tenby and Barry. Saltoun depended on Middlesbrough, and the resorts in South Yorkshire on Hull. In 1851 the largest seaside towns had been Brighton (65,569), Dover (22,244), Hastings (16,966), and Scarborough (12,915). Brighton was still by far the largest in 1901, with a population of 123,478; Hastings (65,528) came next; but Hastings was followed by Southport (48,083), and close behind Southport were Blackpool (47,346) and Bournemouth (47,003), which had easily outstripped Dover (41,782) and Scarborough (38,161). In 1901 three of the seven major resorts were in the north, and Scarborough, which had had more than twice the population of Southport in 1851, was the smallest of the three.[1]

It is not proposed to detail here the vicissitudes in the fortunes of the individual resorts. All did not share to the same degree in the general prosperity. Worthing, for example, had tended to be eclipsed by Hastings and Eastbourne. Gravesend could hardly be described as a watering place any longer. Ryde, despite its famous pier, had actually declined in population. Weymouth was reputed to live too much in its glorious past, symbolized by its bathing machines, which 'as if prepared for illustrious visitors' were 'of aldermanic proportions'.[2]

[1] No account has been taken of boundary extensions in the above statistics and those which follow. To have done this would have been difficult, and it would have greatly complicated comparisons between different resorts. By and large the operation of this factor probably evens out, and while to disregard it involves some distortion, the general picture is not seriously affected. [2] Black's *Guide* (1904), 79.

Nor is it proposed to analyse the gradations in the social standing of the different resorts. These were complex and subtle. To take Kent alone, at one end of the social scale was Sheerness, where a humble family could enjoy as cheap a holiday as anywhere, and apartments could be had for as little as fifteen shillings a week; at the other end was 'Fashionable Folkestone' (30,650), 'one of the most aristocratic watering places on the English coast'.[1] Broadstairs (6,466) was 'a middle-class haunt', appealing 'more particularly to the quiet, respectable, and not too highly cultured middle-class taste'. Westgate was 'something of a prig', and 'nothing vulgar was ever seen'. The character of Herne Bay (6,726) is shown by its nickname 'Baby Bay'; and Ramsgate and Margate, the latter with its 'Bohemian bustle—its coloured minstrels, its clowns and all the kindred elements', which were excluded from its more select neighbour, Cliftonville, were 'the happy hunting ground of the Cockney'. It is a far cry from the homogeneity of the days of Nash and the Prince Regent.

Generally speaking, as might be expected, the resorts which grew fastest were those nearest the more densely populated areas. On the South Coast, still dominated by Brighton, in whose streets all classes mingled, the most spectacular developments were the rapid progress made by Hastings and St. Leonards in the 'seventies and 'eighties; the competition they then experienced from Bexhill, which, thanks to the enterprise of its inhabitants, grew from no more than a village in the 'seventies to a town of 12,213 in 1901 (as compared with nearly 66,000 in Hastings and St. Leonards jointly); the advance, also chiefly in the 'seventies and 'eighties, of Eastbourne, which had 3,433 inhabitants in 1851 and 43,337 in 1901; and the even more striking rise of Bournemouth from a town of 6,000 when it was connected to the railway in the 'seventies to the third largest English seaside resort. Margate and Ramsgate (23,118 and 27,733 respectively in 1901) had grown relatively slowly, but their importance, as the favourite resorts of excursionists from London, was out of proportion to their size.

[1] This and the quotations which follow are taken from A. Montefiore, *The Isle of Thanet* (1893), and W. T. Perkins, *Popular Coast Guide* (1903).

The Isle of Wight had increased steadily rather than rapidly, but boasted in Shanklin (4,533) and Sandown (5,006) two virtually new resorts which enjoyed a good reputation among the discriminating. Farther still from London, Weymouth (19,843) and Torquay (33,625) had respectively doubled and quadrupled between 1851 and 1901, and the other South Devon resorts had held their own. In Somerset the proximity of Bristol had made the fortunes of Weston-super-Mare (19,047), but on the North Devon coast, which the railway had been exceptionally slow to reach, Ilfracombe (8,557) alone was important. Cornwall was still comparatively unknown except to a small minority with a love for the picturesque and romantic, but Newquay (3,115), which was fortunate in its excellent sands, was a rising watering place of the standard type.

The Welsh seaside places fell into two groups. Those in the south—Penarth, Tenby (the 'Madeira of Wales'), the Mumbles, Barry, Saundersfoot and Ferryside—which were small and local in importance, catered for Cardiff and the industrial areas of South Wales. Those in North Wales, which were larger and more widely known, served the industrial towns of the North and the Midlands. These shared in the prosperity which the proximity of the latter brought to the Lancashire coast and the Isle of Man. Llandudno (9,279), Colwyn Bay (8,689), and Rhyl (8,473) had been villages in 1851, but, thanks largely to their cheap and easy accessibility from Liverpool and Manchester by sea and land, had gone ahead with such rapidity that by 1901 they had outgrown Aberystwyth (8,014).

The Lancashire resorts were dominated by Southport (48,083) and Blackpool (47,348). Southport had taken the lead. In 1851 it had 5,000 inhabitants to about 2,000 in Blackpool; its rate of increase was greatest in the 'sixties; it doubled in size between 1871 and 1891, but its growth was slowing down in the 'nineties. As well, however, as being a holiday resort it was an important dormitory of Liverpool, and as an example of the possibilities opened up by the holiday traffic Blackpool stands alone. Its period of most rapid growth did not begin till the 'seventies, it doubled in size in that decade, almost did so in the 'eighties, and doubled

ON THE PIER—A SEASIDE DAY IN THE 'NINETIES

M

again in the 'nineties. The other Lancashire resorts also went ahead; St. Anne's (6,838), which was to Blackpool as Cliftonville was to Margate, the select appendage of a pre-eminently popular watering place, was a new resort; West Kirby and Hoylake were, like Southport, also dormitories for Merseyside. Outside Lancashire but drawing upon a similar clientele and very similar in spirit to Blackpool itself was Douglas in the Isle of Man, which, said Baedeker in 1890, was 'practically one large playground for the operatives of Lancashire and Yorkshire; and their tastes have been so extensively catered for, by the erection of dancing saloons and the like at every point of interest, as to seriously interfere with the enjoyment of the scenery for its own sake'.

On the East Coast Scarborough had grown steadily from about 13,000 in 1851 to 38,161 in 1901, when its population was becoming stationary, and as befitted 'the Brighton of the North', it appealed to all classes. Otherwise the East Coast resorts were with few exceptions quiet and small. North of the Wash were Tynemouth, 'the Brighton of Newcastle', Roker, the seaside suburb of Sunderland, Whitby, Bridlington (12,482), and Cleethorpes (12,578), and of these Whitby was not primarily a holiday resort. Bridlington was thronged in August and September by trippers, chiefly from Hull, but none of the other Yorkshire resorts except Scarborough were more than large villages. The Lincolnshire coast had been particularly late in developing, and neither Cleethorpes, which was virtually a suburb of Grimsby, nor Skegness (2,140), though already in the 'seventies and 'eighties much frequented by excursionists, was separately recorded in the Census until 1881. South of the Wash, the position was much the same. Great Yarmouth (51,316) and Lowestoft (29,850), which were visited by large numbers of day and period excursionists from the Midlands, were not primarily watering places, and the largest of the other Norfolk and Suffolk resorts were Felixstowe (5,815), Cromer (3,781) ('the English Étretrat', as Baedeker called it), and Southwold (2,800).

Even Essex, despite its proximity to London, developed slowly until the outward surge from the poorer districts of the great cities in the last quarter of the century. When this occurred one direction in which the movement from East London naturally flowed was towards the Essex coast, chiefly to Southend-on-Sea and to Clacton-on-Sea. It seems extraordinary now that in 1860 Southend could have been dismissed as 'a quiet flat', 'with its quiet, very quiet ways, and its gossiping boatmen',[1] that its population was less than 3,000 in 1871 and less than 8,000 in 1881, and that it should have been possible for Baedeker to describe it in 1890 as a 'small watering place . . . chiefly patronized by day excursionists from London'. It was not until the 'nineties that its most rapid development began. Its population sprang from just over 12,000 in 1891 to 28,827 in 1901 and by giant strides to nearly 63,000 in 1911; it must not, however, be overlooked that it was also important as a London dormitory. Clacton (7,456) had been unknown in the 'seventies, and like its neighbour, Walton-on-the-Naze (2,014), owed its rise principally to its popularity with both rail and steamer excursionists.

The capital invested in the seaside resorts in this period of expansion was enormous. Large sums were sunk by private persons in hotels, boarding houses, shops, residences and places of entertainment, and private enterprise accounted for most of the capital investment. But municipal activity was by no means negligible. Existing piers were enlarged and new ones built at the public expense; parades, parks, ornamental gardens, were laid out and improved; road and sea defence works were undertaken; baths, bandstands, aquaria and other amenities were provided. In its turn the capital invested gave employment in a hundred different ways—directly in the building industry, to the hotel and boarding house keepers and the domestic staffs who waited upon the visitors, to the shopkeepers, restaurateurs, entertainers, and all the others who attended immediately to their requirements, indirectly on the railways, in the luxury industries, and to all those who supplied the raw materials and the manufactures which were consumed.

Thus what for the want of a better term may be called a great industry had developed. The population figures afford some measure of its importance in relation to the community as a whole;

[1] Thomson, 67.

and if these figures are misleading to the extent that they include persons who lived in the holiday resorts but did not make their living out of them, there were many thousands residing elsewhere who ultimately derived their livelihood in part or in whole from the same source.

There was no change in the mode of life at the seaside resorts to correspond with the tremendous change in their scale and their immensely broadened social basis. As always before, the newcomers were assimilated with little difficulty, the difference which they made at first was in points of detail rather than in essentials, and more remarkable than any changes which occurred was the continuity with tradition. It was characteristic that stories of miraculous sea water cures were still being circulated in 1880,[1] and the belief in the health-giving properties of ozone, in which the sea air was thought to be especially rich, was hardly less credulous than the faith in the drinking of sea water a hundred years before. By the end of the century pride of place for therapeutic virtues was beginning to be given to sunshine, and enterprising resorts were already making use of sunshine statistics for propaganda purposes; but it was inevitable that its value to health should also be exaggerated and there was a large element of ignorance and superstition in the claims made on its behalf.

The indoor bathing establishment still survived, though in so many respects ill adapted to the new requirements. In the same tradition, though decked out to meet modern tastes, were the 'hydropathic' establishments or 'hydros', 'electropathic repertoria' and similar institutions, whose sonorous titles and elaborate equipment gave an impression of novelty and modernity which was sometimes spurious.

'Hydropathy', or 'the water cure', had been imported from Germany in the 'forties. Its German origin gave it a prestige which it did not wholly deserve, its practitioners claimed that it was a specialized branch of medicine, and, however sincere many of them may have been, it provided dangerously easy opportunities for profit-making and commercial exploitation of which there were always rogues and charlatans to take advantage. In the 'fifties,

[1] Murray, *Lancashire* (1880), 150, referring to Blackpool.

BATHING DRESSES, 1905

according to Carlyle, it was 'a prevalent delusion among chronic invalids', and by the end of the century 'hydros' were a common feature of both the inland and seaside watering places. The larger establishments had their resident physicians and provided every kind of medicinal water (light, electric, Turkish, sea water, Russian, radiant heat and other baths, not to mention drinking waters), electrical treatment, massage, 'ozonated' sun lounges, gymnasia, and even billiard rooms as an aid to treatment. In fact hydropathy had outgrown its name and under one roof the hydro set out to provide many kinds of cure. 'Electropathy' was more specialized and less important. It had been foreshadowed a century earlier at Bath, where Jane Austen had commented on the existence of electrical treatment. Refinements apart, hydropathic and electropathic establishments differed from the indoor baths chiefly in being residential, but they belonged to the same genre. Like their prototypes they were to become decreasingly medical in character, and developed from sanatoria into hotels of a somewhat specialized type.

In other respects, too, change was slow. As we have seen, bathing tents and cabins were superseding bathing machines, but mixed bathing was rarely permitted, Bexhill in 1901 being one of the first resorts to allow it. Bathing costumes were by now practically universal for both sexes, and the women's bathing dresses continued to be designed with an eye to modesty rather than to utility. The nigger minstrel, an importation from America in the middle of the century, was a popular seaside entertainer, but the old-fashioned Punch and Judy show did not cease to flourish. Switchback railways, skating rinks and other innovations competed with the merry-go-round and the donkey ride at the larger resorts. The aquaria, modelled on the famous original at Brighton, which was opened in 1872, looked back to the middle of the century rather than forward into the new one. Great dancing palaces at the resorts frequented by working people were up-to-date versions of the Assembly Rooms of earlier days: winter gardens and kursaals were in the same tradition. In the quality of seaside music there seems to have been a certain improvement, associated, for example, with Dan Godfrey at Bournemouth and with the municipal orchestra at Bexhill; but Dan Godfrey was less representative of seaside music than were the military band, the barrel organ and the nigger minstrel's banjo.

LAWN TENNIS PLAYER, 1890

There was one direction, however, in which more fundamental changes were taking place. The new importance which open-air games were acquiring in social life generally was reflected at the seaside. Sport had hitherto had a subordinate part, and the popularity of tennis, golf, and cricket was novel. At Scarborough, for example, the Cricket Festival began in 1871, though there had been a cricket club since 1849; the Yorkshire Tennis Championships were first held there in 1884, and a golf club was opened in 1891. Of the three, lawn tennis—with which its elder sister, croquet, competed for a time—was to play the largest part in seaside life, partly because of its suitability for both sexes. The 'lawn-tennysonian' was becoming a familiar figure on the promenade, in his strange costume, 'a kind of Joseph's coat of divers colours, fearfully and exiguously made' and consisting of 'white flannel trousers or knickerbockers, girt round his waist with a silk handkerchief, like that of a Spanish bullfighter, and a snug little cap pulled down over one eye'.[1]

What of the spas? They cannot be entirely left out of account. There was a small minority of holidaymakers, largely elderly and almost entirely well-to-do, to whom the quiet life and sedate amusements, with or without the spa treatment, still appealed. Most of the spas were congenially situated, and they had the advantage of superior hotel and boarding-house accommodation and other amenities as compared with the average inland town. Capital continued to be sunk in their development. Even at Tunbridge a pumproom was built in 1877. At the end of the 'eighties the Corporation of Bath spent over £25,000 on improvements in two years, and it was claimed in 1891 that the city possessed the finest hydro-therapeutic establishment in the world. At Harrogate the Victoria Baths were built by the Corporation in 1871 at a cost of £30,000, they were supplemented in 1897 by the Royal Baths, which had a winter garden as well as up-to-date medical equipment, and in 1903 the Corporation invested nearly £70,000 in a kursaal. At Bath, though the population was declining, the bathers numbered over 45,000 in 1873-4, 67,500 in 1882-3, and 104,000 in 1889-90; Harrogate had grown to a town of 28,423 inhabitants in 1901; the population of Buxton (7,540 in 1891 and 10,181 in 1901) was estimated by Baedeker in 1890 to double or treble itself in the summer season. A list of English and Welsh

[1] Bernard H. Becker, *Holiday Haunts* (1884), 91.

spas published in 1891[1] included twenty-six names; some of them, such as Purton and Shelfanger, were of no importance, but amongst them were all the great resorts of the past except Epsom. Once again, however, they were more famous for cures than for pleasure.

O's the Ozone that is found by the sea.

[1] Reproduced in Appendix I.

XI

AFTER THE GRAND TOUR

The Revolutionary and Napoleonic Wars interrupted the development of Continental travel to the advantage of the holiday resorts at home—but there was a remarkable rush to France during the first peaceful interval, provided by the Peace of Amiens. It was estimated that in 1802 there were fifteen to sixteen thousand English visitors,[1] more than a thousand of whom were unable to return when war broke out again and ended their trip in internment. There was a still greater rush after the final peace, and if, as was natural, the post-war travellers began by following in the footsteps of their predecessors, this phase was bound to be temporary. The changes in the intellectual and spiritual outlook of cultivated Europe and in the economic and political background were too revolutionary for the return to the past to last long.

There was no catastrophic change. The average traveller tended to be conservative, and the guide books, which mirrored his outlook, continued for many years to speak with the voice of the eighteenth century and to address themselves to the old style tourist. Gradually, however, the new ideas filtered down, and the point of view of Wordsworth and Byron prevailed over that repre-

[1] *The Jerningham Letters*, ed. Egerton Castle (1896), I, 221.

sented by Gray and Horace Walpole. At the same time travel was being transformed by the progress of invention, culminating with the invention of the railway, and by the disappearance of some of the political obstacles to easy movement between States. The growth in the number of travellers led to improved facilities and reduced costs, which in their turn produced a further increase in the number of travellers, while railways opened up ever widening territories and destroyed most of what remained of the Grand Tour tradition.

There were already before the railway age indications of significant changes in the areas most favoured by English tourists. The vogue of the Rhine trip was an unmistakable sign of the changing times, for its appeal was essentially romantic. The increasing popularity of the Riviera was in part due to the same trend, but the outstanding instance is provided by Switzerland, of which, anticipating Leslie Stephen's famous description of it a generation later as the playground of Europe, Dr. Arnold wrote in 1840: 'In fact, Switzerland is to England, what Cumberland and Westmorland are to Lancashire and Yorkshire; the general summer touring-place.'

The story of the Alps as a tourist centre had begun a century earlier with Gray's new vision of the Grande Chartreuse in 1739 as 'pregnant with religion and poetry', and William Windham's account to the Royal Society of the visit which he made to Chamonix in 1741. The interest in the Alps which these events provoked was speculative rather than practical, but they were a portent. Before long tourists began to make their appearance in the mountain valleys to marvel from a distance at the peaks and glaciers of Savoy and the Oberland, but rarely to climb them. The average tourist continued to be more interested in the famous bears at Berne and in meeting Voltaire at Ferney than in the grandeur of the Alps. Until the middle of the nineteenth century the higher slopes of the mountains remained largely virgin territory and the interest lay in the 'sublimity and diversified beauty' of the lakes and glaciers, as seen from the valleys.

But by the time of Dr. Arnold's remark the Swiss tourist industry was already highly developed, and Switzerland was a great tourist centre. Thirty thousand travellers of all nationalities were estimated to pass through Geneva every year. At Interlaken at least two thirds of the summer visitors came from England, and there was a resident English clergyman whose stipend was raised by voluntary subscription. English religious services were also provided at other resorts, including Geneva, Thun, Lucerne, and Lausanne (where an English chapel was built in the 'forties); and the influence of the English was universal. An illustration was the service of a table d'hôte dinner in the late afternoon at most of the large inns, expressly for their English clients.

On the whole, said Murray's *Guide*, no country in Europe was better equipped than Switzerland to supply the needs of the English tourist. It tended to be expensive, the average daily expenses at the best inns amounting to 9s. to 12s. without the cost of conveyances, horses and guides, while hotelkeepers and tradesmen had the reputation of being extortionate; but otherwise travel in Switzerland had everything to commend it. The hotels were numerous and well managed, and yielded to few in France or Germany. Except on the Southern slopes of the Alps and near the Italian frontier, cleanliness could be counted on in the remotest villages. Communications were good and had been greatly improved since the Napoleonic Wars. When to these material advantages were added the therapeutic qualities of the climate and the spiritual exhilaration to be derived from the sublimity of the scenery there was little more that the traveller could desire.

At the same time the more settled political conditions throughout Europe, commercial enterprise, the romantic impulse, and above all the improved facilities for travel combined to bring English visitors in ever growing numbers to other regions hitherto inaccessible. The first steamer passage of the Channel was in 1816; the first regular steamer service began in 1820. In the 'thirties enterprising shipowners were advertising trips to St. Petersburg, Greece, Egypt and the Holy Land. A voyage to Constantinople in 1835 on 'a splendid vessel', a four-hundred-ton steam packet, cost £45 for the single journey, and the advertised amenities included medical attendance on board and a band of musicians between Malta and Constantinople. It was left to the participants in this precursor of the luxury cruise to make their own arrangements for the return journey, but it was suggested that they might come back via Greece and Italy or by the Danube.[1]

Thus the way was prepared for the revolutionary changes which as at home were to be brought about by the railway. As compared with perhaps 100,000 cross-Channel passengers in both directions in the later 'thirties there were more than 500,000 in 1882; and twenty years later the total considerably exceeded a million.[2] These are inclusive figures for all nationalities; the rate of increase for English tourists was probably greater.

Given continued improvements in travel facilities, there seemed to be hardly any limit to the possibilities of expansion. One railway representative giving evidence to the Select Committee on the Channel Tunnel in 1882 forecast that the construction of the tunnel would treble the traffic in eighteen months. The more modest estimate of the General Manager of the Great Western was that it would be doubled in five to seven years and trebled in fifteen years. Sir Edward Watkins, M.P., Chairman of the South

[1] *Manchester Guardian*, 13th June 1835.

[2] The first of these figures is an estimate of the author's: the second and third are based respectively on the *Report* of the Select Committee on the Channel Tunnel (1883) and *Statistical Tables relating to Emigration, &c.* (1904). According to an official source the passengers by the Calais services numbered 38,695 in 1831 and 20,293 in 1840, and those on the Boulogne services 10,937 and 52,807 in the same years. (Select Committee on the Channel Tunnel.) Figures given by the Boulogne Chamber of Commerce to the Select Committee on Postal Communications in 1850 showed the total by all routes in 1842 to be 109,432, made up as follows:

Boulogne	48,254
Ostend	13,780
Havre	23,471
Calais	20,728
Dieppe	3,199.

This list was not comprehensive, but it included all the important ports on the Continental side, and it cannot be far wrong to estimate the total number of cross-Channel passages at about 100,000 in the late 'thirties: this would give about 50,000 passengers making the return journey, assuming no migration in either direction.

Eastern Railway Company and honorary Chairman of one of the rival Channel Tunnel companies, thought in terms of a tunnel with an annual capacity of thirteen to fourteen million passengers, and it was estimated that 1,500,000 a year would be necessary if a 5 per cent dividend was to be paid.

A COCKNEY AT DIEPPE, 1851 (*John Leech*)

Fundamentally, the optimists were right. There was practically no limit to the possible expansion once foreign travel ceased to be the privilege of the leisured and the wealthy. The mechanical difficulties were unimportant, and, Channel Tunnel or no Channel Tunnel, the engineers and the entrepreneurs could between them cater for any conceivable demand. But means was not the only factor. Equally necessary were curiosity about strange peoples and strange lands, and a taste for novelty and change. It was education which mattered most, an educated interest in the culture and customs and manners of other nations, and it was amongst the more earnest of the middle and working classes that Continental travel first found a foothold. Like the Grand Tourists before them, they saw in it an opportunity for self-improvement, of which they were eager to take advantage; and soon middle-aged ladies who in the winter evenings sat at the feet of the Christian Socialist lecturers might be found exploring the Louvre at the heels of a guide, and serious-minded young clerks from the Working Men's College might be seen in their summer vacations at the end of a rope on a Swiss glacier.

This did not come about at once. The transition was not entirely straightforward. The mere existence of facilities for cheap and easy travel was not enough in itself. There was no tradition of travel amongst the newcomers, and there were formidable practical obstacles to surmount—the language problem, prejudice at home and abroad, exchange, passport and other difficulties. To deal with some of these difficulties the rich employed couriers, guides and vetturinos, while the hotels at which they stayed were familiar with their needs and anxious for their comfort. The middle-aged ladies and the serious-minded young clerks could not afford these aids to travel, yet they needed the same kind of help.

The man who gave them it was Thomas Cook.[1] His work in fostering excursions at home was important, but his greatest achievement lay in his share in the popularization of foreign travel. He deliberately set out to be a universal courier, doing for those who could not provide themselves with a courier's services what the courier did for those who could afford to hire him. It was a task which would doubtless have been undertaken by others if it had not fallen to Cook, but hardly anyone could have been better fitted for it than he. Educational enthusiasm and outstanding business capacity were first-class qualifications for one who was to combine the roles of courier and tutor to the new Grand Tourists.

It was appropriate that, like his first major success at home,

[1] As previously stated, the main authority on Cook is Rae, *The Business of Travel.*

Cook's first Continental tour should have been in connection with one of the great exhibitions in which the culture of the age found such characteristic expression. This was an excursion from Leicester to the Paris Exhibition of 1855, the return fare to Calais being only 31s. That there should be such an excursion was no novelty. The Manchester Society of Arts arranged excursions to the same Exhibition for artisans at the extraordinarily low return fare of 13s. 9d. This would not have been possible but for the co-operation of the English and French railways and of the Foreign Office, which, incidentally, offered passports free. It was altogether, as the *Manchester Guardian* said (6th August 1855), 'an event in the history of railway travelling'. Where Cook differed from bodies such as the Manchester Society of Arts was that he did on a larger scale and on a commercial basis what they did occasionally for philanthropic reasons. His originality lay in his methods, his almost infinite capacity for taking pains, his acute sense of the needs of his clients, and the powers of invention and the bold imagination which made him the greatest of all tourist agents. These characteristics are exemplified by such features of his tours as the now universal coupon system, of which he was the inventor, the special guide books which he published for his patrons, and the personal attention in which he took a particular pride.

The French tours—France has naturally always been the country most favoured by English tourists—were the foundation of the success of Cook's enterprise, though the Italian tours which he started in 1863 ran them a good second. The results of opening the London office in 1865 were at first disappointing, but in 1867 another Paris Exhibition gave him an opportunity which he turned to excellent account. He was appointed managing agent of the tourist and excursion traffic of the London, Brighton and South Coast Railway, and he had the support and encouragement both of the French authorities and of the Royal Commission which was responsible for British participation in the Exhibition. Over 20,000 visitors to Paris for the Exhibition passed through his hands, and about half of them were accommodated in the temporary hostels which with his customary energy he had erected in Paris for those excursionists who could not afford to stay in hotels. The minimum all-in cost of four days in Paris, including accommodation and the return fare from London, was 36s. A feature which pleased Cook was the contribution which he was able to make to international understanding.

Building on the experience gained in 1867, Cook surpassed himself when he brought 75,000 visitors to the Paris Exhibition of 1878. Three hundred and twenty-four special trains were run from all parts of the United Kingdom, a cheap express boat service via Dover and Calais was introduced, and the fare by the most popular route—Newhaven–Dieppe—was a guinea return from London to Paris. About 20,000 persons took part in trips which he organized in and around Paris, and he arranged for the accommodation of an average of about 450 persons a night from May to October.[1]

By this time Cook's agency had an international reputation, and the Cook's tourist was as well known in the cities of Italy and France as the *milord* had been a century earlier. It was evidence of his commercial success that other agencies modelled on his were springing up, and evidence of his success as a cultural influence that amongst the more snobbish the Cook's tourist had become a byword for vulgarity. He had succeeded in his aim of enabling the ordinary man and woman to share the joys of foreign travel.

It is not a contradiction of this to add that the charges of vulgarity were in fact superficial. Except on special occasions such as the Paris Exhibitions, when they included a large number of artisans, Cook's patrons were drawn mainly from the middle classes. If they could not claim to be highly refined, they were at any rate highly respectable. They were the poor relations of those who, accustomed to travel from childhood and able to command whatever services they needed, did not require the assistance of a travel organization. And the complaints against them both recall complaints which had been made of their more aristocratic precursors and anticipate similar complaints of their more democratic successors. They rushed from place to place. They were superficial.

[1] *Report* of the Commissioners for the Paris Universal Exhibition of 1878 (1880).

They were preoccupied with the show places. They were insular. As one of their critics, Charles Lever, had said a generation earlier of the Dodd family, they were 'no very unfair sample of a large class of our travelling countrymen'. Like the Dodds, some of them 'had come abroad with crude and absurd notions of what awaited them on the Continent. They dreamed of economy, refinement, universal politeness, and a profound esteem for England from all foreigners. They fancied that the advantages of foreign travel were to be obtained without cost or labour; that locomotion could educate, sightseeing cultivate them; that in the capacity of British subjects every society should be open to them, and that, in fact, it was enough to emerge from home security to become at once recognized in the fashionable circles of any Continental city. They not only entertained all these notions, but they held them in defiance of most contradictory elements. They practised the most rigid economy when professing immense wealth; they affected to despise the foreigner while shunning their own countrymen; they assumed to be votaries of art when merely running over galleries; and last, while laying claim, and just claim, for their own country to the highest moral standard of Europe, they not infrequently outraged the proprieties of foreign life by an open and shameless profligacy.' Profligacy was not by and large a failing of the Cook's tourist, but the new tourists bore a general resemblance to the Dodd family. They were in fact a variation on a recurring theme.

The main point of attack was effectively met by Cook himself, when in reply to Lever he said: 'Let me ask why Mr. Lever's susceptibilities should be outraged, and his refinement trampled on, because thirty or forty Englishmen and Englishwomen find it convenient to travel in the same train, to coalesce for mutual benefit, to sojourn for a like time in the same cities.'

Cook set the pattern for the other travel agencies, but the competition was healthy, and when, as the prejudice against him broke down, his organization tended increasingly to cater for the better-to-do, the scope for his competitors enlarged. Within the same general framework the different agencies were able to experiment and to specialize. Thus the Polytechnic was particularly associated

'DOING' COLOGNE CATHEDRAL, 1854
(*Richard Doyle: The Foreign Tour of Messrs. Brown, Jones and Robinson*)

with the development of holiday hostels such as its chalet at 'Lovely Lucerne'—the latter expression being an early instance of the use of advertising slogans in connection with the organization of holidays. Henry Lunn formed travel organizations especially for members of the Free Churches (1905) and the Church of England, and later still the Hellenic Travellers' Club, famous for its lecture cruises to Greece. The Cyclists' Touring Club arranged their first Continental tour in 1879 and published a Continental Road Book in 1887. In the 'nineties cycling tours were highly popular, and an International Touring Congress which had been formed in 1897 held its first meeting in London in 1899. Sea cruises were becoming less expensive: in the 'nineties the Polytechnic offered cruises to Norway at £8 8s. and to Madeira at £12. Agencies such as the Arlington Travel Club and the Toynbee Travellers' Club which were connected with educational institutions laid particular stress on the cultural aspects of travel: intensive study courses preceded the foreign expeditions from Toynbee Hall. As a further illustration of the diversity there may be mentioned the parties of South Londoners which Canon J. W. Horsley took annually to Switzerland in the 'nineties: the enterprise was so popular that he had to refuse applicants above a maximum figure of 140.

These developments mainly, though not exclusively, affected the middle classes, and the emphasis which was laid on culture showed how the tradition of the Grand Tour was working itself out in a new social milieu. Amongst the leisured classes the eighteenth-century tradition, if not dead, was moribund. Boys and girls might be sent to Swiss finishing schools or to German families as part of their education, adults might perambulate the same museums and admire the same sights as the Grand Tourists, but the novelty of foreign travel had worn off and the social prestige attaching to it had declined. The principal development which affected the upper classes was the emergence of great pleasure resorts frequented not primarily for the sake of the historical monuments, the manners and customs of the natives, natural beauty or health, but in order to follow pursuits different in detail but indistinguishable in kind from those which were followed at Brighton and Bournemouth.

XII

PLAYGROUNDS OF EUROPE

While at home Bath and Brighton were being deserted by people of fashion, and the Grand Tour was in decline, there sprang up all over Europe, and beyond, cosmopolitan resorts whose chief *raison d'être* was the pleasure of the rich. The Continental spas—especially those of Germany and Austria—flourished as never before, but the main interest lies in the new resorts which developed on the sea coast and beside the lakes and in the mountains of Western Europe. As instances of those by the sea may be mentioned Scheveningen, Ostend, Dinard and Deauville in the north, Biarritz in the west, the Lido and the Dalmatian coast in the south-east, with the French and Italian Rivieras pre-eminent amongst them all; while outside Europe or the European mainland the Azores, the Canaries, Tangier, Algiers, and Egypt were favoured especially for winter residence and as places of call on holiday cruises. As for the lakes and the mountains, the choice again was extensive; there were centres of fashion in all the accessible mountain ranges, the Tyrol, the Pyrenees, Bavaria, Savoy, but the mountains and lakes of Switzerland enjoyed an ascendancy comparable to that of the Riviera among the seaside resorts.

We shall confine ourselves here to the French Riviera and

Switzerland, as the main centres of English influence and as the prototypes of all the others.

The popularity of the Riviera with English visitors derived in the first instance from their fondness for Provence.[1] Provence was on one of the main routes from Paris to Italy, and hence was early brought to the notice of English travellers. It made a ready appeal to their tastes; it was wealthy in classical monuments, and its climate was suited to invalids. There were English colonies at Montpellier, Avignon, Toulouse and Aix in the eighteenth century. The Riviera itself was slow to be discovered, and Nice was a small village when Smollett paid his famous visit in 1763. He found no statues and pictures, no public library or bookseller, but he admired the climate and the beauty of the flowers and trees, and he paid it the compliment of staying eighteen months, and the rare compliment of praise in the *Travels*. The time was opportune, peace had just been restored, and at home the rush to the seaside was in its early phases. The Duke of York and later the Duke of Gloucester were the most exalted of those who followed Smollett to the Riviera, and by December 1786 it was possible to say that the neighbourhood of Nice presented 'the air of an English watering place. The town is much enlivened and enriched by the concourse of strangers, who resort hither for the sake of the climate in winter, and great numbers of people are supported by their means.'[2] None the less, visitors were still counted in tens and not thousands; according to Arthur Young, fifty-seven English and nine French families wintered at Nice in 1788. And Nice stood alone. Monaco consisted of 'two or three streets upon precipitous rocks; eight hundred wretches dying of hunger; a tumbledown castle; a battalion of French troops.'[3] Cannes was only a fishing village until Lord Brougham, prevented

[1] A historical study of the rise of the Riviera as a holiday centre appears to be lacking, and the secondary sources are fragmentary. For a detailed account of the different resorts the guide books are a valuable source, though they always tend to be somewhat behind the times and allowance must be made for this limitation.

[2] Sir James Smith, quoted by Constantia Maxwell, 16.

[3] Dupaty, quoted by Mead, 245.

from crossing the frontier to Nice by the outbreak of cholera, discovered it in 1831 and made it famous by returning each winter. Ten years later Mentone had only one well-managed inn.

The position of Nice as a winter residence for the sick, the elderly and the leisured, was consolidated after the Napoleonic Wars, but the transformation of the Riviera into a great pleasure resort did not occur until the railway age. In this transformation the English played a foremost part. Soon a visit to the Riviera came to occupy in the life of the upper classes much the same place as had formerly been occupied by a visit to Bath. That the venue was foreign was largely incidental. It was the natural outcome of improved travel facilities, thanks to which a journey which had formerly taken days could be performed in a matter of hours. In most of the respects for which a seaside holiday was valued the Mediterranean coast had an undoubted advantage over the English resorts, particularly as regards winter climate, while it had in addition the appeal of novelty and social exclusiveness. Later it was popularly associated with gambling, but this aspect of its social life was always of secondary importance and at first seems to have been of little significance.

The period of spectacular growth did not begin until the second half of the century, when the full effect of the introduction of the railway was felt. Nice was still semi-rural in the 'fifties, but, not of course solely because of the tourist traffic, was a great city of 80,000 inhabitants by the 'eighties. Cannes, which was the most fashionable of the Riviera resorts, and Mentone, despite its reputation for gloom, had also grown considerably. On the French side of the frontier, which shifted in 1859, Hyères, Fréjus, St. Raphael and Antibes, and on the Italian side, Alassio, Genoa, Portofino, Bordighera and San Remo, all had their share in the new prosperity and their devotees among the English.

These watering places were on the traditional model. Beside them, in the impoverished principality of Monaco, there was developing a resort of a different type, which in some ways was more characteristic of the age. This is not as paradoxical as it may sound. Monte Carlo, the popular attitude to which was summed up by the writer who said that it had been a 'Southern Hell' in the sixties,[1] stood in the eyes of the average Englishman for a shameless extravagance and an unblushing laxity of moral standards. Yet it provided an outlet for some of the forces which were at work beneath the surface, a vent for some of the impulses which the rigid moral code of the age sought to restrain. In a sense it stood for the older and freer aristocratic tradition which had been temporarily submerged; and the rebelliousness of the very rich against the strictness of middle-class conventions. It pointed the way to the general reaction against Victorianism and to the revaluation of standards which this involved.

More than anywhere else Monte Carlo came to be associated with gambling, of all vices the one perhaps most alien to the spirit of the age. It was due to the accident of Monaco's independence that it became an international gambling centre when the gaming rooms at the great German resorts such as Homburg and Wiesbaden had to close down on their incorporation in the German Empire. Perhaps already sensible of the impermanence of his German investments, one of the brothers Blanc, whose enterprise had been largely responsible for the rise of Homburg, which had been a village when they had obtained permission to set up a roulette wheel there in 1842, had established gaming tables in Monaco in the 'fifties. He began in a quiet way, shunning publicity, of which he may well have been afraid, and it was not until the closure of the German rooms that the great days of Monte Carlo began. The Casino was the foundation on which the life of the resort was built, but its significance in the social history of Europe does not end with its importance as a centre of gambling. Blanc and his successors recognized that this alone would not guarantee permanent prosperity, and they set out to make Monte Carlo attractive to wealthy visitors of all nationalities and all tastes. They appealed above all to the desire for what Thorstein Veblen has called 'conspicuous consumption'. Around the Casino they built superb hotels and sumptuous restaurants. They organized princely entertainments for which Europe's finest artists were engaged. Not least, they virtually took over the administration and in particular the policing of the principality, so that they could

[1] A. I. Shand, *Old Time Travel* (1903), 222.

enforce the discipline and maintain the degree of order and decency which, like Nash at Bath, they saw was essential if the support of the world of fashion was to be held and the suspicion with which their enterprise was regarded by respectable opinion was to be kept within harmless limits. Monte Carlo, like Homburg before it—for the Board of Directors at Homburg had acquired control of the government of the Electorate of Hesse—is an interesting instance on a small scale of the interrelation of economic and political power.

The history of the Swiss resorts is in many ways similar to that of the Riviera.[1] Large-scale development began with the railway age, and the English visitor played the same important part. But the distinctive features of the greatest inland playground of Europe derived from two factors which had little or no significance in the evolution of the Riviera. Both were primarily English in their immediate origin, though both reflected international trends. One was that unreasoning love of the mountains which is amongst the few permanent legacies of the romantic movement: the other was the love of physical activity for its own sake which was an outcome of the Industrial Revolution.

The love of the mountains came first in order of time. In its extreme forms it even yet remains hardly susceptible of explanation in rational terms; the mysticism and the ecstasy which so often accompany it are religious in quality.

'Mont Blanc and the Jungfrau', said Leslie Stephen, 'came in with the renewed admiration for Shakespeare, for Gothic architecture, for the romantic school of art and literature, and with all that modern revolutionary spirit which we are as yet hardly in a position to criticize.' The same point, as he mentioned, had been made by one of the most important counter-revolutionary thinkers, Chateaubriand, who had held that to admire the Alps was a mark of a revolutionist and materialist. To Stephen, said Frederic

[1] As with the Riviera, the guide books are useful sources for the detailed study of particular resorts. There is, as stated in the text, an extensive literature on mountaineering. Special mention should be made of the works of Leslie Stephen and Frederic Harrison, and, as regards winter sports, of Arnold Lunn. (See Bibliography.)

Harrison, the Alps were 'the elixir of life, a revelation, a religion', and Harrison's account of his own reactions to the Alps recalls those of a previous generation to the sea. 'I was carried out of all good sense and self-control by the fascination of this new transcendent world. I deserted my friends and comrades, I raced about the crags and rattled down the snow glissades, tramped through the night, rose to see the dawn in midsummer, and behaved like a youth in a state of delirium.' 'To know, to feel, to understand the Alps is to know, to feel, to understand Humanity.' 'The Alps are international, European, Humanitarian.' 'Bunyan's Pilgrim did not hail the vision of the Delectable Hills with more joy and consolation' than did Harrison the Alps when he revisited them in his old age.

It would be easy to multiply instances of this rhapsodical attitude to the mountains, but we are chiefly concerned with its practical expression. This took several forms; first of all—and before the mystical appreciation of the mountains had fully matured—the tours to the mountain valleys for the purpose of enjoying at a distance the sublimity of the Alpine scenery; next, from the 'fifties and 'sixties onwards, the actual ascent of the mountains themselves by the more adventurous of the enthusiasts; and then, beginning in the 'seventies and the 'eighties, the opening of the higher mountains to the generality of tourists and the discovery of their delights in winter as well as in summer. In each phase Englishmen took a leading part.

A clue to the nature of this strange phenomenon is provided by the fact that unlike visits to the seaside whether at home or abroad, mountain climbing has always appealed particularly to the professional classes, a section of the community which enjoys a high degree of social security without commensurate opportunities for intellectual excitement or physical adventure. Certainly the desire to escape from the security, the tedium and the sophistication of modern civilization ranks high amongst the reasons for the midsummer madness so vividly exemplified in Frederic Harrison. 'We live for the most part in a very iron mask of forms,' he said himself, 'we must be free and simple sometimes, or we break.' The Alps, said Leslie Stephen, were 'places of refuge where we may escape from ourselves and our neighbours. There we can breathe air that has not passed through a million pair of lungs; and water in which the acutest philosophers cannot discover the germs of indescribable diseases.' 'The charm of mountain climbing', Mr. Geoffrey Winthrop Young has said, 'is that it is an adventure; an adventure upright and obvious before our eyes and pleasantly accessible.'

Mountaineering and the other pursuits associated with the mountains provide at one and the same time a sense of escape, an outlet for physical energy, and opportunities for adventure in an environment calculated to make the maximum appeal to the romantic, the sophisticated and the city dweller. And they provide them as it were at every level and for every type and taste. If the ascent of the Matterhorn is for the few, there is no lack of lesser climbs for the inexpert and the timid; if the great ski runs are for the highly skilled, the novice can find adventure enough on the nursery slopes; the beauty of the scenery and the exhilaration of the air are accessible to all.

Active mountaineers have never been more than a minority of the visitors to Switzerland, English or otherwise, but their influence has been entirely out of proportion to their number. It is they who have led the way in both of the great phases in the history of the Swiss mountain resorts, their discovery first as places for summer holidays and then as winter sports centres.

In the first half of the nineteenth century the main Swiss holiday resorts were the cities and the lakes, while those who went to the mountain valleys—there were some three thousand visitors, mostly English, to Chamonix in 1840—came to admire the peaks from a distance. To climb them was looked upon as eccentric at the very least; Murray's *Guide* for 1851 commented on the 'remarkable' fact that a large proportion of those who had made the ascent of Mont Blanc had been persons of unsound mind. Smugglers, chamois hunters, and occasional scientists and explorers composed the small minority who climbed the high mountains.

The new era may be dated from the formation of the Alpine Club in 1857. There were twenty-eight foundation members: by the 'nineties the total had risen to about five hundred. These were the élite, and the influence of the members of this characteristically English institution extended all over Europe and the world. They were aided, it has been plausibly suggested, by the first accident on the Matterhorn (1865), which 'did much to popularize the amusement, which only needed the advertisement of a little hostile criticism'.[1] With growing numbers of fellow-enthusiasts, notably from Germany, they completed the exploration of the Alpine peaks, they perfected the technique of mountain climbing, and they expounded their faith in innumerable publications. Already by 1864 Frederic Harrison was complaining that he was bored to death by every form of Alpine narrative—'serious, comic, scientific, poetical, semi-pseudo-scientifico-poetico-personal'. He may well have been. There is much repetition, and little that is original in the literature of the Alps. But the vast outpouring was both a sign and a cause of the hold which the mountains were securing on the more literate classes, and at its best it is exemplified by Leslie Stephen's classic *The Playground of Europe*, which appeared in 1871 and was dedicated 'chiefly to those fellow lunatics who love the Alps too well not to pardon something to the harmless monomaniac who shares their passion'.

The fashionable physician also helped to popularize the high Alps, and what is at first sight the strangest turn of events of all, their development for winter holidays, was a derivative of the 'mountain air cure'. Earlier in the century the sick had not gone to the mountains except to the spas, such as St. Moritz, but in the middle of the century the medical profession, led by a German doctor, Brehmer, began to recommend tubercular and other patients to take the mountain air. The immense possibilities which this opened up were not appreciated at first, but in fact it was an advance which was comparable in character and importance with the discovery of the seabathing cure. It meant, first, that every mountain village, irrespective of whether it had mineral waters, was potentially a health and hence a holiday resort, and secondly, it was to lead ultimately to an all-the-year-round season. The first winter station for the mountain air cure of consumptives was

[1] Chambers' *Encyclopaedia* (1923), article on 'Alpine Climbing'.

ASCENT OF THE ROTHHORN, 1871
(*Frontispiece to Leslie Stephen's 'Playground of Europe'*)

opened by Dr. Brehmer himself in Upper Silesia, but the 'Görbersdorf cure', as it came to be called, was taken up by English doctors, and as far as Switzerland was concerned, the English were again in the forefront. The appearance in the Swiss mountain villages of small groups of winter visitors from England in the later 'sixties was the beginning of a new chapter in Swiss social and economic history.

The course of events has a familiar ring. The early winter visitors were invalids who came with no other motive but the restoration of their health. They organized their own entertainments, and the more active took part in the traditional winter sports. Soon there came to join them other visitors who had no need of the mountain air cure but were attracted by what they heard of the beauty of the mountains in winter, the invigorating qualities of the climate, the charm of the social life, and the delights of the winter sports. At Davos, the most popular winter health resort, the number of visitors rose from about 70 in 1869 to 200 in 1872-3, 500 in 1875-6, 700 in 1878-9, and 1,700 in 1889-90. St. Moritz began to be frequented in winter at about the same time, and other early winter resorts were Wiesen, Arosa and Andermatt. By the 'eighties winter colonies of invalids were scattered throughout the Alps, and the English element was strong.

According to Robert Louis Stevenson, an Alpine 'sanitarium' was half English, half German, and its diversions reflected the admixture. The German contribution was a band able to play and actors able to act. 'Meantime in the English hotels home-played farces, *tableaux vivants*, and even balls enliven the evenings; a charity bazaar sheds genial consternation; Christmas and New Year are solemnized with Pantagruelian dinners, and from time to time the young folks carol and revolve untunefully enough through the figures of a singing quadrille. A magazine club supplies you with everything, from the *Quarterly* to the *Sunday at Home*. Grand tournaments are organized at chess, draughts, billiards and whist.' Out of doors there was skating, though it was 'curious, and perhaps rather unsafe, for the invalid to skate under a burning sun, and walk back to his hotel in a sweat, through long tracts of glare and passages of freezing shadow'. There was also tobogganing, 'the peculiar outdoor sport of this district'. 'The mad descent' was 'one of the most exhilarating follies in the world, and the tobogganing invalid is early reconciled to somersaults'. The supreme pleasure was to toboggan alone at night; 'this, in an atmosphere tingling with forty degrees of frost, in a night made luminous with stars and snow, and girt with strange white mountains, teaches the pulse an unaccustomed tune and adds a new excitement to the life of man upon his planet'.

The first to join the invalids in the delights which Stevenson described were chiefly attracted by the opportunities for sport, and they were content with the simple life of the Swiss mountain inns. There was as yet little for the lover of luxury and fashion. A visitor to St. Moritz in the early 'nineties has recalled that two hotels were open and that they were, for the most part, patronized by public school masters and boys with relatives and friends, and by a sprinkling of invalids. The sports which were pursued were tobogganing, skating, a primitive version of ice hockey, and curling. A bobsleigh run went down the main street, but the Cresta and Lake runs were already in being. Another visitor added that the indoor committee of one of the hotels produced a concert or general entertainment each week.[1]

Of the winter sports, skating and curling were of ancient origin; tobogganing as a sport is said to date from 1877, when it was practised at Davos, while tobogganing on artificial runs was a development of the 'eighties, chiefly associated with St. Moritz. It was, however, with none of these, but with ski-ing—an importation from Norway—that the future of winter sports was in the main to lie, and it was to a few Englishmen, foremost amongst them being E. C. Richardson, Vivian Caulfeild, and Arnold Lunn, the son of the tourist agent, that this was in large measure due. To these men and the disciples who collected round them, ski-ing was more than a sport, more even than an art; it was a spiritual exercise which brought its reward in an unbelievable exhilaration and exaltation of mind and body. Inspired by the same impulses

[1] Letters to *The Times* from W. J. M., and Francis N. Curzon, 12th and 21st January 1939.

as the early Alpinists, this small group of young Englishmen set to work in collaboration with the Continental pioneers to evolve a scientific technique out of the crude traditional methods and equipment and to propagate their tremendous discovery. The formation in 1903 of the Davos English Ski Club and the Ski Club of Great Britain was a landmark in the history of the Swiss resorts comparable in importance with the formation of the Alpine Club nearly fifty years before.

Little has so far been said of the part of the Swiss themselves in the remarkable story which began with Windham's visit to Chamonix and culminated with the Swiss mountains as a summer and winter playground for all Europe. It was important but secondary. The initiative and the vision came almost exclusively from outside. The Swiss accepted a destiny which was shaped for them by others, and their own contribution lay chiefly in the equipment of their country so that it could fulfil this destiny to the best advantage. Its relative poverty made the part of a nation of hotelkeepers more congenial than it might otherwise have been to a people renowned for independence of spirit, and the honesty, thrift and business skill of the Swiss admirably fitted them for a role in which they were already experienced. In 1853 there were no fewer than 14,500 inns to a population of less than 2½ millions,[1] but there were still many areas which were unknown to foreign tourists. Even Davos was described in 1877 as 'a primitive watering place, frequented almost solely by Swiss',[2] while in 1871 Stephen wrote of 'innumerable valleys which have not yet bowed the knee to Baal, in the shape of Mr. Cook and his tourists', and of retired valleys within a few hours of one of the most frequented routes of Europe where Swiss peasants would refuse money in exchange for their hospitality.

But the retired valleys were fast being invaded, and the shyness of the Swiss peasants was breaking down. In the year in which Stephen wrote, the first mountain railway was built. Regrettable though this might seem to those to whom the actual ascent by their own efforts was of the essence of mountaineering, it marked an

[1] Lambert, 167.

[2] *Holiday Rambles, etc.* (1877), 59.

important step forward in the exploitation by the Swiss of the natural assets with which they were so richly endowed. Mountain railways meant that access to the high Alps was no longer restricted to the energetic and the adventurous. Henceforth the development of the mountain areas proceeded apace. In 1880 the number of inns built specially for travellers was estimated at over 1,000, and their value at nearly £13 million; 283 were at or over 3,400 feet above sea level, and 14 over 6,500 feet.[1] A Swiss historian, Fueter, has estimated that in the same year there were 43,850 beds in hotels catering especially for foreigners, representing a capital investment of 319½ million Swiss francs. The number of beds had doubled by 1894, when it was 88,634, and doubled again by 1912, when it was 168,625, and the capital had risen to 1,136 million francs. During the 'nineties there was a boom in mountain railways; in addition to major railways such as the Pilatusbahn, the Wengernalpbahn and the Jungfraubahn—the first to the really high mountains—there were many rope railways.

Relatively to the Riviera and the great spas, the Swiss mountain resorts were at first simple to the point of austerity. It was impossible that this state of affairs should continue, and before the end of the century there were already signs of two changes which were to assimilate them more closely to Nice and Monte Carlo. They were becoming more luxurious and increasingly cosmopolitan. J. A. Symonds had written in 1882 of the danger of Davos degenerating into 'an ill-drained, overcrowded, gaslighted centre of cosmopolitan disease and second-rate gaiety'. Speaking for the older school of Alpinist, Frederic Harrison in his *Alpine Jubilee* (1908) objected to the 'ultra New York sumptuosity where there used to be plain living', described the visitors as over-civilized, over-dressed and over-fed, and complained that skates and bobsleighs—note that he did not mention skis—had almost superseded ice axes and ropes. He also remarked on the decline in the number of English visitors. In his young days they had come to about three-quarters of the total: now at some of the most beautiful haunts the proportion was only a fifth or even a tenth. It is not credible that there had been an absolute decline in the number

[1] Murray's *Handbook* (1892), 15.

of English visitors. But relatively they were no doubt fewer, as other nationalities, and especially the Germans, followed more and more where the English had led. Even so, as Harrison himself observed, English influences remained marked, being exemplified by such institutions as separate tables for meals, dinner jackets, the rule of no conversation with a stranger, and to greater advantage by such amenities as baths and modern sanitation.

Harrison noticed the tendency for the Alps to be assimilated to the Riviera, except, he said, that there were as yet fewer motors and no gambling hells to speak of. There were other important differences, but broadly speaking Harrison's generalization was sound. Whether they were in the mountains of Switzerland or on the Mediterranean coast, or for that matter in Egypt or Algeria, in the Pyrenees or on the English Channel, the holiday resorts of the wealthy approximated more and more to a universal type, with a strong English line in their ancestry deriving from Bath and Regency Brighton.

walking tour in Holland.

eruption of Vesuvius

XIII

HOLIDAYS WITH PAY[1]

In 1900 the annual holiday had hardly begun to attract the attention of sociologists, still less of politicians. It was taken for granted as a luxury which could be enjoyed at a certain level of income but which there was no special hardship in going

[1] In recent years there have been a number of important reports and surveys on holidays and holidaymaking, and I have made extensive use of them in this chapter: *The Report* of the Departmental Committee on Holidays with Pay (1938): *Planning for Holidays* (Political and Economic Planning ('P.E.P.') broadsheet No. 194, 1942): Elizabeth Brunner, *Holiday Making and the Holiday Trades* (Nuffield College, Oxford, 1945): *Holidays*—a Study made by the National Council of Social Service (1945): *Report* by the Catering Wages Commission on the Staggering of Holidays (1945): *Report* by the Catering Wages Commission on the Development of the Catering, Holiday and Tourist Services (1946). I have also been greatly assisted by material supplied to me by the Industrial Welfare Society, including the *Report* of the Conference on Workers' Holidays in 1938, and the *Report* of the Committee on Workers' Holidays on staggering submitted to the Catering Wages Commission in 1945.

The *Reports* of the Royal Commission on the Distribution of the Industrial Population (1940) and the Committee on Land Utilization in Rural Areas (1942) are relevant and contain some references to holidays. On the position abroad there are a number of reports, etc., by the I.L.O.

without. A few industrialists and social workers were beginning to think differently, but their approach was largely empirical. The industrialists were learning the connection between holidays and productivity. The social workers, preoccupied with the degradation around them, thought in terms of convalescence for the respectable poor of the slums rather than of recreation for the general run of working people; or, like the founders of the Co-operative Holidays Association, saw in the annual holiday a means to some separate end such as popular education. With few exceptions, such public discussion as took place is exemplified by the articles which *The Times* in its lighter vein occasionally published on the oddities of holiday manners and customs, annual variations on similar themes in *Punch*, press reports of congestion at the August Bank Holiday week-end, and the appeals every year on behalf of the Children's Country Holiday Fund and other charities.

More was not to be expected. Inability to take a summer holiday is a secondary consequence of poverty. The graver aspects of poverty called for action, and there was no place for holidays with pay on the immediate agenda of social reform.

Yet there have been few important changes during the present century which could not have been foreseen by a careful observer in 1900. The main trends were settled. Annual holidays were spreading from the middle classes to the better-paid manual workers. A few public undertakings and private firms had granted holidays with pay to their employees. The major seaside resorts of to-day were firmly established. The great tourist agencies, except the Workers' Travel Association, which was founded in 1921, were in being. The railway system was virtually complete, the motor-car was ceasing to be a joke and a nuisance, the bicycle had reopened the countryside to the people from the towns.

If the general standard of life continued to rise, all the ingredients were present for a vast expansion in the number of holiday-makers. The essential requirements were that there should be an increase in the number of persons with a surplus over bare subsistence which they could spend on amenities; and that they should want to spend part of any such surplus on holidays.

Holidays with Pay

Many forces contributed to put holidays high amongst the items on which increased incomes were spent. The faster tempo, higher degree of mechanization, and enhanced scale of modern industry increased the desire for periodical changes from the routine and environment of everyday life. The towns continued to grow until by the 'thirties over two-thirds of the people of Great Britain lived in the seven 'conurbations' of upwards of a million inhabitants, six of them (London, Birmingham, Merseyside, Tyneside, West Yorkshire, and Manchester) being in England itself; and their tendency to sprawl and spread cut off more and more of their population from the countryside.

These imprisoned millions needed little persuasion to escape when they could. The social emulation which comes naturally to the Englishman in itself made a seaside holiday something to strive for. The inhibitions against enjoyment which had survived particularly amongst the Nonconformists—still in the early years of the century a dynamic influence in the lower middle and artisan classes—were fast breaking down, and did not long withstand the skilful commercial interests which traded in entertainment for the newly educated masses. The social and technical upheavals connected with the internal combustion engine and the 1914-18 war stimulated the appetite for change and excitement.

There was no lack of persuasion. All the resources of twentieth-century salesmanship were called into play by the holiday resorts, the transport undertakings, the travel agencies, the hotels, the amusement caterers. The increasing ingenuity which was shown can be traced in the development of their advertising, until in the end skilled practitioners were exploiting almost every human motive in propaganda which year by year grew in scale and intensity.

This is the background to the development of holidays with pay. The decisive factor was the rise in real incomes. Until thanks to rising incomes and successful publicity—some of it organized, some of it the spontaneous expression of their satisfaction by visitors to the resorts—the annual holiday was so widely established that it was looked upon as essential to a reasonable standard of life, there could be no question of claiming that the State should guarantee holidays with pay to every worker, nor any strong incentive in industrial negotiations to prefer them to other improvements in conditions. And until the majority of wage earners were above the subsistence level the claim could hardly be effective. Before he can go away for a holiday the worker must be able to cover not only his regular overheads, including his rent and the keep of his family, but also the extra expenditure which he will necessarily incur on travel, accommodation and amusements. During the rest of the year, he must, therefore, be able to save the difference between his holiday pay and his total holiday expenditure. From this point of view, pay for holidays is an increase in wages which is paid at a particular time in the year for the greater convenience of the worker. Theoretically, the same result could be secured by paying it over the whole year as an addition to wages.

These circumstances may explain why holidays with pay were relatively so slow in spreading, and why they roused so little interest until the 'thirties. It is true that the Trades Union Congress first passed a resolution in favour of paid annual holidays for all as long ago as 1911, and that this was followed up by several later Congresses. But the subject was never in the forefront of the programme of the Congress, and with few exceptions the individual trade unions did not press it.

Under the collective bargaining which settled wages in the organized trades, the connection between holidays with pay and wages was obvious. When the former presented themselves as an alternative to a rise in the weekly rate of wages, it was only in the better paid trades that there was much doubt which would be chosen. There was still less doubt in periods when the trade unions were fighting hard to maintain wages or wages were falling. A few employers considered holidays with pay a good investment which more than paid for itself in terms of output, but the majority were only prepared to concede them as part of a wages bargain. In March 1925, according to a Ministry of Labour estimate, 1½ million manual workers enjoyed holidays with pay under collective agreements; in April 1937, the estimate was 1½ to 1¾ millions. New agreements had been largely offset by the lapsing of old ones. The number who were entitled to paid holidays otherwise than under collective agreements brought the total at the latter date to about 4 millions out of 18½ million workpeople earning £250 a year or less, and in addition there were perhaps another million from the higher income levels.

The number who actually took holidays away from home was considerably greater. *The New Survey of London Life and Labour* reckoned that in 1934 about half the workpeople in London did so. In the North, where the wakes system operated, the proportion was probably higher, and it was estimated that in 1937 the total number of holidaymakers who were away for a week or more was about 15 millions. Most of the increase had taken place since 1919, but it owed little to holidays with pay.

Nor was the question a live issue in the years after the first world war. There was little support for the proposals for additional bank holidays which were occasionally put forward. In 1919 the Swedish Government proposed to the first session of the International Labour Conference that the question of providing regular annual vacations for employees should be on the agenda for the next Session, on the ground that 'it must be considered essential for the physical as well as the psychical health of employees that they should enjoy each year a certain period of absolute rest'. The English translation is curious, but the point is clear, and twenty years later the Swedish Government's view would have had general support. The subject did not in fact appear on the agenda until 1935. The rudimentary state of thought about it at the time it was mooted in 1919 may be illustrated by the proposal of a Committee appointed by the Industrial Council for the Building Industry that every registered worker should have a week's holiday with pay on the same scale and from the same fund as unemployment pay.

In 1925, a Bill for compulsory annual holidays with pay was introduced into the House of Commons, but made no progress. Nineteen twenty-eight saw the first statutory provision, when the Shops (Hours of Closing) Act entitled shop assistants in seaside resorts and seafishing towns to consecutive paid holidays in compensation for working beyond the normal hours during the season. This was an *ad hoc* measure of limited application, without any general significance. In 1929, however, another Private Member's Bill succeeded in getting a Second Reading, before being shelved, after the Parliamentary Secretary to the Ministry of Labour, Mr. J. J. Lawson, M.P., had said that the Government could not find time for its passage, owing to the heavy programme before the House and because they thought that it was necessary to have a full inquiry and consultations with the Unions and interests concerned.

The question was soon overshadowed by the economic depression, and it was not until times were better that—eight years later—the promised inquiry was set up. In the meantime the I.L.O. had had its long-deferred discussion, and in 1936 adopted a draft Convention, by which workers under sixteen years of age were to be entitled to twelve consecutive days of paid holiday each year, and older workers to six. The British Government delegates abstained from voting, after they had failed to persuade the conference to substitute a Recommendation for a Convention on the ground that the draft did not take sufficient account of the widely differing circumstances in practice.

The discussions at Geneva had their reactions at home. The Government was charged with obstructionism. Many who had assumed that Britain was in the vanguard in social legislation were shocked at her apparent backwardness as compared with other countries in which holidays with pay were imposed by law, and disturbed, according to their political outlook, that Communist Russia and Nazi Germany appeared to be showing greater energy. There was also criticism from those who thought that the most hopeful way of curing or alleviating unemployment was to spread it in the form of leisure, through such methods as shorter working hours, the five-day week, raising the school-leaving age, reducing the age of retirement, and compulsory holidays with pay. The latter was one of the remedies for unemployment recommended in 1935 by Sir Malcolm Stewart, the Commissioner for the Special Areas; and Baron von Veitschberger was to submit to the Departmental Committee on Holidays with Pay in 1937 a scheme which held out the attractive prospect that unemployment on the scale experienced in 1936 could be eliminated if everybody had five weeks' paid holiday every year.[1]

The time was thus ripe for the revival of the Annual Holiday Bill, and in November 1936, a Bill introduced by Mr. Guy Rowson, M.P., secured a Second Reading, after a Debate in which he had support from Members of all Parties. The Government opposed the Bill as being impracticable but did not dissent from its object.

This Debate was important. It focused and encouraged the growing opinion in favour of legislation. It attracted additional public attention because of its unusual ending with the rejection of the advice of the Government. It drew from the Government an acceptance of the principle of paid holidays, and during the Committee stage in February 1937, the promise that the inquiry which the Labour Government had foreshadowed in 1929 would be instituted.

In the following month the Departmental Committee on Holidays with Pay was set up—under the chairmanship of Lord Amulree, and with leading representatives of both sides of industry amongst its members—'to investigate the extent to which holidays with pay are given to employed workpeople, and the possibility of extending the provision of such holidays by statutory enactment or otherwise; and to make recommendations'. It lost no time in carrying out its inquiry; but even so it was only by one vote that an impatient House of Commons did not give a Second Reading to another Annual Holiday Bill in November 1937, despite being reminded that the Committee was at work.

The Committee heard evidence from Government Departments, employers, trade unions, the holiday resorts, the transport industry, and the interested voluntary organizations. The chief spokesmen for statutory enactment were naturally the Trades Union Congress. They asked that twelve working days should be granted, to be given as far as practicable between April and October. They based their case mainly on the increased nervous

[1] The scheme was to be financed by the savings on unemployment benefit and assistance in which it would result, the existing expenditure on paid holidays, and the stimulus which it would give to trade.

strain in industry, the advantages to the health and efficiency of the worker, the desirability if only on psychological grounds of removing the unfortunate distinction between the blackcoated and the manual worker, the needs of housewives and mothers, and the slow progress which had been made in default of statutory provision. Regular annual holidays with pay, they said, were 'an integral part of those admittedly necessary regular periods of freedom from daily toil, commonly described as periods of leisure'. They were satisfied that industry could afford the cost, which they estimated at less than 4 per cent of the total wages bill, and they argued that the workers had not yet had their full share of recent increases in industrial productivity.

Few of the employers' representatives directly contested the desirability of holidays with pay. Some employers indeed agreed with the T.U.C., for reasons of social justice, industrial welfare and efficiency, and in fairness to those firms which had given paid holidays. Most of them, however, questioned the wisdom of proceeding by statute, maintained that in the last resort the grant of holidays with pay was an increase in wages, and denied that industry as a whole could afford the cost. Their detailed arguments varied widely in ingenuity and weight. At one extreme was opposition to interference with the worker's freedom to decide how he used his wages. At the other were practical objections to statutory regulation because of the impossibility of covering everybody in industry from the pieceworker and the casual labourer to the hairdresser who was paid partly by tips and the subpostmaster who had to find a substitute when he was away.

The crux of almost all the arguments was the contention that the statutory enforcement of holidays with pay was ultimately the statutory enforcement of an increase in wages. It was wrong to compel the employer to act as the worker's banker for part of his wages. Interference with the established methods of settling wages would undermine the machinery of joint negotiation, cut across collective agreements, and deprive employers and employed of their freedom to decide the order of priority in improving conditions. The burden on industry would be uneven and would vary with the incidence of wage costs, which ranged from less than

5 per cent to about 70 per cent of total costs. Price increases could not be avoided, with possibly serious consequences, particularly to industries exposed to keen foreign competition, and might lead to unemployment. Industries in which it had been assumed that recent wage increases covered provision for holidays would be penalized. There might be labour trouble when, as was inevitable, the grant of holidays with pay had to be taken into account in subsequent wage negotiations.

The Departmental Committee reported in April 1938. They began by analysing the existing position. They estimated that annual consecutive holidays with pay in some form were provided for some 7¾ million workpeople out of a total of 18½ millions earning not more than £250 a year. Three millions of these received paid holidays by virtue of collective agreements, as compared with 1½—1¾ million when the Committee was set up. Usually the entitlement was to a working week plus public holidays, but many manual workers in public utility services and public administration received a fortnight, and in the distributive trades sometimes as much as three weeks. Salaried employees generally received two or three weeks. In some industries proposals for holidays with pay were under consideration. The other workpeople not entitled to them fell into four main categories. In industries such as agriculture, building and shipping, there were difficulties connected with conditions of employment or the nature of the contract of employment. Others such as cotton, wool and coal mining were subject to severe foreign competition, and 'concerned with the problem of passing on to an export market the extra cost which would be involved'. There were the small and miscellaneous industries and industries where industrial organization was weak. Lastly there were workers not in continuous employment. The Committee pertinently commented that in many organized trades neither side had suggested holidays with pay even in recent negotiations. Either no holidays were taken, or it was assumed that the workers could meet the cost from savings. In other cases wage increases had been understood to include payment for holidays.

With a warning against too facile deductions from the practice abroad, the Committee referred to legislation of widely varying scope providing for consecutive paid holidays in some forty countries or territories.

The Committee's recommendations gained greatly from being unanimous. They accepted the principle of holidays with pay but stated their conclusion cautiously. 'It cannot, in our view, be denied that an annual holiday contributes in a considerable measure to workpeople's happiness, health and efficiency, and we feel that the extension of the taking of consecutive days of holiday annually by workpeople would be of benefit to the community.'

Their proposals were a compromise between the employers' and the trade unions' views. While to give a period of more than one week seemed 'not unreasonable', it was desirable to proceed 'judiciously in the matter for reasons connected with production', and it would be wise to start with a working week as the immediate goal. They agreed that holidays had hitherto been regarded as a condition of employment, and, though it would be advantageous if the subject could be removed from the sphere of remuneration, they thought that in the circumstances it was preferable to give industry the opportunity of dealing with the matter for itself before compulsion was applied. They pointed out that the forty-eight-hour week had been introduced by voluntary arrangement. They therefore recommended a probationary period, so that the maximum progress could be made by means of collective agreements, and so that wage readjustments and unrest could be prevented. This probationary period was also needed for working out the details of legislation and administration, and to enable steps to be taken to cope with the great increase in holiday activities which would no doubt result. They referred particularly to the question of 'staggering', and advised the Minister of Labour to set up a Branch 'with a view to supervising the application and observance of the provision of holidays with pay, promoting the adoption of voluntary agreements for paid holidays and the spread over of holidays, stimulating those responsible to make the school holidays to fit in with industrial holidays, and encouraging local authorities in holiday resorts to supervise the provision of accommodation for visitors and various kindred matters'. During the Parliamentary Session of 1940-1 legislation should be passed making provision for holidays with pay in industry generally, but this should be preceded by immediate legislation to give the necessary powers to provide for holidays with pay in agriculture and the Trade Board industries, where wages were regulated under statutory machinery.

The Committee rejected the various contributory schemes which had been submitted to them. They made one express exception to the proposed minimum of a working week: domestic servants in full-time employment should be entitled to a fortnight. They recommended that as far as practicable the annual holiday should be granted between the beginning of Summer Time and the beginning of October. They suggested that the Easter Bank Holiday should take place on a fixed and certain date in the spring.

The Amulree Report settled once and for all the question of State action. The Government accepted it without delay and acted promptly. The Holidays with Pay Act, 1938, gave the proposed powers to wage-regulating authorities, and enabled the Ministry of Labour to help to bring about voluntary schemes under collective agreements. The Ministry of Labour formed the special branch which the Committee had advocated.

There was a remarkable response to the invitation to proceed by the voluntary method. By November 1938, the number of workpeople with £250 a year or less entitled to holidays with pay had risen to about 9 millions, including nearly 4½ millions covered by collective agreements. By June 1939, the total was over 11 millions.

This was in accordance with the expectations of the Departmental Committee. What was unexpected was that there was no corresponding increase in the number of actual holidaymakers. On the contrary the general experience was that 1937 was the peak year, and there was a decline in 1938. One reason may have been the international crisis, and others were the beginnings of a slump in some industries and the high pressure in those engaged in rearmament. It also no doubt showed that for many workers pay during holidays was not enough, and that, as Sir Walter Citrine had told the Departmental Committee, the general introduction of holidays with pay would not lead 'to a sudden rush to the seaside or anything like that. It would be the development of a habit.' Observers agreed that there was much apathy and ignorance amongst those entitled to the concession for the first time.

The respite was, however, useful for those who had to plan for the increase in numbers which was bound to come. The Government, the resorts, the railway companies, the travel agencies, the voluntary societies, were all impressed with the urgency. In the period before the war important preliminary work was done, in which the Ministry of Labour collaborated with a representative Committee on Workers' Holidays formed with Government encouragement by the Industrial Welfare Society in 1938.

The war brought most of the planning to a sudden end, and in 1940 and 1941 graver matters preoccupied the country. When the worst of the crisis passed, it became clear that a difficult situation threatened as soon as the war was over. Conditions during the war were a foretaste of things to come. The closing down of coastal areas vulnerable to bombing and invasion, the occupation of hotels and other premises by the Services and Government Departments, shortages of supplies, equipment and labour, transport difficulties, resulted in inconveniences which were only tolerable because of the emergency. But it was evident that when the war ended there would be a vastly increased demand for a reduced volume of accommodation. The number entitled to holidays with pay was rising rapidly. By March 1942, between 6 and 6½ millions were covered by collective agreements, and 2—2½ millions in agriculture and the Trade Board industries. In 1945 it was estimated that no fewer than 14 million workpeople or about 80 per cent of the total were entitled to holidays with pay. And to a growing extent provision was made for a fortnight instead of a week. On the other side, there was a considerable reduction in the available accommodation; the National Council of Social Service estimated in 1945 that it might be down to 75 per cent of the pre-war level in the first year after the war.

The problem which had to be tackled may be simply stated. It was a question firstly of numbers, and secondly of poverty. How could the millions of new holidaymakers be accommodated? What could be done for those still unable to afford to go away for holidays? P.E.P. estimated that in the first year after the war thirty million holidaymakers, or twice as many as in 1937, would have to be provided for, and that this number would rise to 45 millions in succeeding years: the estimate of the National Council of Social Service was 26 millions. These figures were certainly not reached in 1946, partly because of accommodation difficulties, and it may be that they did not allow sufficiently for the innumerable personal circumstances which prevent people from taking a holiday in a particular year, for those who do not want to go away for holidays, and for the substantial number who lack the means to do so. But the forecast of a considerable increase was clearly sound.

The problem of numbers could be solved in one or both of two ways. The accommodation already available could be made to go further; or it could be increased.

Though still practised, some of the traditional methods of making the accommodation go further were no longer adequate or acceptable. Such devices as the conversion of billiard tables or baths into beds and the segregation of the sexes by screening off part of a bedroom commended themselves to nobody except landladies anxious for the maximum profit and lodgers compelled to cut their expenditure to the minimum or faced with the alternative of no accommodation at all.

None the less it was the extension of another of the traditional methods which offered the obvious and most hopeful line of advance. 'Staggering'—or 'spread-over'—had long been practised in the North of England; in 1938 over 100 towns in Lancashire and Yorkshire staggered their holidays between June and October. It was taken for granted in most offices and some factories. And it had long been favoured by the holiday resorts and the railways, both of which suffered from the compression of the peak holiday period into a few weeks.

The problem itself is old. Eighteenth-century Bath and Brighton were congested in the season, gentlewomen had to sleep in garrets, every fisherman's cottage was filled to capacity, and prices soared.

It was in August that Dickens's 'clerks madly in love' flocked to the sea, and one of the reasons for choosing the month for the new bank holiday in 1871 was its holiday associations. Whether or not, as was suggested in the House of Commons in 1938, the origin of the practice of going away in August was that the London season lasted until July, this was certainly important. In August the Court was away, Parliament had usually risen, Society had departed, the leaders of commerce had followed its example, the lawyers were in vacation, the schools were closed; and the clerks in Whitehall, the City and the Inns of Court took the earliest opportunity of going away before the summer was over. The August bank holiday made things worse, especially when the manual workers began to go away as well. They became accustomed to think of the bank holiday as the official starting point for the annual holiday; it followed immediately after the closing of the elementary schools; and since they would usually receive no pay for the bank holiday it was economical to include it in their own holiday week or fortnight.

But it is only recently that the problem has been considered as one which is social as well as personal and that serious thought has been given to 'staggering' as a matter for communal action. The greater attention which it began to receive in the 'thirties was partly due to the immensity which by this time it had assumed, and partly no doubt to greater readiness to think in collectivist terms.

By this time the situation was becoming critical, and it was evident that the existing facilities could not keep pace with the growing demand. The extent of the concentration upon a short period in the second half of July and in August was examined by the Catering Wages Commission in their Report on the Staggering of Holidays (1945). The railway statistics for 1938 showed that 22·5 per cent of the total passenger journeys in the year were made in July and August, and 31·5 per cent of the journeys other than excursions; during the four weeks ended 6th August, the number of coaching train miles was 24 per cent greater than in February. The Commission also gave the proportion of accommodation taken up in two unnamed resorts during the summer of the same year. They differed in the extent of the concentration on the peak period, but in each the peak was marked.[1]

Ministry of Labour figures for 1938 (England and Scotland excluding London) analysing the dates at which holidays were given showed an even greater concentration. As compared with nearly two million people who had their holidays in the first two weeks of August, there were about a million for the five weeks of July, nearly half a million for the last three weeks of August, and 100,000 for the first week of September.

As the Catering Wages Commission pointed out, precise evidence is scanty. The examples they gave no doubt represented the general trend, but there are many variations of detail. The season tends to be shorter in the North. Some resorts make greater efforts than others to cater for the out-of-season visitor. The spreadover is longest amongst the well-to-do and hence amongst the more exclusive resorts and more expensive hotels.

The arguments for staggering are obvious. In the first place, it relieves congestion at the resorts and on the railways and roads. Representatives of the railways told the Amulree Committee that they had almost reached maximum capacity with the existing permanent way. If the pressure increased further all that they could do would be to put on still earlier and later trains at times inconvenient to the public. They might even have to ration places; in 1938 Mr. Roland Robinson, M.P., told the House of Commons that it had in fact been necessary to do so at Blackpool.

Secondly, staggering reduces costs to the holidaymaker and those who cater for him. In normal conditions prices are forced up in August by competition and because the resorts have to compen-

[1] At one, it rose from 25 per cent and 33 per cent of total capacity in May and June respectively, to 50 per cent in the first half of July and 75 per cent in the second half and to 90-100 per cent in August; it fell to 75 per cent in September and 50 per cent in October. At the other, numbers increased fairly steadily from about 6,000 to 10,000 a week in April to 50,000 in the third week of July; there was a steep rise to 75,000 in the last week of July, 80,000 in August, and 75,000 in the first week of September, followed by a sharp decline from 55,000 in the second week and 35,000 in the third week, to 15,000 in the first week of October and 3,000 in the last week.

sate for the shortness of the season by making high profits while it lasts.[1] For the rest of the year capital equipment ranging from boarding houses and furniture to railway stock and pleasure steamers is idle or only partially employed. The use of labour is also uneconomical. Extra employees have to be taken on for a few weeks, overtime has to be worked, the heavy pressure imposes an unnecessary strain on health and efficiency, wages go up. Those who look after the visitors have less incentive to raise their standards, and, moreover, in an average year the visitor would enjoy more sunshine, more daylight, and less rain in June than in August.[2]

Individual holiday resorts have for long attempted to popularize themselves out of season. The lower prices which are charged are an inducement to prefer the less favoured months, except so far as they confirm the impression that because the latter are less favoured they are also less desirable. Yet neither the resorts nor the railway companies have had much success in persuading the public to change its habits, and the Amulree Committee were told of the lack of a marked response to the Earlier Holidays Movement propagated by the railways. The response to the Com-

[1] The *Report* of the Catering Wages Commission on the *Staggering of Holidays* gave the following four examples of the cost a week for board residence in 1938. ((d) refers to a holiday camp.)

	April	August
(a)	£3 8 6	£4 17 6
(b)	£1 15 0	£2 10 0
(c)	£2 7 6	£3 5 0
(d)	£2 12 6	£3 13 6

[2] The averages for England and Wales as a whole, quoted by the Catering Wages Commission, are:

	June	*July*	*August*
Rain	2·43 ins.	3·06 ins.	3·40 ins.
Temperature	57·4° F.	61·1° F.	60·5° F.
Sunshine	6·60 hrs.	5·71 hrs.	5·40 hrs.

mittee's own references to the subject was more encouraging. In April 1938, immediately after their Report had appeared, the House of Commons carried a Motion advocating greater spread-over. The Government and the voluntary societies gave urgent attention to the question. The railway companies and the holiday resorts intensified their propaganda, and renewed efforts were made to improve the out-of-season attractions at the latter. Blackpool, for example, spent £4,000 in 1938 on a national advertising campaign for June holidays and offered its attractions at half price during the month.

The war came before it was possible to judge how far these measures were likely to be successful. It is doubtful, however, if they made much difference. The only major advance was the decision at Coventry in 1938 to change the annual holiday from August Bank Holiday week to the last week in June. This showed what could be done where the local leadership was sufficiently energetic, but it also showed how great were the difficulties. It was only after prolonged discussions that agreement was reached, and it had no binding authority.

The progress which, judged by results, had been made before the war was thus slight, and in 1945 the Catering Wages Commission described staggering as the 'most important and urgent' of all the questions connected with holidays. They themselves undertook a special investigation into the subject, in which they had the help of a report from the Committee on Workers' Holidays. So impressed were the latter with the difficulties that they even recommended a limited and temporary measure of compulsion, if voluntary methods proved ineffective.

The difficulties were indeed formidable. Inertia and tradition are serious obstacles. The belief that August is the best holiday month does not easily yield to rational arguments: the experience of one bad June and one fine August is more persuasive than averages and statistics. August is the least attractive summer month in the great cities, and there are many who think that other things being equal it is preferable to take the annual holiday as near as possible to the winter, but while the days are still long. The ordinary man seeks the company of large numbers; and many of his entertainments—dancing, the theatre, concerts, amusement parks—gain from or depend upon big attendances. In these respects he does not differ from people of fashion either in the past or in the present.

It is necessary, therefore, to make holidays at other times as satisfying psychologically as holidays at the peak period. But to the extent that this is bound up with the presence of crowds its solution depends upon the success of the policy of staggering. There is a vicious circle. It seems to be agreed that the most promising ways of breaking it are by careful publicity—to which the Catering Wages Commission attached great importance—and by making the resorts more attractive in the other summer months. It was with these considerations in mind that the Ministry of Labour conducted a publicity campaign in 1946 with the slogan 'It's better, remember, in June and September!' Propaganda by the railways and the resorts supplemented the Government campaign, but the year was abnormal and provided no reliable guide for the future. The most favourable circumstance, as the Catering Wages Commission had pointed out, was that as a result of the war 'so many customs are in the melting pot and people have learned to accept a holiday at some time other than July or August because of war-time conditions'. It was thus a matter of holding ground which had already been gained as well as of gaining new ground. And the risk of recession was illustrated by the experience at Leicester and Northampton, where, after a ballot taken on the initiative of employers and trade unions, the holiday week was moved in 1945 from the August Bank Holiday week and in 1946 it was decided to revert.

Many practical questions have also to be answered. Is it better to stagger by towns—on the wakes system—or by firms or by individual employees? The general opinion, endorsed by the Catering Wages Commission, has favoured town holidays, the dates of which could be varied in different years. But there are the inevitable exceptions, firms which are interdependent with firms in other towns, public services and utilities which have to carry on all the year round, individuals whose private circumstances do not fit into a general scheme, and not least the great cities, in which the closing of every factory in the same week would aggravate the very evils it was intended to remedy. For the latter the Catering Wages Commission recommended staggering by industries or by areas.

Should there be a new bank holiday, say in September, and should the August Bank Holiday be abolished? The Commission thought that, where the town holiday week did not include the August Bank Holiday, this holiday should be transferred to the holiday week. The Amulree Committee had advocated a fixed Easter or holding what is now the Easter Bank Holiday at a fixed date. What should be done about school holidays, which in one investigation 40 per cent of those questioned gave as their reason for choosing August? The Catering Wages Commission recommended that schools should close during holiday weeks and that the external school examinations should be removed from the holiday period. Over what period should the staggering of town holidays extend? The Commission thought that it would be unwise to aim at a longer period than June to September. How could the pressure on transport be relieved? The most practical suggestion which was made was probably that mid-week travel should be encouraged, and the Commission commended this idea to the consideration of those concerned. It is obviously far from straightforward.

All the investigators have agreed upon the uselessness of looking for watertight arrangements into which all areas, all firms and all individuals can be fitted. Less emphatically, they have agreed that public opinion is not ripe for regimentation, and that, while positive obstacles such as the holding of school examinations in the summer can be removed, progress is most likely to come from the discovery by trial and error of the arrangements suitable for particular localities and firms.

'Staggering' is the most effective but not the only form of spreadover, and, on the most optimistic view, it would not suffice on its own. P.E.P. calculated that if there were no more staggering than in 1937, the peak number seeking accommodation at one time would be in the neighbourhood of 5 millions. This number, they thought, could be reduced to between 2 and 4 millions (a wide range which may illustrate the difficulty of any precise estimate) by spreading holidays between May and October, as compared with a pre-war peak of around 1¼ million. If the latter figure is taken as the maximum pre-war capacity, the 30 million holidaymakers P.E.P. expected to see immediately after the war could only have been accommodated with the pre-war facilities if staggering had covered 24 weeks at August pressure. This would obviously have been impossible.

The figures given by the Catering Wages Commission led to a similar conclusion. If the two resorts cited by the Commission are representative, at full capacity the holiday resorts could accommodate about 50 per cent more visitors during the months from June to September than they actually did in 1938. If an allowance of 10 per cent is made to account for the reduction in pressure which is one of the objects of staggering, but no allowance for a reduced volume of accommodation, the possible increase would be about 40 per cent. If they were filled to capacity during May as well, they could take about three-quarters more people than in 1938, or with a 10 per cent reduction in pressure, about 60 per cent.

These are guesses, as are the estimates of potential demand. But the gap is clearly considerable, and in practice an even staggering over the whole summer will certainly not occur. The gap will partly be made up by individual staggering outside the main holiday months. For the rest it must be filled by other methods, including holidays at home for those who are crowded out.

The obvious alternative solution is to increase the volume of accommodation, by adding to existing resorts and developing new ones. This is more easily said than done. The main short-term difficulty is that new building for this purpose will be restricted until more urgent needs have been met; and in any event development, however carefully planned and controlled, must consume irreplaceable capital of another kind—the coast and the countryside themselves.

Extensive building will certainly be required, but the order of priority will necessarily be, first, staggering, secondly, the full use of resources already available, including the development of alternative forms of holiday which do not involve substantial additions to existing accommodation, and, only lastly, new building.

Holidaymakers can be encouraged to go to existing accommodation which is not fully used. Holidays in the country and in suitable inland towns can be fostered. Stratford-on-Avon is an example of what can be done by a town with a readily marketable cultural asset. The Malvern Drama Festivals show how it is possible to develop new assets. London itself has much to offer the visitor from the Provinces, and to large sections of the population our historic cities are as unknown and potentially as attractive as the Continental cities which are traditional resorts of British tourists.

Camping and caravanning have immense possibilities. The Camping Club of Great Britain estimated that in 1938 half a million people had camping holidays of three days upwards. Holidays of this kind are not suitable for everybody, but they are cheap and require little permanent accommodation. The resumption of motor touring—there were two million private cars and motor cycles before the war —will help to transfer the pressure from the coast. Holiday cruises will revive in due course. The reopening of travel abroad made some difference in 1946 and will make more in the future, though the gain will be offset by the increase in the number of foreign tourists here which it is hoped to bring about.

It remains to be seen how far the gap will be closed by these means, but the outlook is less unfavourable than is sometimes suggested. Inability to find room at the popular resorts will be a powerful encouragement to look for alternatives and will help to build up new habits and traditions. All the time, however, numbers may be expected to be growing, and as the gap is closed it may tend to be forced open again by increases in real earnings, the breakdown of inhibitions against leaving home, and—perhaps most important of all—the extension of the normal period from one week to two. This is to say nothing of the complications which would result if the spread of a five-day week led to the growth of the habit of going away for week-ends.

Ironically, too, the more effective holidays with pay become the worse will the congestion tend to be, and the more the poorer workers are enabled to take their holidays away from home, the greater the tendency for prices to rise against them, unless accommodation keeps pace with demand.

It was estimated before the war that the minimum cost of a week's holiday at the seaside for a man and his wife and two children was about £10, inclusive of home rent.[1] This was too much for the majority of the 13 million workers earning £4 a week or less. A British Institute of Public Opinion survey in 1939 found that while nine out of ten persons earning £4 a week upwards went away for holidays, only one in three of those earning less did so. An investigation in one of the poorest London Boroughs, Shoreditch, in 1938, showed that despite the better facilities for children and young people than for adults, more than half the junior boys and girls (whose average age was twelve years) had not been away for as much as a week, and about four-fifths and two-thirds respectively of the senior boys and girls. On the other hand, as will be recalled, *The New Survey of London Life and Labour* had estimated that in 1934 about half the workpeople in London went away for holidays.

Theoretically there are two ways in which those who find it difficult to pay the extra cost of a holiday can be helped. They can be given the extra sum they need or assisted to save it: or the cost can be reduced.

There have been experiments on these lines over many years. The activities of the charitable agencies have been described in an earlier chapter: they still do good work.[2] Theirs is the method of direct subsidy, and its scope is necessarily small. Self-help through savings schemes has been the most successful of the existing methods. Holiday savings clubs, which, as we have seen, flourished in the last century, particularly in the North, have multiplied, and probably embrace most wage-earners. In some cases the em-

[1] *The New Survey of London Life and Labour* had estimated in 1934 that for a family of two adults and two children the median rate was about £5 5s. a week in June and £6 6s. in July and August, for board and lodging alone, i.e. exclusive of home rent, travelling expenses and pocket money.

[2] Some at least of the non-commercial travel agencies, e.g. the Holiday Fellowship and the Workers Travel Association, make limited provision for holidays free or at reduced charges for people in need.

ployers have taken the initiative and the workers have no direct share in the management. The modern view, which the Industrial Welfare Society have been prominent in fostering, is strongly in favour of their participation, and the model schemes which the Society have recommended have contributed much to the development of properly organized arrangements. Trade unions, cooperative societies and other working-class bodies have also provided holiday savings facilities on a large scale, and the National Savings Movement has stressed the advantages of saving for this purpose.

For those who cannot afford to save enough, a large proportion of them men with families, the alternatives are holiday pay at a rate higher than the normal wage, a direct subsidy, or reduced costs, with or without a subsidy from public or private sources. The I.C.I. factory at Winnington paid double wages for holidays after an incident in the early years of the century when during the factory holiday the heads of the firm—Dr. Ludwig Mond and Mr. Brunner—met an old labourer who told them that he had still got to keep up his home and on his ordinary pay could not afford to go away. In a few firms bonuses are paid at holiday times, but on the whole the precedent has not been followed. Nor are there any signs of its general adoption. The present trend is towards two weeks' holiday with pay rather than extra pay for one week.

Direct State subsidies to individuals have not been seriously suggested, and the practical point is whether costs can be sufficiently reduced. Staggering will help, as will the taking of holidays in the cheaper areas such as the country. Many get over their difficulties by staying with friends or relatives. But no major advance can take place without radical cuts in capital and labour costs in connection with facilities suitable for the mass of holiday-makers. The prospects of substantial reductions in commercial charges are not good, especially as long as there remains an unsatisfied demand from those able to pay. The situation may possibly get worse. The Catering Wages Commission were told that there was an increasing tendency for boarding and apartment houses to be unwilling to cater for families with young children, and that the restriction of service to 'bed and breakfast' was becoming more widespread. While supplies remain short, labour is difficult to get, and the pressure for accommodation is high, this tendency is unlikely to be reversed.

For the young and active and for some older people, one excellent solution is provided by cycling, rambling and camping, which involve accommodation of the simplest kind and minimum demands on labour. Much is due to the Boy Scouts, boys' clubs, and other youth organizations for popularizing open-air holidays, for removing the anxieties of parents about allowing their children to go away without them, and for training the public in the way to enjoy the countryside and how to behave in it. Before the war camping sites belonging to the Camping Club of Great Britain, which had been founded in 1901, could be hired for 8d. a night or 3s. a week. By 1939 the Youth Hostels Association, which had begun modestly in 1929, had nearly 80,000 members of all ages in England and Wales, and provided a bed for 1s. a night, with cooking facilities for those who could not afford the reasonably priced meals which were supplied. Guests at the hostels were expected to help with the cleaning, the preparation of meals and other domestic work. The national cyclists' organizations, the Cyclists' Touring Club and the National Cyclists' Union, represented some 3,500 clubs with nearly 60,000 members in 1938. Reference has already been made to their work in the last century in bringing tourists back to the roads of Britain, and they provide for the cyclist much the same services as are provided for motorists by the A.A. and the R.A.C.

Many young people found a satisfactory alternative to the conventional holiday at the work camps organized by the Ministry of Agriculture during the war, and this type of holiday, which is not merely free but provides its own pocket money, may have a future, if only amongst a small minority. Another interesting suggestion is that cheap cruises on tramp steamers should be organized for young men, who would do most of their own domestic work and could even help with the running of the ship.

There is already no reason why any young wage-earner who is energetic and self-reliant should go without a holiday for lack of means. The facilities are ample and varied, and the opportunities are attractive.

Families and old people present the really difficult problem. The more primitive forms of accommodation are unsuitable for the family, and some relief from household chores and cares must be given to the mothers of young children. But the accommodation need not be elaborate, and labour costs can be kept down by arrangements for self-service without making too heavy a tax on the guests. Capital outlay can be cut by choosing sites in the least expensive areas, adapting premises which are no longer required for other purposes, building new accommodation on economical lines, and organizing on a communal system. Overheads can be reduced by making full use of the accommodation for the whole of the summer. At the Conference on Workers' Holidays organized by the Industrial Welfare Society in 1938, it was stated that to be economic a workers' holiday centre needed a minimum season of twenty weeks.

In practical terms, holiday camps, guest houses, and camping sites are the most promising possibilities; and much experience has already been gained by the various non-commercial agencies which have experimented with them. Amongst the pioneers were the Co-operative Holidays Association, the Holiday Fellowship, which was founded in 1913 as an offshoot of the Association, and the Workers' Travel Association. Some firms have acquired or built holiday homes, guest houses, camps and other premises and placed them at the disposal of their workers at prices much below commercial rates. The trade unions do not seem to have entered this field, but some co-operative societies have provided holiday accommodation for their members, and in 1939 Travco Ltd., which had been formed jointly by the Co-operative Wholesale Society and the Workers' Travel Association, opened its first holiday camp, as a non-profit-making venture. Another interesting development which the war interrupted was local authority enterprise in the provision of holiday camps. The Lambeth Borough Council, with the help of the National Fitness Council, were planning to spend nearly £50,000 on a camp for 400 people at Herne Bay. The Chesterfield Borough Council were making similar plans, and in the summer of 1939 had invited a number of local authorities to send representatives to a conference to discuss possible collaboration.

Two major difficulties have emerged in the experiments hitherto conducted. It is difficult without a substantial subsidy to reduce prices sufficiently to help those who are in greatest need; with no profits, £2 a week all in was about the lowest economic rate before the war.[1] Secondly, no satisfactory method has yet been devised of preventing those who can afford to pay more from making use of the cheaper accommodation. It is universally agreed that a means test or similar condition would be objectionable and that in any case the segregation of the poorer holidaymaker is undesirable. A solution for the exceptionally difficult problem of old people seems to be still more remote.

What of the future? Though holidays with pay have not been made obligatory, they are all but universal already. In December 1946 the *Ministry of Labour Gazette* recorded that agreements for holidays with pay were in force in almost all industries in which conditions of employment were determined by collective bargaining, and that there were between 11 and 12 million wage-earners entitled to them under agreements or orders, apart from the large numbers, such as the salaried, who enjoyed them otherwise. And there was a marked trend towards a fortnight as the normal period. The majority of the agreements were for twelve days, including the six public holidays, but a considerable and growing number provided for eighteen days. Though the details varied greatly, normally the only important condition was twelve months' qualifying service.[2]

But there is an important distinction between holidays with pay for all, and holidays for all. For Great Britain as a whole the P.E.P. broadsheet spoke as though there might soon be 45 million holidaymakers, or nine out of every ten persons. This seems an overestimate, and may never be reached. There will always be

[1] In 1946 the Holiday Fellowship charged 55s. a week at a few centres, and 67s. 6d. at most. At the Travco holiday camp the range was from £3 to £4 according to the date.

[2] See Appendix II for a summary of this article.

some who do not want to go away—many aged people, for example—and many more who cannot for personal reasons, such as sickness, private ties, and individual financial difficulties. There are the shiftless, people in institutions, and eccentrics who do not follow the main stream of social opinion. Rising real incomes will extend the number of actual holidaymakers more effectively than anything else, and the incentive to save for holidays will be increased as they become more and more part of the life of all classes. But both processes will be gradual, and neither will do much to reduce the number of those who do not go away for other than financial reasons. In a sense, therefore, there may never be holidays for all. Yet there are few who do not sometimes go away for holidays, and the summer holiday, so recently the privilege of a minority, has already become 'the prerogative of the million'.[1]

trouble with the authorities

[1] Mr. Roland Robinson, M.P., in the House of Commons, 6th April 1938.

XIV

TWENTIETH-CENTURY HOLIDAYMAKING[1]

If in the present century holidays have become a social problem, they have also become a cult. For many they are one of the principal objects of life—saved and planned for during the rest of the year, and enjoyed in retrospect when they are over.

As Mr. J. L. Hammond has said, 'We are trying the experiment of universal education, universal leisure, universal suffrage.'[2] There are some who think that on balance the increase in leisure has not been advantageous, and it has inevitably produced extravagances which only time will correct. Social traditions are not created in a day, advance is by trial and error, and equilibrium has not yet been reached.

The problem of leisure, of which so much has been written, will

[1] In this chapter I have made considerable use of: E. W. Gilbert, 'The Growth of Inland and Seaside Health Resorts in England' (*Scottish Geographical Magazine*, January 1939): Elizabeth Brunner, *Holiday Making and the Holiday Trades* (Nuffield College, 1945): the other surveys referred to in the last chapter: and on foreign travel F. W. Ogilvie, *The Tourist Movement* (1933), A. J. Norval, *The Tourist Industry* (1936), and R. G. Pinney, *Britain—Destination of Tourists?* (Travel Association, 2nd edition, 1944). I have also drawn a good deal on the press, guide books, publicity material, etc.

[2] J. L. Hammond, *The Growth of Common Enjoyment* (1933), 17.

not be solved in the study, but ultimately—for good or ill—by the people themselves. While, however, the majority of holidaymakers are not consciously influenced by considerations other than the desire for enjoyment and the improvement of health, the gropings towards what may be called a philosophy of holidays have had important practical results.

The idea that holidays may be best employed not in mere relaxation but, as the Trades Union Congress told the Amulree Committee, for 'the freely chosen development of the human personality', bears little relationship to present realities as far as the mass are concerned. It has, however, influenced a considerable and growing minority, chiefly of young people. That this should be so is largely due to the youth movements and other voluntary organizations—foremost amongst them the Co-operative Holidays Association, the Holiday Fellowship, the Workers' Travel Association, and the Youth Hostels Association—which have taught them that holidays are opportunities for discovery and adventure, study and community service, and have educated them in enterprise and self-reliance. The positive approach for which these bodies stand is illustrated by the objects of the Holiday Fellowship—'To provide for the healthy enjoyment of leisure; to encourage love of the open air; to promote social and international friendship; and to organize holidaymaking and other activities with these objects.'

This may prove to be the most significant development of the century, but the most spectacular change has been the vast increase in the number of holidaymakers. To the fifteen million persons who were estimated to have spent at least a week away from home in 1937 must be added several times that number for the countless excursionists who also visited the holiday resorts. Many of them do not strictly come within the province of this book because their excursions were not part of their annual holidays, but the two categories cannot be easily separated, and both made their contribution to the life of the places to which they went.

Before the war Blackpool was reported to have seven million visitors every year, and—incredible though this may sound—to be able to accommodate half a million in a single night. Southend had 5½ millions, four-fifths of them between Whitsun and the end of September. Nearly 3 millions were said to visit Hastings, 2 millions Bournemouth and Southport respectively, over a million Eastbourne, and 1 million Ramsgate.[1] This gives a total of well over 20 millions for seven resorts, excluding some of the biggest; and making every allowance for possible exaggeration the figures remain impressive, not to say astonishing. It is not clear how they were calculated, but, when all the excursionists—by road as well as rail—are taken into account, they may not be far wrong, and they tend to be confirmed by the pre-war estimate that the railways carried 20 million more passengers in August than in May or October.

What we have called the 'holiday industry' has grown correspondingly. 'Evidence suggests', said the Royal Commission on the Distribution of the Industrial Population (1940), 'that the growth of the services represented by such [seaside and other holiday] resorts, including the service of transport, has been among the most rapid forms of economic growth since the [1914–18] war, and that its effect upon the movement of population has been of the first importance.' The percentage growth in the number of people employed in providing entertainments—48·7 per cent—was greater between 1931 and 1939 than for any other industry.

In 1931 the 105 English towns whose population exceeded 50,000 included eight places which were primarily holiday resorts, and two—Bath (68,000) and Poole (57,000)—which fitted more readily into this than any other category. Brighton (147,000) was still in the lead, without taking into account its neighbour, Hove (54,000); and it was followed by Southend (120,000), Bournemouth (116,000), Blackpool (101,000), Southport (78,000), Hastings (65,000), and Eastbourne (57,000). The inevitable allowances have to be made. Brighton, Southend, Southport and Hove in particular were also dormitory towns; in 1938 there were 10,500

[1] These figures are taken from Gilbert, except the Ramsgate figure, which was given by the Mayor in a speech in 1939 (*The Times*, 8th March, 1939).

London season ticket holders at Southend, and nearly 2,500 at Brighton and Hove. All these resorts had substantial residential populations; in Bournemouth, Hastings and Hove in 1931 more than one in every ten males over fourteen years of age had 'retired from previous gainful occupation', as compared with percentages ranging from 6·9 per cent (Brighton) upwards in the others, and an average of 5·5 per cent for England and Wales as a whole. But these factors were more than offset by the towns and villages outside the municipal boundaries which formed part of the same economic unit. Thus the Brighton 'conurbation' (Brighton, Hove, Portslade-by-Sea and Southwick) comprised 218,000 people; in the Bournemouth area (Bournemouth, Poole and Christchurch) there were 183,000; in the Blackpool area (Blackpool, Fleetwood, Lytham St. Anne's and Thornton Cleveleys) 160,000; and in Southend-on-Sea with Shoeburyness 127,000. And these figures take no account of a number of resorts which were hardly less important—Torquay and the Torbay 'conurbation', Scarborough, Margate and Ramsgate, Worthing, are a few obvious examples—, nor of the hundreds of smaller ones and the long stretches of coast where development was practically continuous.

What these vast concentrations of population with their elaborate and costly capital equipment mean in terms of economic effort can be imagined; and Miss Elizabeth Brunner in her study for Nuffield College (1945) made the first attempt at the difficult task of analysing and measuring the 'holiday trades'. She divided them into two classes. Firstly there were 'the primary holiday trades' or 'the direct consumptive trades of Entertainments and Sport and Personal Service which cater directly for the holidaymaker in his role of one who has money to spend on leisure and luxuries. They include a great number of enterprises in holiday areas which shut down completely out of season. The secondary class consists of the trades of building, decorating and contracting, gas, water and electricity, transport and communication, and the distributive trades. These are the trades stimulated by the tourist traffic rather than the tourist industry itself, they provide the means to the end rather than the end of holidaymaking.'

But, as Miss Brunner pointed out, the extent to which a particular trade is dependent on the holidaymaker is largely a matter of guesswork. The complications are endless.[1] A seaside public house may cater almost exclusively for local residents: workers in a factory inland may be largely engaged upon the manufacture of souvenirs or sweetmeats for sale at the seaside. It has been estimated that during the agricultural depression of the 'thirties some Devonshire farmers derived as much as 50 to 75 per cent of their income from the tourist trade—by the sale of teas, by providing board and lodging, by letting camping sites.[2] A complete list of people drawing part or all of their livelihood from the holiday traffic would include sailors and railwaymen, clerks in London travel offices, draughtsmen in advertising agencies, journalists, military bandsmen, and, amongst a host of others, the enterprising landowners who charge for access to beauty spots or the use of private roads.

No clear-cut picture can be drawn, but there are certain features which are common to most holiday resorts. First is naturally the preponderance of Miss Brunner's 'holiday trades', with a corresponding absence of manufacturing industry. In Brighton before the war there were 2,100 recognized lodging and apartment houses and 205 hotels in the built-up area: only thirty acres in the borough were set aside by the Corporation for industry. In Blackpool in 1931 there were nearly 4,000 lodging and boarding house keepers and 240 inn and hotel keepers. At Margate in 1939 6,540 or nearly 50 per cent of the 14,000 rateable properties were normally used for the accommodation of visitors—30 first-class hotels, 60 smaller hotels, 150 private hotels, 1,300 boarding

[1] An analysis of tourist expenditure in the United States and Canada gave the following result—in percentages of the total: merchandise 26·0: restaurants and cafés 20·5: hotels and rooms 17·3: petrol and other motor requisites 11·5: theatres and amusements 8·5: transport 7·0: confectionery and incidentals 5·9: tramcar fares, taxis, etc. 3·3 (Ogilvie, 33–4, quoting *Board of Trade Journal*, 6th March 1930). Sir Frederick Ogilvie thought that this was probably fairly representative, except that in poorer countries the proportion spent on maintenance and transport would be higher.

[2] Brunner, 61. Report from C. Martin.

houses, 1,500 apartment houses, and 3,500 private houses which catered for visitors.[1]

Distribution is also of special importance at places where there are great transient populations bent on enjoying themselves. The proportion of shops at Brighton in 1937 was reckoned to be nearly double the average (1 for every 47 people as compared with 1 for every 80 in the country generally). At Torquay even in July 1940 a total insured population of 16,000 included 4,000 persons in the distributive and 3,000 in the hotel trades, not to mention those who were outside insurance.[2]

Two other features of the resorts are a high average age, due to the large retired element, and a high proportion of women, due in part to the age distribution and in part to the exceptional demand for female labour. Widows and women with dependent husbands are naturally attracted into keeping boarding houses, and the letting of rooms in the season is a convenient method of supplementing the family income in other cases. Married women form a valuable labour reserve, but labour has also to be imported for the busy period, and the holiday resorts have usually been characterized by seasonal unemployment.

The chief holiday trades are highly individualistic; in a place like Brighton there are thousands of separate units. But ultimately their survival is bound to an exceptional degree with the maintenance and development of natural and other assets over which they have no direct control. Except in the simplest cases, where, for example, one landlord owns a whole town or a famous beauty spot is on a single estate, the full task of replenishing and adding to capital is beyond the capacity of a single individual. Often it is beyond that of groups of individuals or is commercially unprofitable. Hence, as we have seen, the holiday resorts were pioneers in municipal enterprise, and from the earliest days found it necessary to assume responsibility for essential undertakings which private enterprise would or could not finance.

The share of the municipality has grown with the years. Coast protection, promenades, public gardens, bandstands, illuminations,

[1] Brunner, 53, quoting *The Times*, 30th August 1943.

[2] Brunner, 59. Report by C. Martin.

have long been accepted as the almost exclusive province of the local authority; piers, concert halls, sports facilities, bathing pools, beach huts are probably more often municipal than private; theatres and restaurants are examples of public enterprises which are the exception rather than the rule. Good will is one of the most important forms of capital, and is accepted as a special charge of the municipality. Beau Nash may be said to have been his own public relations officer. Richard Russell, Granville and other pioneers were skilled in the same art. To-day every important resort has its own publicity department, either organized directly under the local authority or, where it is provided by voluntary arrangements, sponsored by them. Limited powers to advertise were conferred by the Health Resorts and Watering Places Act, 1921, but they were confined to advertisements in newspapers, by handbooks or leaflets, or by placards at railway stations, and to the expenditure of profits from the provision of entertainments or recreation for visitors. Even so the expenditure could not exceed the equivalent of the revenue from a penny rate. These restrictions bore most heavily on the resorts which were trying to establish themselves, and in 1936 power was granted to draw upon the rates, the upper limit of expenditure was raised to the receipts from a rate of 1⅓d.,[1] and all forms of advertising were permitted. Local authorities were also allowed to combine for advertising purposes with other local authorities and organizations—a provision of which a number of them took advantage.

And only the local authority or groups of local authorities, with the assistance of the State, can attend to the most important matters of all—the preservation of the coast and the countryside and the orderly development of the resorts. Only they can plan comprehensively for the future.

The scale of municipal action may be illustrated by a few examples. At Blackpool between the wars seven miles of promenade were built, with sunken gardens and other amenities, at a cost of over £1,500,000; in 1921–3 nearly £100,000 was spent on an open-air bath; in 1926 a park which had cost over £250,000 was

[1] Blackpool is specially favoured, as a result of other legislation, and can levy a 2⅓d. rate. (*Municipal Year Book* 1946.)

opened; another £250,000 was spent on improvements to the Winter Gardens; and in 1939 an indoor sea water bath was completed at a cost of £300,000. During the same period large sums were also spent on capital development by the Blackpool Tower Company. At Hastings over £100,000 went into the White Rock Pavilion, which was opened in 1927, £180,000 into a new promenade with an underground parking station which was ready in 1931, and nearly £100,000 into baths which were completed in the same year. The total capital cost of the pier and two municipally owned pavilions at Worthing was given as about £80,000 in 1946. £175,000 was spent at Hove on a building which comprised swimming and other baths, a restaurant, an underground car park and indoor bowling greens. The revenue from beach rents and tolls at Great Yarmouth was given in 1946 as over £11,000 a year.

So has it been with all the resorts; and, in addition to capital expenditure, great sums are spent on maintenance and administration. The municipal property has to be kept up, the public gardens have to be stocked and tended, trading rights on the beach and public land have to be farmed out, bands and concerts organized, advertising placed, inquiry bureaux staffed, transport and public utility services related to the needs of the visitors.

Then there is the much greater capital and current expenditure of private enterprise on accommodation, entertainments, shops and so on, and also—in what may be called the pipeline between the resorts and the holidaymaker's home—on facilities such as transport and travel agencies which exist to get him there.

Each side in this curious partnership is essential to the other, but only the public authority can effectively co-ordinate the many strands which compose it. Hence, as numbers have grown and the relationship between the consumer and the supplier has increased in complexity, the role of the municipality has steadily enlarged. If it is energetic and imaginative it can do much to mould the character of the resort. Experience has shown how easily decline can set in where it is careless or neglectful. Blackpool is an outstanding example of what an active local authority with a determined policy can achieve. Sidmouth and Frinton-on-Sea are examples of resorts which have succeeded in the opposite aim of excluding the masses.

Yet there is a point beyond which the most dynamic municipality cannot advance. It can advise, persuade, stimulate, plan, but except in purely negative respects it cannot compel the individual citizens who provide the staple services such as accommodation and catering. And it is at this level that the English holiday resorts have been least successful. There is substance in the evergreen complaints of high prices, poor food, incivility, congestion and dreary appointments. The reasons are various. The poor standards are an inevitable result of the concentration of trade in a short season during which demand exceeds supply. In part they may reflect inadequacies of English housekeeping in general. To some extent they are due to ignorance and lack of foresight; most apartment and many boarding house keepers are amateurs; large numbers of hotel keepers are untrained. To a great extent the cause is lack of capital to make improvements which are admitted to be desirable.

There is not much that local authorities can do to remove these conditions. At most they can take the lead in building up a tradition of better service and adopt such largely negative measures as the registration of apartments. Where they cannot help directly—though they may come to this—is in the provision of capital for the improvement of the accommodation for visitors; and staggering, which offers the most hopeful approach, can only be a partial solution.

It is only in the last few years that there has come a serious reaction against the inconveniences which had previously been taken for granted. There has emerged the most significant innovation of the century—the holiday camp—and with it the prospect of radical changes in popular holiday-making.

The holiday camps are the result of an entirely different approach —the provision of capital and the reduction of overheads through large-scale organization and communal living. The idea is not novel. It represents the application to holiday catering of accepted business methods. It has underlain the experiments of the Co-operative Holidays Association, the Holiday Fellowship, the

Workers' Travel Association, and other non-commercial agencies in providing facilities for the poorest workers. But it was not until the late 'thirties that it was applied in a big way to the middle group of holidaymakers, in whom the non-commercial agencies were not primarily interested and who could not afford to stay in hotels.

The origin of the holiday camp, as of most social discoveries, is complex. Its ancestors include the camps of the youth organizations, the guest houses of the Co-operative Holidays Association and other voluntary bodies, and the more or less permanent camping sites for motorists, cyclists and pedestrians which sprang up in increasing numbers particularly after the 1914–18 war. Its title reflects its ancestry but is otherwise misleading. Holiday camps take different forms. Their common feature is that they are self-contained settlements in which the guests' needs are supplied for an all-in charge. They provide sleeping accommodation (usually in separate chalets), communal dining arrangements, and organized amusements; dance halls, bathing pools, sports fields, nurseries and playgrounds are part of the standard equipment of the more elaborate. They are more than camps. They are more than popular hotels. They are miniature holiday resorts,[1] and potentially they threaten not only the boarding and apartment houses but the resorts themselves.

The New Survey of London Life and Labour stated in 1935 that holiday camps run on commercial lines had recently appeared and seemed to be popular with young people who did not want the trouble of camping on their own account. In fact some of them went back many years, but it was not until 1937 that the growth of the holiday camps attracted much attention. This was due in the main to one man, William Butlin, a South African by birth, and a Canadian by upbringing, who from small beginnings had made a fortune as an amusement park proprietor and had little to learn about the technique of popular entertainment. He it was who put holiday camps on the map. Consciously or otherwise his timing was admirable; his first venture—the opening of a luxury camp at

[1] It was announced in 1947 that Butlin's had appointed resident Church of England chaplains at two of their camps and that churches were to be built.

Skegness—coincided with the peak holiday year, 1937. This was so successful that in the following year it had to be considerably enlarged, and work was started on new camps at Clacton-on-Sea and at Filey near Scarborough. The Clacton camp was opened in 1939, Filey was ready soon after the outbreak of war but not used for holidays till 1946, and during the war a further camp was completed at Pwllheli in Snowdonia. Mr. Butlin's flair for publicity was no less remarkable than his judgment of the public taste. 'Butlin's' was soon a household word; and 'Butlinism', 'Butlineer', and other derivatives have since been added to the language.

The main respects in which the Butlin holiday camps differed from their predecessors were in size—they accommodated upwards of two thousand people and two of them now take 5,000 each—their luxurious and comprehensive character, first-class publicity and the exceptional efficiency with which they were organized. They claimed to provide everything that a popular holiday resort could offer, and a good deal more—such as arrangements for looking after children, free tuition in different sports, and an active community life.

It was obvious that a highly profitable discovery had been made, which also met a latent public need. A number of other camps on the same model were quickly established; the most interesting were the camp opened at Prestatyn in 1939, jointly by Thomas Cook's and the L.M.S., and two camps, only one of which was completed, which were projected by Travco Ltd. The Travco camps were to accommodate 500 persons, which was considered the maximum number with which a community spirit could be created. And, as mentioned in the last chapter, the Lambeth Borough Council approved plans for a municipal holiday camp for 400 persons, and another local authority, Chesterfield, were exploring the idea. It has been estimated that by 1939 there were altogether perhaps 200 holiday camps with room for 30,000 people a week. These included not only the few large luxury camps of the Butlin type, but medium-sized camps for 200–500 people offering similar though simpler facilities, and a greater number of small camps for twenty or so people upwards which did not pretend to be luxurious and were sometimes quite primitive. The charges were rarely less than £2 10s. a week. At Butlin's and Prestatyn they were £3 to £3 10s. according to season, and after the war (1946) £5 5s. to £6 16s. 6d., when the charges were £3 to £4 at the Rogerson Hall holiday camp run by Travco. The Butlin camps had 100,000 visitors in 1939; in 1946 about a quarter of a million stayed at them, mostly for a week, and thousands had to be turned away. Most of these were black-coated workers, and though there were some manual workers it is difficult to explain why there were not more. Certainly the reason was not solely financial. Travco had the same experience. Perhaps it lay in a mixture of social shyness and conservatism.

The holiday camps evoked all the attention which was due to them as an outstanding commercial success, an experiment in large-scale mass entertainment, and a potential threat to important vested interests. The publicity has not yet died down, and controversy about them is still acute.

'Another development', said the Scott Report on Land Utilization in Rural Areas (1942), 'expressing in a different form the physical impact of the town on the countryside has been the establishment in country places, and especially along the coast, of permanent and semi-permanent camps for urban populations on holiday. Several hundreds of the camps had been set up before 1939. They varied greatly in size and character. Some were very large, accommodating thousands of people: they were almost towns in themselves—summer-time towns providing for a brief season the pleasures not ordinarily obtainable in the everyday towns. Some were small and provided quieter and more intimate conditions. Some were well designed for their purpose, laid out in an orderly way, built of trim semi-permanent materials; while others were squalid and disordered in the extreme. But whatever their size and condition they all reflected clearly still another new aspect of the urban impact on the countryside, and one indicative of other similar developments yet to come.'

'There seems no doubt that the public demand will lead to an increase in the number of holiday camps in the future', said the Catering Wages Commission (1945). 'In so far as there is such a demand we see nothing in this development about which to be apprehensive, and, indeed, we welcome it as a means of providing on a large scale the type of holiday which will attract more and more people.' The National Council of Social Service (1945) thought that this 'new idea in holidays' showed every sign of growing and that the camps were 'a typical product of the last ten years, a time when entertainment has come to centre increasingly round the first-class dance band, the cinema, the "lido", and the loud speaker'. P.E.P. had commented (1942): 'These holiday camps have received some merited criticisms, but they are popular and they have definite potentialities as a means of providing really refreshing holidays for the great numbers who like a sociable holiday, and they can give a respite from domestic cares to the mother of the family that no other form of holiday can offer. It is therefore vital that they should be developed on sound lines under enlightened management. They will then become an important national asset, not least as places where young men and women who may have few social opportunities in their daily lives can meet, mix, and plan to marry. To achieve this end, the first essential is that profit making should not be their primary motive force, the second that they should not be too large.'

There is no serious doubt that holiday camps have come to stay, nor—whatever their demerits may be—as to the substantial advantages they offer. To those mentioned by P.E.P. may be added the inclusive charges—within the pockets of many manual workers—relief from worrying details, and the guarantee of comfort and efficiency. To point the contrast it is only necessary to refer again to what is so often the alternative—gloomy apartments, surly and inefficient service, lack of society outside the family itself, the constant company of the children, queues, congestion, long walks in all weathers to and from the sea.

The controversy over 'Butlinism' raises some important issues. Admitting the advantages, it is asked, is not the social cost too high? Does it not entail regimentation and standardization to a degree which is unhealthy in a free society? Are there not dangers in the sacrifice of privacy and individual initiative? Is it not inevitable that as in the cinema the cultural level should fall to the lowest common denominator and be determined by purely commercial considerations?

Some of the accounts[1] which have been published of life at the holiday camps have lent colour to these apprehensions. They were not removed by the cautious verdict pronounced by Dr. C. E. M. Joad, in the *New Statesman*, that on balance we should be 'grateful to the man who has done more to increase the happiness of his fellow men than any of us, and in making the millions happy, has helped to bring a few, a very few, under the spell of natural beauty'.

They were reinforced by a succession of accounts of the Butlin camps which stressed just those features which were most likely to perturb the more intellectual and fastidious of the critics. The picture which emerged was one of all-pervasive heartiness and schoolboyish immaturity.

The campers were divided into 'houses', which competed in athletic and other competitions, and it was a point of honour not to let the house down. There was a Butlin anthem: 'Now we're at Butlin's, jolly old Butlin's.' One visitor told how the day opened at 7.45 with the many loud speakers broadcasting the rousing song:

Roll out of bed in the morning
With a great big smile and a good good morning—
Get up with a grin
There's a good day tumbling in!
Wake with the sun and the rooster,
Cock-a-doodle-do like the rooster use'ter,
How can you go wrong
If you roll out of bed with a song?

[1] The public interest in the holiday camps, in particular Butlin's, was shown by the large number of articles about them in 1946. That the *New Statesman*, the *News Chronicle*, *Picture Post*, the *Illustrated London News*, the *National Geographical Magazine*, *Pilot Papers*, *The Observer*, *Tribune*, the *Daily Worker*, for example, all had articles is evidence of the wide interest they evoked in different sections of the community. In 1945 the B.B.C. had a programme on holiday camps in its series *People's Pleasures*.

It ended with another song: 'Good night, Campers.' And so on throughout the day. No detail was overlooked, every hour was planned, and 'Radio Butlin' kept the 'happy campers' constantly informed of the programme. The bathrooms and lavatories were unconventionally labelled 'Lads' and 'Lasses'. The 'Butlin Buddies' or 'red coats'—a picked team of athletes and expert social mixers—mingled with the guests and helped to keep their spirits up to the desired temperature. It was their job to make sure that at Butlin's holidays were truly 'jollidays'. Of one of the camps it was reported that 'Jovial Joe', the cook, walked round the dining-hall to make sure that everyone was enjoying his food; and that a now celebrated official punctuated the meals with calls of 'hi-de-hi', and insisted that the Campers should shout back 'ho-de-ho'. Before the war there was a weekly magazine, the *Butlin Times*, which played its part in maintaining *esprit de corps* by recording such occurrences as 'the blooming of romance' at Skegness, 'where two happy Campers have this week tied the nuptial knot at the conclusion of their holiday'. And the 'campers' are invited to join Butlin's Physical Recreation and Social Club, the object of which is to provide 'healthy recreation and social enjoyment in London and the Provinces during the winter months—to stimulate and encourage the Butlin Spirit amongst all members and to keep in touch with old Campers'.

There is much in this of which it is easy to be scornful. There is much which is not to everybody's taste. But criticism is dangerously easy, personal distaste is too slender a ground for condemning any popular institution, and there is another side to the case.

The holiday camps deny the charge of regimentation. They claim that they cater for every taste and that their guests are free to decide for themselves in which of the many activities to participate. One of the main appeals made in Butlin's publicity is to those for whom 'the chief joy of a holiday is a rest': Prestatyn has been at pains to point out (1946): 'Now . . . don't—please don't—get the idea that you've GOT TO BE GAY at Prestatyn. You can take part in the fun or if you choose be a spectator—whichever attracts you. No compulsion. No chivvying you to do this or that. Nor should there be; you are the guest—and it's *your* holiday!' A carefully regulated programme is essential for activities such as team sports and competitions, but there is something for everybody—bathing, bowls, billiards, table tennis, gardens, lounges, dances, boating, tennis, cricket, concerts, beauty contests, physical training, the amusements of the fun fair, putting, riding, excursions, including for those who want them amateur theatricals, brains trusts, discussions and debates. In 1946 Butlin's engaged the San Carlo Opera Company for a short season, and it was ironical that they had to defend themselves against the criticism that their clients would not appreciate grand opera.

Ultimately, too, it may be asked, is not comparison with the traditional holiday the true test? There is no doubt where the superiority in comfort and convenience lies, and, as regards amusements, why should a holiday camp set a different standard from Blackpool or Margate? Butlin's can claim that the entertainments they provide are the best of their kind. Amongst the artists engaged before the war, for example, were Gracie Fields, George Robey, Elsie and Doris Waters, Vic Oliver and Frances Day.[1]

Most of the holiday camps are on the coast, and during the present century the seaside holiday has maintained its popularity. There is nothing to suggest that its ascendancy will be seriously threatened in the foreseeable future. This is an international phenomenon, but it is particularly characteristic of a people who live on an island and never many miles from the sea.

There is still a peculiar fascination about the sea. The custom of visiting the seaside is deep-rooted. Medical authority and popular belief agree on its health-giving properties. No natural playground offers more varied opportunities to more people of all ages; and for a century and a half the seaside resorts have been without serious competitors as specialists in the entertainment of holidaymakers.

The ingredients of the seaside holiday are much the same as they always were. Beneath a façade of modernity, in the shadow of the illuminations, in the Victorian streets behind the luxury hotels,

[1] I reproduce in Appendix III my notes of a visit to Messrs. Butlin's holiday camp at Clacton-on-Sea.

amongst the giant racers, the 'dodgems' and the other electrical marvels of the amusement parks, there is on every hand evidence of a lasting conservatism.

The pier is perhaps as good an example as any of this fundamental tendency. Except in so far as it is used for its primary purpose as a landing stage, it is in large measure an anachronism, and is no longer well adapted to be either an amusement centre or a focal point of social activity. Yet it is hardly less indispensable than fifty years ago. The same point is illustrated by the adherence of the pierrots and other seaside entertainers to traditional forms and patterns. An extreme case is the Punch and Judy show, which has almost disappeared elsewhere.[1] There are many other instances. Witness the continuity of design and character in the ornamental china and other souvenirs, which, like their predecessors for generations, the visitors—especially working people—buy in large numbers for the adornment of their homes. The crude vulgarity of the comic postcards which sell no less freely has the flavour of the Victorian music hall. Seaside 'rock'—that oddest of sweetmeats—would surely have died out but for its traditional associations. The system of accommodation in furnished apartments goes back to the earliest days. Beach photographers, refreshment booth proprietors, sand modellers, evangelists, weighing machine men, the men who hire out telescopes or donkeys; these familiar seaside figures have changed little with the times.

The persistence of traditional forms and institutions at the seaside is doubtless connected with its special associations with children. Children are conservative beings. They look for the scenes and personalities to which they are accustomed. They love a ritual in which each item recurs exactly as before. At the same time, the adult often associates the seaside with memories of youth, of happiness, adventure, and romance, which add a sentimental value to things as they are. The tendency for the newcomers to imitate and to emulate their predecessors operates in the same direction; for them the traditional institutions have a prestige value. The bathing machines and the assembly rooms have

[1] The Christmas pantomime, which is a holiday entertainment in a different sense, offers a close analogy.

Showing the brave effort of a poster-artist to do justice, in the limited space at his disposal, to the various attractions advertised by the Municipality and Sports Committee of Mixingham-on-Sea.

'MIXINGHAM-ON-SEA', 1912

vanished, but the piers live on, the endless perambulations on the promenade continue, and the scene on the beach has changed least of all, a confused whirl of humanity in the mass engaged upon the timeless seaside activities—building, flirting, eating, paddling, bathing, shrimping, reading, sleeping—simple pleasures that do not grow stale.

It is unnecessary to say much of the spas. Relatively to the seaside resorts they are likely to remain unimportant. They have by now fully adjusted themselves to this state of affairs. Once again they make their main appeal to those in need of treatment, and secondarily to those in search of rest and recreation in quiet and beautiful surroundings. Yet the ten years before the war saw a remarkable revival of enterprise and vitality at the spas, in which, aided by the economic depression and the consequent reduction in foreign travel, they vigorously challenged their continental rivals. They called the science of hydrology to their assistance in asserting the claim that they were able to compete with the Continent in treatment and service. The slogan, 'Health comes happily at British Spas', was used in a national advertising campaign launched by six of the most famous—Bath, Buxton, Cheltenham, Droitwich, Harrogate and Leamington. For the invalid there were the waters, applied at moderate cost by 'the most modern hydrological methods known to modern science'. For sick and whole alike happiness was to be found in 'the contentment and refreshment of mind and body' to be derived from the beauty of the surroundings and from the other amenities—notably music, sport and drama. In short, as a Buxton hotel advertised, they offered 'Relaxation, Recreation and Restoration'. And more splendid days were recalled, perhaps rather pathetically, by the cocktail parties which were held at Droitwich, where the bathers bobbing about in the brine served their own drinks from floating tables.

Of much greater significance than the revival of the spas as such was the rediscovery of the countryside and the historic inland towns, in which the spas of course shared. Fifty years ago Scotland, the Lake District and North Wales were the only important inland touring areas. By 1939, thanks largely to the motor-car and the bicycle, there was hardly a village which did not provide some facilities for holidaymakers—teas, bed and breakfast, camping sites or a garage—while in the hilly districts and in most of the hinterland of the coast holiday catering had become an important source of income. Derelict hotels and inns were rejuvenated, cottage parlours blossomed forth as tearooms, the village blacksmith became a motor mechanic and a petrol station sprang up where once the village smithy stood.

The cyclists and the youth organizations had pointed the way. The motorists followed, and of over 2,000,000 private motor-vehicles in 1939 there were few which were never used for touring. Bus services opened up new country every year. 'Pleasure coaches' were estimated to have increased their receipts by about 20 per cent between 1932 and 1935, and to have earned nearly £5,000,000 in the latter year; in 1936–7 the number of passengers exceeded 82 millions and the receipts reached £5,400,000. Not all of these coaches were going to the country; many went from town to town or from town to coast, but all of them passed through the country. 'Make your journey part of your holiday', they advertised; and touring coaches provided all-in tours under luxury conditions. Stimulated by the competition, the railways also improved their facilities for tourists by foot, by cycle, even by car. Circular tour tickets, holiday seasons (giving seven days' unlimited travel in a selected area), special tickets for ramblers and cyclists, these were some of the innovations. Motorists were encouraged to send their cars to their holiday destinations by rail. Camping coaches, which were corridor railway carriages converted into caravans and left in sidings by the sea or in the country, were a successful invention of the 'thirties, and in 1939 the four main line companies had no fewer than 434 of them.

Scotland, the Lakes and North Wales retained their pre-eminence, but the new tourists were to be found wherever there was beautiful country. Towns which were favourably situated as touring centres and were convenient stopping places on the main roads shared in the benefits. Cook's *Holiday Guide* for 1946—admittedly an abnormal year—listed 53 inland resorts in England and 7 in Wales as compared with 71 seaside resorts. Their variety is illustrated by the dozen first on the list: Ambleside, Bovey Tracey, Bradford-on-Avon, Brotherswater (Westmorland), Burford, Buxton, Caterham (with 'rural delights that can be swiftly exchanged for the pleasures of the capital'), Chagford, Cheltenham, Chester, Chiddingfold (Surrey—'a splendid centre for a walking holiday', 'proud of its fourteenth century inn and its twentieth century unsophistication'), and Coalbrookvale (Shropshire). The others included Crowborough, Dulverton, Ely, Evesham, Haywards Heath, Ilkley, Lechlade, Ludlow, Lyndhurst, Ross-on-Wye, Stratford-on-Avon, Tewkesbury, Woodhall Spa, and Yeovil. Stratford-on-Avon is of special interest. Within half a century it had turned its Shakespearian associations to such good account that it had built up an international reputation. 1,500 people attended the first Shakespeare Festival in 1879, which lasted ten days, over 4,000 in 1894, 14,000 in 1904, and about 200,000 in 1938, when the season lasted over twenty-four weeks.[1]

And these are only a sample out of hundreds of inland towns and villages which in varying degrees are holiday resorts. Numerically they far exceed the seaside places; in the total number of guest weeks, to use the technical term, they are still far behind them, but even in this respect London, the outstanding inland holiday resort, may well be on a level with Blackpool or Brighton.

The invasion of the countryside by townspeople produced a tension which is not yet wholly relaxed. The boisterous and curiously clad cyclists of the 'nineties were coolly enough received: the motorist, leaving behind him a trail of dusty hedges, strange odours, slaughtered poultry and frightened animals, was still less popular. There was much to be learned on both sides. The countryman's first reaction was to protect his property by every means at his disposal—from barbed wire to threats of prosecution and the closing of rights of way. The townsman asserted his right as a free citizen of a free country to go where he liked, did thoughtless damage, and showed deplorably bad manners. The Boy Scouts, the Council for the Preservation of Rural England,

[1] The story of Stratford-on-Avon is amusingly told by Ivor Brown and George Fearon, *Amazing Monument. A Short History of the Shakespeare Industry* (1939).

the Youth Hostels Association, the cycling organizations and other bodies have helped to educate the visitors from the towns: the discovery that there was money to be made has mellowed the country people. Relations have become less strained, but, said the Scott Report, 'there is much yet to be done to create the mutual understanding and sympathy that are necessary if all sections of the community are to enjoy the countryside, which, if it is the heritage of all, is in the guardianship of the countryman'.

The countryside is a national heritage which all should enjoy, but, as the Scott Committee pointed out, this also means that it should be safeguarded as the precious asset which it is. The English landscape, with its fields and hedges, its farms and cottages, its woods and parks, owes as much to man as to nature, and man's carelessness can quickly destroy the beauty which he has helped to create. Restraint must be exercised, agriculture must be protected, indiscriminate development must be checked, wild life must be preserved. The townsman's rights carry corresponding duties.

The dilemma was well illustrated by the controversy about the Butlin Holiday Camp at Pwllheli in 1945. Was Mr. Butlin to be condemned for spoiling the Welsh mountains or to be praised for introducing thousands of his fellow citizens to them? The problem was stated by the Scott Committee. The growth of holidays 'would lead to a need for more accommodation in existing holiday resorts; the creation of further holiday resorts; the building of holiday camps; the provision of additional Youth Hostels; the catering for the needs of week-enders—all of which would mean a very considerable building programme. While these needs should—and indeed must—be provided for, the building which would result, if such development were unregulated, would ruin many more districts of the beautiful land of Britain, particularly along stretches of the coastline. It would also have very harmful effects on agriculture.'

Even at the best the problem is difficult. An ugly vision of what is possible at the worst was seen after 1918. Lovely stretches of the coast were irremediably spoiled by indiscriminate and unsightly building; settlements of insanitary shacks, huts and caravans sprang up around the holiday resorts; ill-sited, aggressive and often vulgar, petrol stations, cafés, refuse dumps, pylons, advertisement hoardings, intruded into the most beautiful scenes.

Much of this damage was merely thoughtless, and, thanks in particular to the Council for the Preservation of Rural England and the SCAPA Society for the Prevention of Disfigurement in Town and Country, there was a marked improvement in standards between the wars. The public conscience was quickened, the powers of local authorities were extended by private Acts of Parliament, the Town and Country Planning Act, 1932, and the Ribbon Development Act, 1935; and some big firms, notably Shell Mex, the banks and the brewers, set a good example in civilized and sensitive building. The privately owned North Wales resort, Portmeirion, was an object lesson in what could be done by thoughtful and imaginative planning.

But a great deal remained to be desired. According to the Scott Committee, 'the story of the 1932 Act is one of high hopes and subsequent disappointment. . . . It was discovered that the Act regarded the countryside as a mere appanage of the town, an appanage with scenic values for the townsman'. The powers under the Act were not fully used, and even against the more obvious nuisances the local authorities were sometimes impotent and sometimes inactive.

On the more positive side, some progress was made in the reservation of country and coastal areas as open spaces, national parks and nature reserves. Since 1865, the Commons, Open Spaces and Footpaths Preservation Society have been fighting, on the whole successfully, for existing rights of way and access to common land. In 1939, after half a century of agitation in Parliament and outside, the Access to Mountains Bill at last reached the statute book; by this time it was, however, regarded as inadequate by the Ramblers' Association and similar bodies. The National Trust, which was founded in 1894, after a slow start went rapidly ahead between the wars, aided by the high level of death duties: in the eleven years before 1945 its subscription income was almost trebled, and the area it held for preservation was quadrupled.

The Town and Country Planning Act, 1932, gave power to local authorities to reserve open spaces either permanently or temporarily. Torquay, Eastbourne, Margate and other far-seeing authorities acquired adjacent coastal strips as permanent open spaces. Three National Forest Parks were established by the Forestry Commission before the war—Argyll (54,000 acres), Snowdonia (20,500 acres) and Dean Forest (23,000): these were areas belonging to the Commission in which all the land was not suited to forestry and the Commission provided simple accommodation for campers. National Parks as such—areas to be kept as far as possible in their natural state—have been much discussed. A Departmental Committee recommended their establishment in 1931; the Scott Committee advocated a National Parks Authority to be responsible for areas of natural beauty, perhaps including the whole coast, as national recreation zones, and the Government accepted the idea of National Parks in principle. An important report by Mr. John Dower was referred in 1945 to a Committee under the chairmanship of Sir Arthur Hobhouse for further examination of the details. Mr. Dower recommended that the Lake District, Snowdonia, Dartmoor, the Peak District and Dovedale, the Pembroke Coast and parts of the Cornish Coast should become the first National Parks, and that the Craven Pennines, the Black Mountains, the Brecon Beacons, Exmoor and the North Devon Coast, and the Roman Wall should be added later. And the comprehensive town and country planning measures of 1944 and 1947 have begun a new era in the ordered development of the countryside.

The period between the wars was on balance favourable to the spread of the last of the main categories of English holidaymaking—holidays abroad. The discouraging effect of political and economic difficulties was more than offset by improved travel facilities, the energetic steps taken by foreign Governments, especially in the 'thirties, to attract tourists, the widespread belief in the value to international relations of intercourse between peoples, and the traditional love of the English for travel. British subjects, not all of them tourists, nor all of them domiciled in the United Kingdom, leaving the country for Europe numbered 761,019 in 1913, 553,099 in 1921, 639,050 in 1922, and passed the million in 1928 and 1929. Then came the great depression. A million was not reached again until 1936, but in 1937 all records were broken with a total exceeding 1,400,000.[1]

In 1929 881,000 out of nearly 2,000,000 foreign tourists in France were estimated to have come from the United Kingdom; 133,000 out of over 1,200,000 in Italy; over 200,000 out of about one and a half million in Switzerland; 110,000 out of nearly a million in Germany. But there was no country in Europe and few in the world to which British tourists did not go. Already before the 1914–18 war a few foreign countries and resorts had travel offices in London. In the 'thirties official and semi-official tourist organizations of the following countries at least were represented—Austria, Belgium, Czecho-Slovakia, Eire, France, Greece, Germany, Hungary, Italy, Japan, Jugo-Slavia, New Zealand, Norway, Portugal, Roumania, Spain, Southern Rhodesia, Sweden, Switzerland, the United States and the U.S.S.R. In addition there were tourist offices of officially recognized organizations connected with Albania, Algeria, Australia, the Bahamas, Barbados, Bermuda, the Canary Islands, China, Denmark, Estonia, Egypt, Finland, India, Luxemburg, Madeira, Malta, Persia, Poland, Scotland, South Africa and the Straits Settlements.

The scope was enormous. It embraced day trips to Boulogne and cruises round the world, pilgrimages to Lourdes and University Vacation courses, big game shooting organized by Messrs. Cook's Field Sports Department and bear hunting under the auspices of Intourist. Some went to Ostend or Dinard for holidays which differed little from those which they would have had at home; in August 1937 there were said to be 15,000 English people at Dinard and St. Malo. There were others who went to the Continent for a fling which out of prudence or modesty they refrained from enjoying in England. For many the main attraction was the Mediterranean sun, and the Riviera came into fashion for

[1] Most of the figures in these paragraphs are taken from Ogilvie. Sir Frederick Ogilvie was the pioneer in the scientific study of the tourist industry, and all subsequent work on the subject is greatly indebted to him.

summer as well as winter holidays. A veritable philosophy of life is summed up by the word 'lido' which entered the language between the wars. For the musical there were Salzburg and Bayreuth, for invalids the spas, for lovers of art the treasures of the Louvre and of Rome.

The main concentrations of English tourists were still in the traditional holiday centres of Belgium, France, Italy and Switzerland, but the range was vastly extended. In the 'thirties, to take two extremes, a two weeks' all in tour to Russia cost as little as £17; and Transatlantic fares came swiftly down until the round trip to New York on the *Queen Mary*, with everything found for a stay of three or four days in the United States, cost less than £37. Between 1924 and 1934 British tourists in Jugoslavia increased from 450 to 7,000 a year; in 1930 there were 6,000 in Sweden, including those who came on pleasure cruises; in 1934 there were 28,000 in Norway, of whom 10,500 were on cruises. And these figures must have been greatly exceeded in the later 'thirties.

The programmes of one of the most enterprising of the travel agencies, the National Union of Students, included amongst many other possibilities riding in the Balkans, canoeing on the Danube, climbing and winter sports for all grades of skill in almost every mountain range from the Pyrenees to the Caucasus, yachting in the Adriatic, tours to Persia, India and across the American Continent.

Motoring from being an adventure became humdrum enough —there were said to be 17,000 British motorists in France in August 1937—but there were still opportunities for the hardy and enterprising. Motorists who completed the Arctic Circle tour which ended at Liinahamari in North Finland were rewarded with the polar bear badge of the Suomi Touring Club. The West Indies—where, said the advertisements, 'the trade winds blow, the flying fish play, and the sugar cane grows'—were a favourite alternative to the Mediterranean amongst the wealthy. Palestine, Egypt, North Africa, Greece, the Canaries, the Balearics, all built upon the reputations they had previously established, despite the political and economic vicissitudes to which they were exposed.

The popularity of Russia with the intelligentsia in the 'thirties was due to the new respectability of the Soviet experiment, the curiosity about which was stimulated by the world depression, and to the energetic and skilful publicity of Intourist, the Russian State travel agency, with its 'trouble-free touring'. As it advertised in 1935: 'The U.S.S.R. is different, its peoples take a different view of life and try to live it in a different way (therein lies its supreme interest for the foreigner).' Hitherto unimaginable new possibilities were opened up by the development of air travel in the years before 1939.

Nothing was more characteristic of the age than the winter sports holiday, which despite its origin earlier was for practical purposes an innovation of the twentieth century and did not fully establish itself until after the 1914–18 war. A guide to its popularity with the British is provided by the numbers passing the tests of the Ski Club of Great Britain; these were a small *élite* but it may be supposed that they were a fairly constant proportion of the total. From 19 in 1905 and 44 in 1910 they rose to 83 in 1913, and after falling to 59 in 1921, to 294 in 1924 and 435 in 1927. In the meantime ski-ing technique had been perfected. 'It is with these things as it is with whisky,' said a pioneer in 1901, 'one never knows how to stop and when!'[1] In later years every winter sports resort had its own ski-ing school in which qualified teachers gave carefully graded courses in a standard technique, and provision was made for everybody from the incorrigible novice to the international champion.

We have seen how amongst the enthusiasts ski-ing was more than a pastime, more than an art. It had an element of the transcendental. 'The love of the mountains is like the love of music,' said Mr. Arnold Lunn in his *History of Ski-ing* (1927), and the climber learns 'in the mountain school lessons of courage and endurance and initiative and good humour under adversity, lessons of imperishable value not only to the individual but to the race.'

But the winter resorts did not make the mistake of relying upon the enthusiasm which the ascetic few transmitted to the many. To

[1] Article by *The Times* Swiss correspondent, 6th February 1939.

the disgust of the more austere they also attended to the creature comforts and the social foibles of weaker vessels. The Prince of Wales did for winter sports much what the Prince Regent had done for the seaside, and the famous winter resorts of Switzerland and Austria came to share the place of the Riviera as cosmopolitan centres of luxury and fashion.

Superficially so different, the holiday cruise had much in common with the winter sports holiday. The sea in its grandeur, beauty and mystery took the place of the mountains. Skill and danger were lacking, but the active social life and luxurious conditions were points of resemblance. Above all, both offered escape into a dreamland of glamour and romance.

There have been pleasure cruises for more than a century. But it was not until firstly the 1914–18 war left the shipping companies with a surplus of shipping, and secondly the depression of the early 'thirties brought them face to face with ruin that they really set out to provide for holiday cruises on a large scale. 'Cruising', said the *Daily Telegraph* with some exaggeration in a special supplement (25th February 1935) which listed nearly 400 cruises, 'was a word which until four years ago meant practically nothing to the British public.' It stated that about 70,000 passengers travelled on holiday cruises in 1931, about 125,000 in 1932, and about 165,000 in 1933; figures quoted by Miss Brunner were 50,000 persons travelling on British ships to Mediterranean and European ports in 1936 and 55,000 in 1937, and in the latter year nearly 25,000 to other non-European ports. It is not clear in what the discrepancy lies, but a substantial number went on cruises which did not call at any ports, and others on foreign ships. The range may be illustrated from the cruises in Cook's list for 1939, which numbered nearly 250 up to 7th October: Cook's representatives accompanied more than half of them, and charges were as low as £3 5s. 6d. for a week-end cruise to Northern France, Belgium and Holland and £6 6s. for a six-day cruise to Norway.

Sunshine, the sea, comfort, social life, entertainments, interesting and beautiful ports of call, prestige—the appeal of cruising to the average holidaymaker was obvious. For most the gaiety and the luxury were the main attractions but there was something for almost everyone. An interesting variant of the main type was the study cruise, in which so to speak two traditions converged. It was a kind of Grand Tour afloat. The most famous were those organized by the Hellenic Travellers' Club, in which distinguished lecturers took part. The same idea in a more popular form was exemplified in *Cruising—with a Hobby*, which was featured by the Wayfarers Travel Agency just before the war. It was, they said, 'a new idea in holidays'. 'Cruise with Music . . . chamber music and madrigal parties, lectures, discussions, gramophone recitals, and all on the open sea! Plenty of scope for holidaymaking—deck games, dancing on deck, fancy dress carnivals, shore excursions.' 'Cruise with Books. . . . All the advantages and gaiety of a sea journey, but the dull hours filled up with readings and discussions on books of all kinds, lectures and competitions.' 'Cruise with Drama. . . .'

The affinity between the holiday cruise and the holiday camp will be observed. Each is characterized by a high degree of organization and the acceptance by the individual of community living, a superimposed routine, and an external discipline. 'Life afloat has few idle moments.' 'A round of social interest and enjoyment.' 'Banishing taciturnity.' 'Every hour of a cruise is full of interest.' 'Varied entertainments to suit all tastes.' 'Breaking down our British reserve.' These are headlines from the *Daily Telegraph* cruising supplement of 1935, when the luxury holiday camp was yet unknown. But the spirit is essentially the same. Everything possible is done to take the individual out of himself. Only he is to blame if he is bored. He can forget the troublesome details of everyday life as a unit in a smoothly run machine. He is encouraged to sink into a world of make-believe.

Is this the key to the holidaymaking of the future? There is much to suggest that it is. There are similar developments abroad; it corresponds with other trends in popular entertainment; it fits in with the social and political ideas of the age; and in a sense it would be a reversion to the older tradition of Bath and Brighton, where convention prescribed the daily routine, a Master of the Ceremonies presided over the entertainments, and one of his first duties was to introduce new arrivals to the rest of the company.

The road from Nash to Butlin has been winding and long, but as the crow flies the distance is not great. The individualistic holiday may prove to have been the aberration, and the communal holiday the norm.

The next few years are likely to provide the answer. They are certain to be crucial. As Mr. J. L. Hammond said in 1933, the mass of people to-day have 'leisure without the traditions of leisure'.[1] But there cannot be a vacuum. Either the old traditions are followed, or by departing from them the people create new traditions. Post-war conditions are bound to compel radical departures from the past. There are reasons for thinking that the communal holiday will prevail, but this does not mean that the pattern need be stereotyped or that there cannot be the widest diversity. The commercial holiday camp is very different from the guesthouse of the Co-operative Holidays Association; there is not much resemblance between a Summer School and a Cook's conducted tour, or between a boys' club camp and a holiday cruise. Yet they are fundamentally similar in that those who take part live in common and the arrangements are made for them by others. Nor is there any reason to suppose that the individually organized holiday will cease to be important. The alternatives are not mutually exclusive, and in a free society the new holidaymaking will reflect the diversity of tastes and standards of the whole community.

Left to itself, the pattern will be shaped by many influences—commercial interests, the leadership of public-spirited individuals and voluntary associations, the system of education, the cinema, the wireless, the traditions of the past, the policy of the State and the local authorities on a wide range of subjects from town and country planning to liquor licensing and exchange control.

One of the most important recommendations of the Catering Wages Commission was that the Government should set up a non-governmental body to foster the development of the catering, holiday and tourist services. This recommendation was adopted, and it was announced in Parliament on the 10th December 1946 that the Government proposed to appoint for this purpose a Board consisting of twelve members, together with a chairman

[1] J. L. Hammond, *The Growth of Common Enjoyment* (1933), 19.

and a chief administrative officer. The Board would include representatives of the touring, catering, home holiday and hotel services, and Scotland and Wales, the Trades Union Congress and the Co-operative Movement would also be represented. Sir Alexander Maxwell, who had been Tobacco Controller, was appointed Chairman of the Board.

The British Tourist and Holidays Board will no doubt make an important contribution to the future pattern of the Englishman's holiday. The local authorities will do so in a variety of ways, from the development of amenities and the control of apartments to the establishment of holiday camps and the arrangement of 'holidays at home'. The voluntary organizations which deliberately set out to improve the general standard of holidaymaking will continue to play their part in the same process.

These public and voluntary bodies on the one hand and the commercial interests on the other are doing for the masses what—to return to the past—Richard Nash did for people of fashion in the eighteenth century. They are helping to form the new tradition. But in the outcome the shape which the new holidaymaking will take will depend upon the development of society itself, upon the complex of forces, moral, social, economic, political, which will determine the quality of its culture, its standard of life, and the nature of its social organization. In the short run certain predictions seem safe. There is no sign that the sea and the mountains are losing their hold upon the public. The trend towards communal holidays shows every sign of accelerating. It is unlikely to be many years before a fortnight has become the normal period for the summer holiday. But to ask what in the longer run the future of the Englishman's holiday is likely to be would be to ask—at a critical point in the history of the country—what will be the future of our society and our civilization.

APPENDIX I

(*See footnote to page* 185)

The forty-eight seaside resorts listed by the 1871 Census Report were as follows:

Deal
Dover
Folkestone
Herne Bay
Margate
Ramsgate
Walmer
Bognor
Brighton
Eastbourne
Hastings
Hove
Littlehampton
St. Leonards
Worthing
East Cowes
Newport

Ryde
Sandown
Shanklin
Ventnor
West Cowes
Southend
Lowestoft
Yarmouth
Lyme Regis
Weymouth and Melcombe Regis
Dartmouth
Dawlish
Exmouth
Ilfracombe
Sidmouth
Teignmouth

Torquay
Penzance
St. Ives
Weston-super-Mare
Blackpool
Fleetwood
Southport
Scarborough
Whitby
Tenby
Aberystwyth
Rhyl
Bangor
Llandudno
Beaumaris

By 1901 the following resorts at least were of sufficient importance to warrant their addition to the above list:

Bournemouth
Broadstairs
Clacton-on-Sea
Cleethorpes
Colwyn Bay
Cromer

Felixstowe
Hoylake and West Kirby
Leigh-on-Sea
Newquay
New Shoreham

Paignton
Portslade-by-Sea
Redcar
Lytham
St. Anne's-on-the-Sea
Skegness
Walton-on-Naze

Appendix

Seaside Watering Places (1896-7 ed.) listed the following seaside resorts in England and Wales:

The North-East

Spittal
Bamburgh
Alnmouth
Whitley-by-the-Sea
Cullercoats
Tynemouth
South Shields
Roker
Ryhope
Seaham Harbour
Seaton Carew
Redcar
Coatham
Marske-by-the-Sea
Saltburn-by-the-Sea
Staithes
Runswick
Sandsend
Whitby
Scarborough
Filey
Bridlington Quay
Hornsea
Withernsea

The East Coast

Great Grimsby
Cleethorpes
Mablethorpe
Sutton-on-Sea
Chapel St. Leonards
Skegness
Hunstanton
Holkham
Wells-next-the-Sea
Sheringham
Cromer
Overstrand
Sidestrand
Trimingham
Palling-on-Sea
Great Yarmouth
Lowestoft
Southwold
Aldborough
Felixstowe
Harwich
Dovercourt
Walton-on-Naze
Frinton-on-Sea
Clacton-on-Sea
Brightlingsea
Bradwell-on-Sea
Southend-on-Sea

The South-East

Sheerness-on-Sea
Whitstable
Herne Bay
Birchington-on-Sea
Westgate-on-Sea
Margate
Broadstairs
Ramsgate, with St. Lawrence-on-Sea
Deal
Walmer
St. Margaret's Bay
Kingsdown
Dover
Folkestone
Sandgate
Hythe

The South Coast

Hastings and St. Leonards
Bexhill-on-Sea
Eastbourne
Seaford
Newhaven
Brighton
Shoreham-on-Sea
Lancing-on-Sea
Worthing
Littlehampton
Bognor
Hayling Island
Southsea
Lee-on-the-Solent
Southampton
Mudeford
Southbourne-on-Sea
Bournemouth
Parkstone
Studland
Swanage
West Lulworth
Weymouth
Bridport
Charmouth
Lyme Regis

Isle of Wight

Ryde
Sea View
Bembridge
Brading and Yarbridge
Sandown
Shanklin
Bonchurch

Appendix

Ventnor
Freshwater
Totland Bay
Yarmouth
Cowes

The South-West

Seaton
Sidmouth
Budleigh Salterton
Exmouth
Dawlish
Teignmouth
Torquay
Paignton
Brixham
Dartmouth
Torcross
Salcombe
Hope
Bantham
Plymouth
Downderry
East and West Looe
Polperro
Fowey
Mevagissey
Portscatho
Falmouth
Gunwalloe
Porthleven
Prussia Cove
Marazion
Penzance
Scilly Isles
St. Ives
St. Agnes
Perranporth
Newquay
Padstow
Tintagel
Trebarwith Strand
Boscastle
Bude
Clovelly
Westward Ho!
Bideford
Instow
Saunton Sands
Croyde
Woolacombe
Morthoe
Lee-on-Sea
Ilfracombe
Combe Martin
Lynton and Lynmouth
Porlock
Minehead
Blue Anchor
Watchet
Burnham
Weston-super-Mare
Clevedon
Portishead

Wales

Penarth
Porthcawl
Port Talbot
Swansea
The Mumbles
Horton
Porteynon
Pembrey
Burry Port
Ferryside
Llanstephan
Pendine
Amroth
Saundersfoot
Tenby
Manorbier
Milford Haven
Dale
Little Haven and Broad Haven
Solva
St. David's
Goodwick
Fishguard
Newport
The Gwbert and the Poppit
Cardigan
Aberporth
Llangranog
New Quay
Aberayron
Aberystwyth
Borth
Aberdovey
Towyn
Barmouth
Harlech
Criccieth
Pwllheli
Nevin
Clynnog Fawr
Dinas Dindlle
Carnarvon
Beaumaris
Holyhead
Bull Bay
Cemaes
Bangor
Llanfairfechan
Penmaenmawr
Llandudno
Colwyn Bay
Pensarn (Abergele)
Rhyl

The North West

Hoylake and West Kirby

New Brighton
Southport
Lytham
St. Anne's-on-the-Sea
Blackpool
Fleetwood
Morecambe
Silverdale

Arnside
Sandside
Grange-over-Sands
Seascale
St. Bees
Allonby
Silloth
Skinburness

Isle of Man

Douglas
Port Erin
Peel
Ramsey

The 1871 Census Report singled out eight inland watering places, Bath, Tunbridge Wells, Cheltenham, Malvern, Leamington, Buxton, Matlock, and Harrogate. In addition to these, *Inland Watering Places* (1891) mentioned the following:

Ashby de la Zouch
Askern
Boston
Clifton
Croft
Dinsdale-on-Tees

Droitwich
Gilsland
Ilkley
Llandrindod Wells
Llangammarch Wells
Llanwrtyd Wells

Nantwich
Purton
Shelfanger
Southborough
Tenbury
Woodhall Spa

Yeo, *Climate and Health Resorts* (1890 ed.), referred also to Shapfell, Nottington near Weymouth, and Builth.

APPENDIX II

Holidays with Pay: December 1946

The following is a summary of the main points in the analysis given in the *Ministry of Labour Gazette* for December 1946 of the provision made for holidays with pay.[1] This was the first full account of the position after the war: the previous analysis had been published in September 1944.

Numbers entitled to holidays with pay. The Ministry were aware of over 1,100 collective agreements made between employers or employees' organizations and trade unions providing for holidays with pay for wage-earners: about 900 were general or district agreements and over 200 were agreements covering individual firms.

These agreements operated in practically all the industries in which conditions of employment were determined by collective bargaining. In addition orders having statutory force directed that holidays with pay should be granted to workers for whom statutory minimum wages had been fixed by Wages Councils in various industries, by the Agricultural Wages Boards, the Road Haulage Central Wages Board, and the Wages Board established for industrial and staff canteen undertakings under the Catering Wages Act, 1943.

It was estimated that between 11 and 12 million wage-earners were covered by these agreements and orders, apart from the many other workers, e.g. clerks and the salaried generally, to whom holidays with pay were granted under other arrangements.

[1] See page 236.

Appendix

Length of the Holiday. In most of the agreements provision was made for 12 days with pay, but in a considerable number the period was 6 days or a week, and in nearly as many—notably in public utilities and distribution—it was 18 days or 3 weeks. Twelve days normally meant 6 consecutive days plus 6 public holidays; 6 days or a week normally meant a week's annual holiday with pay without payment for public holidays; and 18 days or 3 weeks that there was pay for public holidays and 12 days or a fortnight of annual holiday. Since the publication of the previous article in the *Ministry of Labour Gazette* (September 1944) there had been an increase in the period granted in many industries.

Qualifications for Full Holiday or Full Payment. Nearly all the agreements laid down qualifying conditions, normally twelve months continuous service, not necessarily with the same employer. Workers with less than the full qualifying period were usually entitled to a shorter holiday, or, if the full holiday was granted, to less than the full amount of holiday pay.

A few agreements stipulated that the worker must not have lost, through his own fault, more than a specified number of days during the qualifying period. A few made paid holidays conditional upon good conduct, satisfactory service or good timekeeping.

Payment of wages for public holidays was not usually made dependent on length of service.

Time of Holidays. Many of the agreements specified the period during which the annual holiday was to be taken—normally during the summer months—but it was usually left to the employer to decide when within this limit it should take place; often, however, phrases such as 'unless otherwise agreed' or 'as far as possible' gave additional latitude. Sometimes provision was made for consultation with, or due notice to, the workpeople.

Rate and Form of Payment. Many agreements referred to holidays 'with pay' or 'with full pay' without further definition. Others contained definitions of varying degrees of complexity, especially in regard to piece-workers. One system was to pay them the appropriate time rate. Another was to calculate average earnings, sometimes subject to a maximum or a minimum. Some agreecrents provided for the annual holiday payments to be made from medits provided weekly by the employer and accumulated in a special fund, thus relating the individual's holiday pay strictly to his record of attendances.

In the boot and shoe manufacturing industry a contributory scheme was in force, equal contributions being paid by employer and employee.

Other Provisions. Many agreements provided for holiday payments to workers who had ceased to be employed before they had taken their holiday. A few prohibited the taking of employment with another firm during the holiday period. Casual, temporary, and part-time workers were not usually covered specifically, though sometimes the conditions were such that they could benefit to some extent. Some agreements specified when the holiday payment was to be made: ordinarily this was to be before the holiday, but there were a few exceptions, e.g. 'at times to suit local arrangements, but preferably on the first working day after the holiday'.

Statutory Orders. The article also summarized the provisions of the various statutory orders relating to workers covered by wages councils and boards.

APPENDIX III

Notes of a Visit to Butlin's Holiday Camp at Clacton-on-Sea on Thursday 29th August 1946

It is a good indication of the importance of the Camp that Colchester railway station is now labelled: 'Colchester—Junction for Clacton, Frinton, Walton and Butlin's Holiday Camp.'

Situation and Layout

The Camp is at the end of the Clacton Front and forms a self-contained settlement on the outskirts of the town. You pass an amusement park belonging to a separate Butlin Company, and then come to the spacious entrance to the Camp, with a uniformed porter on duty and notices about the days on which the Camp is open to visitors. (Twice a week at 2s. 6d. a head, and yet, I was told, several hundreds, mainly people staying at Clacton, come each time. Of course they can reckon to get their money's worth in free entertainment.)

A short drive leads past the swimming-pool (heated to 65 degrees and thoroughly cleaned by up-to-date methods—it is no wonder that few campers prefer to bathe from the nearby shore) to the main building, with the camp office, billiards-room, Palm Court tea lounge, gymnasium, 'Jolly Roger' bar (the title referring to the style of decoration) and shops.

Behind lie the rows and rows of brightly coloured wooden chalets, which are separated by well-kept flower gardens. The effect is pleasant. The typical chalet has three beds (sometimes including a two-tier bunk), with a wardrobe, cold water laid on, and folding chairs for use on the balcony. Bathrooms and lavatories—labelled 'Lads' and 'Lasses'—are interspersed amongst the chalets.

The other main buildings are the ballroom (with extensive galleries for spectators) and the two dining-halls—one for Gloucester House and one for Kent House, each (with two sittings for the meals) accommodating over 600 people at a time. Both halls have stages for concerts, etc.

Then there are a 'Kiddies' playroom', a cocktail bar (in a modernistic style), a 'Smugglers' Cave' bar, and a nursing and medical unit with sick bay (kept very busy with minor accidents and ailments), more shops and so on.

Out of doors are two playing-fields, two sets of tennis-courts, a bowling-green and a children's playground.

Organization

The Camp takes 2,500 campers (as compared with 5,000 at Filey and Skegness). 'Kiddies' are from 2 (the minimum age) to 7: 'Junior Campers' from 7 to 14: 'Senior Campers' over that age. All are included in the generic term 'happy campers'. Dogs are not allowed. Each camper is assigned to one of the two Houses.

The season lasts from early April to November. The charges range from £5 5s. a week before 1st June and after 19th October to £6 16s. 6d. from 6th July to 14th September, but the attractions keep going all the time. Children up to ten are half price.

The most important extra is afternoon tea. Other extras are 'elevenses', drinks and snacks, the shoe shine service (2s. a week), riding and excursions. Practically everything else—concerts, dancing, competitions, instruction, billiards, sport—is free. Campers provide their own towels and soap.

The large majority come for a week only and the programme is organized accordingly. A small minority stay longer than a fortnight. Most come from London, and special fast trains are run on Saturdays.

The camp is in the charge of a Camp Commandant, assisted by

various specialist managers and the house captains. These, in their turn, are helped by the 'Red Coats', so called from their blazers, whose main job is to organize the entertainments. I saw several of them at work and met some of them. One was looking after the billiard tables. Another was taking a health and beauty class. A third was giving instruction in the 'Lancers' in anticipation of the 'Old Fashioned' night in the ballroom. Several were on duty for the fancy dress parade in the afternoon. And so on. They get up teams for athletic contests, act as dancing partners, arrange the campers' concerts. They are the non-commissioned officers in the somewhat military hierarchy, and mostly seemed to be of the N.C.O. type rather than the high-powered entertainment organizers I had been led to expect. Several of them, I was told, were ex-army P.T. instructors, and others included professional dancers and sportsmen.

But the staff are nothing if not varied. The most highly paid are the Squadronnaires Dance Band, which has a national reputation. There is a second orchestra which specializes in light rather than dance music, and other full-time entertainers include the Frogmen (under-water swimmers), a theatre organist, 'Uncle Mac' (entertaining the 'Kiddies'), and a camp cartoonist. The chief radio announcer (formerly on the B.B.C.) and his assistants are responsible for 'Radio Butlin', which has an important role in the whole organization.

There are a number of other entertainers, apart from visiting artists, and a whole host of employees are engaged upon catering, cleaning, maintenance and administration. Work goes on by night as well as by day. Much of the cleaning including window-cleaning has to be done at night, as has most of the preparation for breakfast.

Discipline does not present a serious problem. On the whole the campers are well conducted, but at the least signs of rowdiness or other misconduct a firm hand is applied, and where necessary the camper's money is returned and he is told to leave.

The Day's Programme

I was at the camp for the week's 'Carnival Day', which was

unfortunately spoiled by the weather. But the programme as it was meant to be was as follows:

'9.30 a.m. Kiddies' Playtime in the Playroom (Parents' Free Hour).

9.45 a.m. Special Motor Coach trip to the Norfolk Broads, including a motor Launch trip on the Broads—Arrive back in Camp by 9.15 p.m.

10.00 a.m. You should be getting really fit by now! How about coming along and have some more Games and Exercises on the Sports Field.

10.30 a.m. Butlin Beginners' Swimming Class at the Pool. Two more days now to get that Certificate.

10.30 a.m. Uncle Mac will entertain children of all ages on the Playground.

10.45 a.m. Organized Amble. A pleasant walk along the Coast. Meet at the Pool.

11.00 a.m. Final rehearsal for Campers' Concert in the Kent Theatre. Your last chance to mount that ladder to the stars!

11.00 a.m. Special attraction!! Lads' and Lasses' Softball Match. The Campers of Kent *v.* Campers of Gloucester.

11.00 a.m. Boxing Instruction in the Gym. Some last-minute tips from Reggie Meen for to-night's contests.

11.00 a.m. In a few hours' time Harry Davidson and his Orchestra will be playing for you. Come along and learn the Fifth and Last Figure of the Lancers, with Arthur Wood at the Compton Organ.

11.15 a.m. Kiddies' Fun and Games on the Green (Under 7's).

11.45 a.m. Health and Beauty class, for 16's to 60's, on the Green.

2.30 p.m. Butlin's Grand Carnival! There will be a Grand Parade of Decorated Motor Cars, Decorated Bicycles, Decorated Juvenile Bicycles—Adults', Junior Campers' and Kiddies' Fancy Dress Parade (Best Costume, Most Original and Most Humorous). Also Junior Campers' Inter-House Dancing Competition. The Parade will be headed by the Holiday Lovely of the week, the most charming Junior Camper and the Kiddies' Holiday Lovely, on the Sports Field. Alvin Gould and his Carnival Band will be there too. Followed by the world famous Frogmen at the Pool, and a Swimming Gala, at approx. 4.30 p.m. Events: 1 Length

Free Style; 1 Length Breast Stroke; Diving Competition; 1 Length Backstroke; 6 x 1 Length Inter-House Relay; Veterans' 1 Length.

4.00 p.m. Toddlers' Tea Time, in the Noah's Ark.

4.30 p.m. Uncle Mac with Punch and Judy on the Playground.

8.00 p.m. Inter-House Novices' Boxing Competition in the Gym. And an exhibition bout: Reggie Meen, Heavyweight Champion of Great Britain, 1931 and 1932; and Ray Salmon, Army Heavyweight Champion, Western Command.

8.30 p.m. Campers' Concert in the Theatre.

9.00 p.m. Special attraction! Old Fashioned dancing to Harry Davidson and his Orchestra.

10.15 p.m. Arthur Wood on the Compton Organ will take over until 10.45 p.m.

10.25 p.m. Penny on the Drum.

10.45 p.m. Old Fashioned Dancing Again with Harry Davidson and his Orchestra.

11.00 p.m. A Demonstration of the Lancers will be given by members of the Entertainment Staff.

11.45 p.m. Good night Campers.'

Some Impressions

Owing to the weather, there was little doing out of doors. A few hardy bathers and a few children on the playground were exceptions. The crowds were indoors—in the ballroom practising the Lancers or watching, in the Palm Court and elsewhere having mid-morning tea or coffee, later on in the bars, though these were by no means crowded. I saw little evidence of regimentation or organized 'jollying' and heard little of 'Radio Butlin'. The proportion of campers engaged on anything active was small. The billiard tables were fully occupied—mainly by youths. The health and beauty class consisted of perhaps twenty 'lasses'. There was a fair crowd on the dance floor. A small group was rehearsing for the campers' weekly show.

Lunch was an impressive demonstration of efficiency. I ate at the Kent House second sitting—in a huge well-lit restaurant with separate tables. The service was speedy, and the food was good. Soup—meat pie and vegetables—steamed pudding—it was a mass-produced meal but substantial and well enough prepared. No bread—owing to rationing. Tea to drink afterwards, and I was told that tea is served at every meal. (More remarkable still, beer had never run out at the bars during the whole season.)

There were no 'hi-de-hi's and 'ho-de-ho's, but Radio Butlin made some announcements. Owing to the weather the outdoor carnival was off, but the fancy dress parade would still take place. Campers whose names began with certain letters should take their ration books along between such and such hours. There were telegrams for Mr. A. and Mrs. B. A small child had been lost. Uncle Tommy told the children of the afternoon's arrangements.

The company looked unremarkable—a good solid mixture of respectable people of all ages with none of the ostentatious jollity of which I had read—at a guess clerical workers, shop assistants and similar folk. Few of them were in holiday attire, still fewer could be said to be smartly dressed, and the general impression was rather drab.

The chief event in the afternoon was the fancy dress parade and competition in the ballroom, and several hundred campers turned out. About a hundred of them went in for the competitions in the three classes—Kiddies, Junior Campers and Senior Campers. The chief radio announcer was in charge, and the judges were the 'Holiday Lovely' of the week, and one representative of each House. Once again the impression was one of informality rather than of high-powered organization. Prizes were given in each class for the best, the most original and the most humorous fancy dresses, and the winners gained points for their Houses. The standard, of course, varied greatly, but a good deal of ingenuity was shown and there were some excellent entries. The humour was somewhat obvious—favourite themes being clothes rationing, queues, and the English summer. Cheers and counter cheers greeted the names of the Houses to which the winners belonged, but mainly, I thought, from the children.

High Spots in the Rest of the Week

The following items from the printed programme for the week seemed to me to be of special interest.

Appendix

Sunday

10 a.m. 'The Campers' Gathering', on the Sports Field. 'We would like to see ALL the Campers from sixteen to sixty so that we can all 'Get Together' and start the week with a swing. The Squadronaires with Jimmy Miller will be there too!'

10.45 a.m. Grand March Past.

11.45 a.m. 'DIVINE SERVICE, conducted by the Rev. H. G. Redgrave, of St. James' Church, Clacton, is held in the Ballroom. The Rev. Redgrave wishes to stress that Campers, if they wish, may attend the Service in Holiday attire.'

2.30 p.m. 'HOLIDAY LOVELIES'. 'The premier contest of the week at the Pool.'

8.0 p.m. Whist drive in the Palm Court.

8.20 and 10.5 p.m. All Star Variety in the Theatre.

Monday

10.45 a.m. 'Special attraction'! 'Sing with the Squadronnaires' Contest to discover the 'Girl with the Silver Voice' (first heat). The winner of this week's contest will receive the Squadronnaires' Silver Cup and will be entitled to enter the All England Finals of our 'Girl with the Silver Voice' contest at the Albert Hall next February.

'The National winner will receive £100 in cash and the offer of a contract with the Butlin organization for the 1947 Season.'

4 p.m. 'Special Mannequin Parade, when Mayfair Mannequins will show this year's summer and the coming winter's Fashions. Included in the programme will be a competition, "I want to be a Mannequin"—Four Prizes. Also a special Mannequin Competition for the Junior Lasses. With Alvin Gould and his Orchestra.'

8 p.m. All Star Wrestling.

Tuesday

10 a.m. Audition and Rehearsal for Campers' Concert.

4 p.m. 'Bring Your Beauty Problems! Two well-known experts from the Icilma Company, Ltd., will give a Beauty Culture Lecture and Demonstration.'

Friday

3.30 p.m. 'The Funniest Face' Competition.

4.15 p.m. 'The world famous BRAINS TRUST—Professor Joad, Commander Campbell, with Denis Yates as Question Master.'

These are only a selection from the entertainments, and in addition provision was made for organized instruction in boxing, swimming, softball, and dancing, and for competitions (counting for house points) in snooker, table tennis, seven-a-side football, tennis, bowls, dancing, darts, athletic sports, softball, boxing, billiards and netball. There was a separate programme for the children.

BIBLIOGRAPHY

I. General

For the political and economic background use has been made of the standard secondary authorities, notably Lecky's *History of England in the Eighteenth Century*, G. M. Trevelyan's works, David Ogg's *England in the Reign of Charles II*, J. H. Clapham's *Economic History of Great Britain*, C. R. Fay's *Life and Labour in the Nineteenth Century*, Elie Halévy's *History of the English People*, and the later volumes of the *Oxford History of England*. None touches more than cursorily on holidays and holiday resorts.

Except as regards social life at the fashionable watering places, much the same is true of the social histories, of which use has in particular been made of *Shakespeare's England* (1916); J. B. Botsford, *English Society in the Eighteenth Century, As Influenced from Overseas* (1924); *Johnson's England* (1933); A. S. Turberville, *English Men and Manners in the Eighteenth Century* (1926); M. Dorothy George, *London Life in the XVIIIth Century* (1925); E. S. Roscoe, *The English Scene in the Eighteenth Century* (1912); W. C. Sydney, *England and the English in the Eighteenth Century* (1891), and *The Early Days of the Nineteenth Century in England* (1898); John Ashton, *The Dawn of the XIXth Century in England* (1886); E. Beresford Chancellor, *Life in Regency and Early Victorian Times* (1927); and G. M. Young (ed.), *Early Victorian England* (1934). Mona Wilson has an interesting chapter on travel and holidays in the latter, but it does not pretend to be more than a sketch. There is a short but entertaining and informative account of the history of bathing costumes in James Laver's *Taste and Fashion* (1937). J. L. Hammond's lecture *The Growth of Common Enjoyment* (1933) is a stimulating essay on the problem of popular leisure.

Secondary authorities dealing with the history of holidaymaking as such or of the holiday resorts as a whole are few in number. Not on this account alone, Reginald Lennard's essay on the watering places in *Englishmen at Rest and Play: Some Phases of English Leisure*, 1558–1714 (edited by him, 1931) is of outstanding importance. E. W. Gilbert's essay on the *Growth of Inland and Seaside Health Resorts in England* (*Scottish Geographical Magazine*, January, 1939) is shorter but extends to the present day. Illustrated with maps, diagrams and statistics, it approaches the subject from the point of view of a historical geographer, and is original and thought-provoking.

Mrs. Stone, *Chronicles of Fashion* (1845), and George Roberts, *The Social History of the People of the Southern Counties in Past Centuries* (1856), are of interest as being amongst the earliest works to treat the rise of the seaside resorts from the historical point of view, though neither deals with them at any length.

George Ryley Scott, *The Story of Baths and Bathing* (1939), which covers bathing in all its aspects in different parts of the world, is necessarily cursory on the English watering places.

Harold Clunn, *Famous South Coast Pleasure Resorts Past and Present* (1929), is concerned more with the present than the past, but traces the rise of Brighton, Bournemouth, Hastings, Eastbourne, Torquay, Folkestone, and Worthing. *Beside the Seaside* (ed. Yvonne Cloud, 1934) is a collection of essays by the editor and other well-known writers on the seaside in general, and on five resorts, Southend, Brighton, Bournemouth, Blackpool, and Margate in particular. For *Holidays Abroad* see the separate heading; and see *Topographical* for histories of particular resorts.

Hutton Webster, *Rest Days* (University of Nebraska, 1911), is useful on holidays in the ancient world.

Richard Russell's *Dissertation on the Use of Sea Water in the Diseases of the Glands* (1752) is for obvious reasons of unique importance. It was foreshadowed by Sir John Floyer, *An Enquiry into the Right Use and Abuses of the Hot, Cold, and Temperate Baths in England* (1697), and Floyer and Edward Baynard, *The History of Cold Bathing, Both Ancient and Modern* (various editions, 1702 onwards).

The following are notable recent surveys of popular holiday-making and the problems arising out of holidays with pay: Political and Economic Planning (P.E.P.) broadsheet No. 194, *Planning for Holidays* (1942); Elizabeth Brunner, *Holiday Making and the Holiday Trades* (Nuffield College, Oxford, 1945)—a pioneer study in the economics of the holiday trades; and the National Council of Social Service, *Holidays* (1945), which was based upon the work of a post-war holidays group set up by the Council.

On travel and communications the secondary authorities are good. For the period before the railway, R. M. C. Anderson, *The Roads of England* (1932), is a useful survey; Gilbert Sheldon, *From Trackway to Turnpike* (1928), which deals with roads in Devonshire, is of special interest because of the attention which the author gives to the seaside resorts; Joan Parkes, *Travel in England in the Seventeenth Century* (1925), is well documented and authoritative. For the railway age the following are important: W. M. Acworth, *The Railways of England* (various editions); W. T. Jackman, *The Development of Transportation in Modern England* (1916); C. E. R. Sherrington, *A Hundred Years of Inland Transport 1830–1933* (1934); and the histories of the great railway companies: G. H. Grinling, *History of the Great Northern Railway* (new ed. 1903); E. T. MacDermot, *History of the Great Western Railway* (1927); C. F. Dendy Marshall, *A History of the Southern Railway* (1936); Clement E. Stretton, *The History of the Midland Railway* (1901).

None of these works deals more than incidentally with the development of railway excursions, and for information on this important subject it is necessary to supplement them, notably from the official reports on railways and on social conditions.

James T. Lightwood, *The Cyclists' Touring Club* (1928), which surveys the Club's first fifty years, is valuable for the early history of cycling. On the National Sunday League there is a pamphlet produced by the League in 1903: *The Aims, Objects and Work of the National Sunday League*. For the main sources on the travel agencies see *Holidays Abroad.*

There is an extensive literature on town and country planning and related subjects including the preservation of coast and countryside.

It has seemed more convenient to classify the other sources by their character—literature, topographical, etc.—than by the subjects on which they are most useful, since so often they throw light on a number of different subjects; an exception has been made for holidays abroad which have been treated separately in the text.

II. Literature (including memoirs and correspondence)

The wealth of literary material is almost embarrassing, as is only natural with a study in the use of leisure. From the middle of the eighteenth century onwards there is hardly a volume of memoirs or correspondence which has not some contribution to make, whether, for the eighteenth century, it is gossip about Bath, or, in the nineteenth century, reminiscences of a holiday by the sea.

The literary material is especially rich for the eighteenth and early nineteenth centuries, when the watering places were at their zenith as social centres. Goldsmith's *Life of Richard Nash of Bath* (1762) is still the main authority on Nash, and an important authority on the spas. Other literary sources of special value include the novels of Smollett (especially *Humphry Clinker*), Fanny Burney (especially *Evelina*, which is set at Clifton), and Jane Austen (including the little-known sketch for a novel to be called *Sanditon* (1817) which was to have been about a rising seaside resort of that name), and the plays of Sheridan. The famous passage on the rush into the sea from Cowper's *Retirement* (1782) has been quoted in the text. Amongst writers of letters, diaries and memoirs, first place must be given to Horace Walpole, but special mention should also be made of the correspondence of Jane Austen, Fanny Burney, and Elizabeth Montagu (the 'Queen of the Blue Stockings'), Southey's fictitious *Letters from England by Don Manuel Alvarez Espriella* (1807), and, amongst less well-known writers, *Catherine Hutton's Letters* (ed. Mrs. Catherine

Hutton Beale, 1891), James Lackington's *Memoirs* (1791), the *Jerningham Letters* (1780-1843) (ed. Egerton Castle, 1896), and the *Correspondence of the Countess of Suffolk* 1712–1767 (1824).

Of the great Victorian novelists Thackeray and Dickens were conspicuous for their love of the seaside, and this is amply reflected in their works, especially their non-fiction writings; Thackeray's name is chiefly associated with Brighton, and Dickens's with Broadstairs. Walter Dexter's *England of Dickens* and other works by the same author provide a convenient index to the main references to the holiday resorts in Dickens. *Jorrocks's Jaunts and Jollities* and other writings by Surtees, the letters of the Brontës and Jane Welsh Carlyle, and R. L. Stevenson's works all contain material of special interest. H. G. Hutchinson, *The Life of John Lubbock, Lord Avebury* (1914), and *The Life Work of Lord Avebury* (ed. the Hon. Mrs. Adrian Grant Duff, 1924) describe Lubbock's activities in connection with bank holidays.

Osbert Lancaster's *Progress at Pelvis Bay* (1936) is an entertaining and penetrating satire on the modern seaside resort in the form of a history of a fictitious resort. It is convincingly illustrated.

III. Newspapers and Periodicals

On matters which constitute news or for which publicity has to be bought, the press—and pre-eminently perhaps the advertisement columns—is one of the most useful sources of information. Such matters include excursion and other holiday travel, the development of the travel agencies, the manner of celebrating bank and other popular holidays, e.g. the wakes weeks, and the accommodation, amenities, etc., at the resorts. Though by no means negligible in the eighteenth century, this class of material is most important for the nineteenth century and since. Its quantity is indeed inexhaustible, and it has not been practicable for the present volume to do more than skim the main periodicals—*The Times*, the *Manchester Guardian*, the *Gentleman's Magazine*, the *Illustrated London News*, *Punch*, and the *Lady*, for example. A more thorough study of the press would be richly repaid, especially if it extended to local newspapers.

IV. Official Reports and Social Surveys

Until the last ten years there was no official inquiry into annual holidays or the ways of spending them, but the numerous official reports of the nineteenth century none the less form one of the most important sources, particularly on the extent to which manual workers had holidays, on what they did with them, and on excursion travel. The other sources tend to be mainly concerned with the upper and middle classes, and as regards working people the official reports are the main authorities on many points.

The *Census Reports* are of course of primary importance for the growth of the holiday resorts, and, as explained in the text, the *Reports* for 1851 and 1871 contained comparative surveys especially germane to our subject. On the other hand, the *Reports* of the Royal Commission upon the Boundaries and Wards of Certain Boroughs and Corporate Towns (Municipal Corporation Boundaries) (1837) and the various *Reports* on Harbours, though not entirely barren, are disappointing.

Except for the civil service, information about the incidence of holidays has to be pieced together from the reports on labour conditions in particular industries and in industry in general, of which there were many. There is much detail about working-class holidays in the evidence collected by, and the *Reports* of, the Royal Commissions on Children's Employment (1842 onwards), Child Employment (1862), and Labour (1892-4); the voluminous reports of the Sub-commissioners appointed by the first of these bodies to make local inquiries on its behalf are particularly valuable. The Civil Service Inquiry Commission (1875), apart from collecting information about civil service holidays, obtained for comparative purposes information about other blackcoated workers in analogous employment.

The innumerable reports on railways are chiefly useful as regards excursions, not the least valuable being the reports of the routine inquiries into accidents, because they so often contain details, e.g. about the number and conduct of the passengers, not easily obtainable elsewhere.

There is much that is of value in the *Reports* of the Inspectors of Factories. The *Reports* on the Exhibitions of 1851 and 1862 are important in connection with excursion travel. The Parliamentary Debates and the *Report* of the Select Committee on the Bank Holiday Bill of 1868 are amongst the chief authorities on bank holidays.

Other groups of reports which are helpful, particularly on excursion travel and popular holidaymaking, are those dealing with the conditions in the great towns, the problem of open spaces, and the drink question.

There is useful topographical material in a few of the *Reports* of the Historical Manuscripts Commission (e.g. the *Verulam*, *Carlisle*, *Bath* and *Hare* MSS.) but none of them is of special interest.

On the position in the last ten years, there are three important official reports dealing directly with annual holidays. The *Report* of the Departmental Committee on Holidays with Pay (1938) is of course of exceptional importance; it has a useful summary of the history of holidays with pay. The evidence given before the Committee is also valuable. The *Report* of the Catering Wages Commission on the *Staggering of Holidays* (1945) is sufficiently explained by its title. The Commission's *Report* on the *Development of the Catering, Holiday and Tourist Services* (1946) does not deal with holidays at any length, but makes some important proposals for their development.

As explained in the text, the *Reports* of the Royal Commission on the Distribution of the Industrial Population (1940), and the Committee on Land Utilization in Rural Areas (1942), and Mr. John Dower's *Report* on National Parks (1945) are relevant. The *Ministry of Labour Gazette* is the main source for information about entitlement to holidays with pay: the issue for December 1946 included the detailed analysis of the position at that time, which has been used for Appendix II. The International Labour Office has published several reports on the subject. *Hansard* is important for the various Parliamentary debates on holidays with pay and staggering.

Complementary to the official reports is Charles Booth's invaluable survey of the *Life and Labour of the People in London* (1889-1902), which is much more useful on holidays and holidaymaking than the contemporaneous *Report* of the Royal Commission on Labour. B. Seebohm Rowntree, *Poverty: A Study of Town Life* (1901), which deals with York, is also useful; *Poverty and Progress* (1941) based on a second social survey of York by Rowntree, has, however, practically nothing on annual holidays. Of the same genre is G. von Schulze-Gävernitz, *Der Groszbetrieb, ein wirtschaftlicher und sozialer Fortschritt* (1892), which, apart from other interesting material, contains the analysis of working-class budgets of which use has been made in the text. There are a number of more recent surveys, the most valuable of which from the present point of view is the *New Survey of London Life and Labour* (1930–5). On the whole they are disappointing in the amount of attention given to holidays.

V. Topographical

This is an almost inexhaustible category, and the list below gives only the main sources of which use has been made for the purpose of this volume. For fuller bibliographies on particular places, reference should be made to works about them. It is emphasized that the present list is incomplete: thus Margaret Barton, *Tunbridge Wells*, names twenty-two works referring to Tunbridge in their title, as compared with six mentioned here. There is of course a good deal of information about the resorts in the literary and other sources which have been mentioned under the previous headings; authorities already referred to have not been repeated.

The utility of guide books and other topographical volumes is great and obvious, but their limitations should not be overlooked. Except where their authors are persons of rare originality, curiosity, or insight, they tend to be superficial and to reproduce secondhand information; special care is necessary where they are camouflaged propaganda for particular places or interests.

(*a*) *General*

John Aikin, *England Described* (1818).

Baedeker's *Guides*.

George Beaumont and Captain Henry Disney, *A New Tour thro'*

England perform'd in the Summers of 1765, 1766 *and* 1767 (undated).

Bernard H. Becker, *Holiday Haunts* (1884).

Black's *Guides*.

E. D. Clarke, *Tour through the South of England in* 1791 (1793).

Harold Clunn, *The Face of the Home Counties* (1936).

W. Cobbett, *Rural Rides*, during the years 1821 to 1832 (various eds.).

(Cobbett's comments are usually trenchant and original, and, though he was unfriendly towards the watering places and what he says about them must be considerably discounted, it is useful to have a critical contemporary view.)

D. Defoe, *Tour through the Whole Island of Great Britain* (1724).

Alphonse Esquiros, *Itinéraire Descriptif et Historique de la Grande Bretagne et de l'Irlande* (Paris, 1865).

John Evans, LL.D., *An Excursion to Brighton, a Visit to Tunbridge Wells; and a Trip to Southend* (1821).

(This useful volume, the scope of which is shown by the title, contains much useful detail about the three resorts with which it is mainly concerned, but it is also valuable for the annotated list of mineral waters and seabathing places which is appended to it.)

Celia Fiennes, *Through England on a Side Saddle in the Time of William and Mary* (ed. the Hon. Mrs. Griffiths, 1888).

(An indispensable seventeenth-century source which is one of the main authorities for the spas, especially the minor ones. Celia Fiennes combined to an unusual degree curiosity and an eye for significant detail, and that she was rather naïve is in some ways an advantage.)

Arthur Freeling, *Picturesque Excursions* (1839).

A. B. Granville, M.D., F.R.S., *The Spas of England and Principal Sea-Bathing Places* (1841).

(Perhaps the most important work ever published on the English spas, and also useful, though less complete on the seaside resorts, Granville's survey is invaluable because of the standing which he enjoyed as a specialist in the mineral water cure, his acute powers of observation and love of detail, and the comprehensive character of the work.)

Bibliography

A Handbook of Travel round the Southern Coast of England (1849.)

Sir George Head, *A Home Tour through the Manufacturing Districts of England, in the Summer of* 1835 (1836).

(Head had a good eye for interesting detail, and his *Home Tour* is one of the main authorities on the seaside resorts of the North, notably Southport, on the eve of the railway age. The sequel—*A Home Tour through Various Parts of the United Kingdom* (1837)—does not deal with the holiday resorts.)

Inland Watering Places (1891 ed.).

Malcolm Letts, *As the Foreigner Saw Us* (1935).

Dr. William MacRitchie, *Diary of a Tour through Great Britain in* 1795 (ed. David MacRitchie, 1897).

Murray's *Guides*.

W. T. Perkins, *Popular Coast Guide* (1903).

(An informative handbook to the South-East Coast resorts, published by the South Eastern Railway.)

Valérie Pirie, *A Frenchman Sees the English in the 'Fifties* (adapted from the French of Francis Wey) (1935).

Dr. Richard Pococke, *Travels through England* 1750–1757 (Camden Society, 1888–9).

Seaside Watering Places (Various editions, 1876 and later).

Rev. S. Shaw, *A Tour to the West of England, in* 1788 (Pinkerton's Voyages).

Stanford's *Guides*.

Spencer Thomson, M.D., *Health Resorts of Great Britain; and How to Profit by Them* (1860).

Mackenzie Walcott, *Guide to the South Coast of England* (1859).

Mackenzie Walcott, *The East Coast of England* (1861).

J. Burney Yeo, *Climate and Health Resorts* (1890 ed.).

(*b*) *Particular Areas*

The following list should be read in conjunction with (*a*): in a number of instances one of the general works there mentioned is also an important source for a particular resort. Conspicuous examples are Evans, Granville, Head, Thomson and Yeo. The standard series of guide books—notably Black's, Murray's and

Stanford's—between them cover the country pretty thoroughly, but have not been mentioned at all below.

Cornwall

A. K. Hamilton Jenkin, *Cornwall and the Cornish* (1933).

W. H. Tregellas, *Tourist's Guide to Cornwall and the Scilly Isles* (1878).

Derbyshire

William Bray, *Sketch of a Tour into Derbyshire and Yorkshire* (1797) (Pinkerton's Voyages).

Devonshire

Handbook for Torquay (1854).

Llewellyn Jewitt, *History of Plymouth* (1873).

John Presland, *Torquay. The Charm and History of its Neighbourhood* (1920).

J. T. White, *The History of Torquay* (1878).

Dorset

C. Wanklyn, *Lyme Regis. A Retrospect* (1922).

Essex

W. H. Lindsey, *A Season at Harwich, with Excursions by Land and Water* (1851).

Gloucestershire

Bristoliensis, *The Bristol Guide* (1815, 4th ed.).

Chilcott's *New Guide to Bristol, Clifton and the Hotwells* (1826).

Edith M. Humphris and E. C. Willoughby, *At Cheltenham Spa* (1928).

(A useful modern history of Cheltenham as a watering place.)

Hampshire

Horace Dobell, M.D., *The Medical Aspects of Bournemouth and ts Surroundings* (1885).

Charles H. Mate and Charles Riddle, *Bournemouth* 1810–1910 (1910). (A useful quarry of information.)

Bibliography

Kent

Margaret Barton, *Tunbridge Wells* (1937). (An entertaining modern history of the spa as a social centre.)

E. W. Brayley, *Delineations of the Isle of Thanet and the Cinque Ports* (1817).

T. Benge Burr, *History of Tunbridge Wells* (1766). (Still the main authority for the early days of the spa.)

Walter Dexter, *The Kent of Dickens* (1924).

C. G. Harper, *The Kentish Coast* (1914).

Kidd's *Picturesque Companion to the Isle of Thanet* (? 1840).

S. J. Mackie, *A Descriptive and Historical Account of Folkestone and its Neighbourhood* (1856).

Margate Delineated (10th ed. undated, probably 1820's).

Lewis Melville, *Society at Royal Tunbridge Wells in the Eighteenth Century—and After* (1912). (A popular but well-documented study of the social life at the spa, mainly in the eighteenth century.)

Arthur Montefiore, *The Isle of Thanet* (1893).

W. C. Oulton, *Picture of Margate* (1820). (An informative illustrated account of Margate.)

Robert Hutchinson Powell, *A Medical Topography of Tunbridge Wells* (1846).

The Tunbridge Wells Guide, 1780, *and a Description of Tunbridge Wells in its Present State*, 1785.

Lake District

W. Hutchinson, *An Excursion to the Lakes in Westmorland and Cumberland, etc.* (1776).

West, *A Guide to the Lakes* (1784, 3rd ed.).

Lancashire

Joseph Aston, *The Lancashire Gazetteer* (1808).

F. H. Cheetham, *Some Old Books of Southport* (reprinted from the Transactions of the Historical Society of Lancashire and Cheshire, 1908).

Henry Fishwick, *History of Lancashire* (1894).

William Hutton, *A Description of Blackpool*, 1788 (ed. R. Sharpe France, 1944). (This short essay, written because Blackpool 'has merit, which is little known', contains one of the earliest detailed accounts of seaside life.)

A New Description of Blackpool (undated, probably 1830's).

Somerset

A. Barbeau, *Life and Letters at Bath in the XVIIIth Century* (1904). (A thorough and well-documented study by a French social historian which has become a standard authority on the life at the watering places.)

P. Rowland James, *The Baths of Bath in the Sixteenth and Early Seventeenth Centuries* (1938). (A careful and scholarly study of Bath in the early phases of its revival as a health resort.)

Lewis Melville, *Bath under Beau Nash* (1907). (A companion volume to the same author's works on Tunbridge Wells and Brighton (q.v.).)

Edith Sitwell, *Bath* (1932).

R. A. L. Smith, *Bath* (1944).

Surrey

Gordon Home, *Epsom* (1901).

Henry Pownall, *Some Particulars Relating to the History of Epsom* (1825).

Sussex

J. Ashton, *Florizel's Folly* (1899).

W. H. Attwick, *Brighton since the Grant of the Charter* (1929).

Margaret Barton and Osbert Sitwell, *Brighton* (1935).

Brighton As It Is (1828, new ed.).

G. F. Chambers, *A Handbook for Eastbourne* (1876, 8th ed.).

William Harwood, *On the Curative Influence of the Southern Coast of England; especially that of Hastings* (1828).

Lewis Melville, *Brighton, Its History, Its Follies, and Its Fashions* (1909). (See the note on Melville's similar volumes on Bath and Tunbridge Wells.)

Wales

Jenkinson's *Practical Guide to North Wales* (1878).

S. Lewis, *A Topographical Dictionary of Wales* (1833).

Isle of Wight

Barber's *Picturesque Illustrations of the Isle of Wight* (1845).

J. Hassell, *Tour of the Isle of Wight* (1790).

Thomas Roscoe, *Summer Tour to the Isle of Wight* (undated, 1840's).

Worcestershire

John Chambers, *A General History of Malvern* (1817).

G. W. Hastings, *The Story of the Malverns* (1911).

T. Nash, *Collections for the History of Worcestershire* (1789).

Yorkshire

J. S. Fletcher, *Harrogate and Knaresborough* (1920).

Arthur Rowntree (ed.), *The History of Scarborough* (1931).

J. Schofield, *An Historical and Descriptive Guide to Scarborough and its Environs* (1787).

Thorpe's *Visitor's Handbook for Harrogate* (1859, 3rd ed.).

VI. Holidays Abroad

On the whole the secondary authorities are good for the age of the Grand Tour but not for the subsequent period. On the former, see E. S. Bates, *Touring in 1600* (1911), 'a study in the development of travel as a means of education'; W. E. Mead, *The Grand Tour in the Eighteenth Century* (1914); A. Barbeau, *Les Voyageurs en France de la Renaissance jusqu' à la Révolution* (Paris, 1885); C. H. Lockitt, *The Relations of French and English Society* (1763–1793) (1920); Constantia Maxwell, *The English Traveller in France* 1698–1815 (1932); and R. S. Lambert (ed.), *The Grand Tour* (1935), which is more popular. There is in addition an extensive literature of foreign travel from the eighteenth century onwards, and correspondence, memoirs and fiction are rich in allusions to the Grand Tour and trips to the Continent. Smollett, Sterne, and, for the latter days of the Grand Tour, Charles Lever may be specially mentioned. Out of the mass of guide and travel books of one kind and another, that remarkable volume, *The Gentleman's Guide in his*

Tour through France, 'wrote by an Officer in the Royal Navy' (1770), may be singled out. It was highly popular, running into many editions, and it is most revealing of both the point of view and the practice of the English visitor to France in the middle of the eighteenth century. For fuller information on sources reference should be made to Bates, Mead, and Maxwell. None, however, is by any means comprehensive: the extent of the available material may be illustrated by the fact that the present writer has traced more than two hundred accounts—some, of course, only incidental—of visits to France between 1763 and 1789.

For the later period there seems to be no secondary authority which covers more than part of the ground. The stimulating and entertaining essay by Mona Wilson in *Early Victorian England* (mentioned under I) is only a sketch. There is, however, an abundance of primary material, and on at least one aspect of the subject —the vogue for the mountains—ample secondary material. Important examples of the rich literature on mountaineering and winter sports are John Ball's *Guide to the Western Alps* (1863), Leslie Stephen's classic *The Playground of Europe* (1871), Frederic Harrison's *My Alpine Jubilee* (1908), *The Englishman in the Alps* (ed. Arnold Lunn, 1927, 2nd ed.), Arnold Lunn's *A History of Skiing* (1927), and the Lonsdale Library volumes on mountaineering and winter sports.

The guidebooks—Baedeker and Murray may in particular be mentioned—are indispensable, especially since there are few other sources in English for the development of individual Continental resorts. Bradshaw's *Dictionary of Mineral Waters, Climatic Health Resorts, etc., of the World* (1882 ed.) and J. Burney Yeo, *Climate and Health Resorts* (1890 ed.) are particularly useful.

On the travel agencies there are a number of useful works. W. Fraser Rae, *The Business of Travel* (1891), is a competent record of Cook and his agency, of which extensive use has been made in this volume. Ethel M. Wood, *The Polytechnic and its Founder* (1932 ed.), contains an account of the origin and rise of the Polytechnic Touring Association. Sir Henry Lunn tells of his experiences as a travel agent in his autobiography, *Nearing Harbour* (1934), and John Frame of his in *My Life of Globe Trotting* (1931). T. Arthur

Leonard, *Adventures in Holiday Making* (1934), is the story of the Co-operative Holidays Association and the Holiday Fellowship. *Geoffrey Franklin* 1890-1930 (privately printed, 1933) is a memoir of the founder of the Wayfarers' Travel Agency. Lightwood (see p. 286) is interesting on cycling tours on the Continent. J. A. R. Pimlott, *Toynbee Hall* (1935), refers to the origin and activities of the Toynbee Travellers Club. The advertisements, pamphlets, etc., of the travel agencies are also valuable, and like the works about the agencies themselves throw light on other points as well.

On the history of Switzerland in the second half of the last century use has been made of Eduard Fueter, *Die Schweiz seit 1848* (1928).

The treatment of holidays abroad in this volume owes much to Sir Frederick Ogilvie's *The Tourist Movement* (1933), which is an important study of the economic significance of foreign touring in the period after the 1914-18 war. A. J. Norval, *The Tourist Industry* (1936), relates particularly to South Africa, but it contains a useful introductory review of the position elsewhere, and a summary of tourism in the Roman Empire. R. G. Pinney, *Britain—Destination of Tourists?* (1944, 2nd ed.), a slight volume produced for the Travel Association, brings Ogilvie's figures up to date on some points.

VII. Illustrations

This bibliography would be incomplete without a reference to the illustrations which are one of the most important sources for the history of holidays. The volume is considerable. The quality with some notable exceptions is poor, but this does not necessarily make the material less useful to the historian.

Most of the topographical works are illustrated—on the whole disappointingly. There are a great many prints in the national and other collections, particularly of the resorts in the eighteenth and early nineteenth centuries. For the subsequent period their place is increasingly taken by the illustrated magazine and, with the development of press photography, the newspapers. Holidays and holiday resorts have been a favourite subject for caricaturists and have often served them as a background for political satire. The outstanding name is Thomas Rowlandson, whose cartoons are most illuminating on the details of holidaymaking: this also applies, though to a lesser extent, to Gillray and Cruikshank. For the middle of the nineteenth century John Leech is most useful: there can be hardly any facet of mid-Victorian holidays which is not illustrated in his numerous cartoons on this theme. But he is only one of many *Punch* cartoonists down to the present time whose work is valuable. The *Punch Almanack* and *Summer Number* are particularly so. David Low has used a holiday camp as the setting for at least one of his cartoons.

Fashion plates, music title pages, book illustrations, and to a growing extent posters and other pictorial advertisements all contain much useful material. What may be called legitimate art is somewhat unrewarding, though there are naturally a large number of landscape and topographical works which depict holiday resorts. An outstanding case is Turner, who did several pictures at Brighton. Frith's famous *Ramsgate Sands* should also be mentioned.

Paul Martin, *Victorian Snapshots* (1939), contains some interesting photographs of holidaymakers. Alan Bott, *Our Fathers* (1931), and Alan Bott and Irene Clephane, *Our Mothers* (1932), which are collections of illustrations from the *Graphic* and the *Sketch*, are also useful.

VIII. Some Suggestions

The Bibliography seems to be an appropriate place in which to refer to gaps in the existing sources and to make—for what they are worth—some suggestions as to possible subjects for further study. I apologize in advance if, as may well have happened, I have overlooked any work which has already been done.

(*a*) The holiday resorts are no exception to the general neglect of local history. As will have been seen from the text, there are some excellent histories of a few of the principal resorts, but even they concentrate upon certain aspects, notably fashionable social life, to the subordination of others of at least equal interest, such as—to mention a few examples—the number of visitors at different times, the arrangements for their accommodation, the economics of the holiday trades, and local government. Still more conspicuous is the absence of up-to-date and authoritative histories of some of the greatest resorts, including Blackpool, Bournemouth, Eastbourne and Margate. The general tendency, too, amongst such works as there are is to taper off into silence by the middle of the nineteenth century.

(*b*) There is little secondary material on railway and other excursions, the history of which would make an excellent subject for a book.

(*c*) There is no comprehensive account of the development of weekly holidays—the half holiday, the week-end, and more recently the Saturday holiday, as a result of the spread of the five-day week.

(*d*) An interesting book could be written on holidays abroad after the age of the Grand Tour.

(*e*) The open-air movement, cruising, cycling, holiday camps, and other subjects touched on in this book would repay more detailed study than they appear to have received.

(*f*) The vogue of Scotland as a touring place for the English would be a fascinating study, which would lead into several exciting historical by-ways such as the Romantic Movement and the neo-Jacobitism of the nineteenth century.

INDEX

(Resorts appearing in the lists given in Appendix I but not mentioned in the actual text have not been indexed.)

Index

Index

Index

Index

Index

Index

Index

Index

Index